Washin  ry

BUCKEYE REBIRTH

URBAN MEYER,
AN INSPIRED TEAM,
AND A NEW ERA AT
OHIO STATE

BILL RABINOWITZ

TRIUMPH
BOOKS

Library of Congress Cataloging-in-Publication Data

Rabinowitz, Bill, 1964–
    Buckeye rebirth : Urban Meyer, an inspired team, and a new era at Ohio State / Bill Rabinowitz.
        pages cm
    ISBN 978-1-60078-905-2
1. Ohio State University—Football. 2. Ohio State Buckeyes (Football team) 3. Meyer, Urban. 4. Football coaches—United States. I. Title.
    GV958.O35.R335 2013
    796.332092—dc23
    [B]
                                                                    2013013947

This book is available in quantity at special discounts for your group or organization. For further information, contact:

Triumph Books LLC
814 North Franklin Street
Chicago, IL 60610
(312) 337-0747
www.triumphbooks.com

Printed in the United States of America

ISBN: 978-1-60078-905-2
Design and editorial production by Alex Lubertozzi
All photos courtesy of the Columbus Dispatch

To my dad, born on the day Ohio State's marching band first performed "Script Ohio," who taught me to love sports. And to my mom, who tolerates that love.

I wish that everyone could see everything we did and how close we became as a family. Every guy on this team always will have a place for this team in his heart. Everyone truly loves each other. A lot of times on college teams you have guys you don't even talk to. There are 105 guys, and you stay in your own little clique. But everyone knew each other's names and where everyone was from. That's what makes great teams rare, and that's what we had this year. We'd gone through so much together. As a team we made the conscious effort to get that close. I think that's what made the team great. We took that extra step. No one rejected anyone. We embraced the idea of becoming one big family.

—Zach Boren
Senior Fullback/Linebacker, 2012 Ohio State Buckeyes

CONTENTS

FOREWORD

WHEN A UNIVERSITY loses a great coach, it must replace him with an even greater coach. That's what Ohio State did when it lost Jim Tressel and hired Urban Meyer. My history with Urban goes back more than 25 years. Back in 1986, I asked my trusted friend and assistant coach Tom Lichtenberg to find me new graduate assistants. He brought back Urban, joining a GA group that included Tim Hinton. Little did I know then, but both would become very successful coaches. Hinton is now OSU's tight ends/fullbacks coach. Urban brought with him to the job a passion, knowledge of the game, determination, and work ethic that I knew would take him places.

When I was at Colorado State, I hired Urban as my wide receivers coach in 1990. You could see that he was a cut above most of the other assistants, maybe all of them. He had ideas. He had a great mind for offensive football. I was always impressed with his innovative play calling and willingness to go the extra mile. He could have been a coordinator right after his first year there, if I'd had an opening. He has a true love of coaching and mentoring young players to become the best they can be, and that is what makes him a great coach.

I'm honored that he considers me a mentor, and I've watched his coaching career with pride. When, during Ohio State's difficult 2011 season, it became apparent that the Buckeyes would be looking for a new coach, I knew who the ideal person would be. But I did not discuss it with Urban. I figured if he was interested, all he'd have to do is say he was interested, and he'd have a great shot at the job.

That's what happened. After his hiring, he lived with me for a short time, though I hardly saw him. We chatted during breakfast at 5:00 AM and talked for a few minutes when he returned late at night from the Woody Hayes Athletic Center. He was going on adrenaline. He was moving and shaking and baking, mainly concentrating on recruiting. He was a focused guy, all on one thing—to make Ohio State a great football team and to get the best players he could get.

Football requires a year-round commitment from players as well as coaches. It takes the body (weight training, speed, agility, etc.), the mind (education and coaching), and the community to be a success. Toughness is developed through the training room, weight room, and conditioning on the practice field. The 2012 team met many stiff challenges. Urban, with much help from the hard work and leadership of Buckeyes seniors, met every one and persevered to have a perfect season. The kids needed the discipline and the hard work. They thrived on it and took the bit and ran with it.

I was fortunate to have an inside view for much of what happened. Urban allowed me to watch practices and sit in on coaches meetings. The meetings were well-organized. The practices were outstanding. All that translated to the field on Saturdays.

This book covers everything about the 2012 season, from Urban's arrival in Columbus to the climax of the final weeks of the season and beyond. Ohio State football has been around since 1890, and this was only the sixth time the Buckeyes went undefeated and untied. That is how hard it is to go undefeated in major-college football. It was a pretty special feeling watching Urban's team go undefeated in his first season at Ohio State. It brought back many memories from my first season in 1979 as head coach at Ohio State. I was so proud to see my alma mater and one of my closest coaching friends do Columbus proud.

This is the story of that remarkable season and how it sets up the foundation for the Urban Meyer era at Ohio State. Go Bucks!

—Earle Bruce

PROLOGUE

GENE SMITH SAT in his black Buick Enclave in disbelief. His car was parked in front of Ohio State president Dr. E. Gordon Gee's house in Bexley, a few miles from campus. It was shortly after 7:00 AM on December 20, 2011.

For months, the Ohio State athletics director had staked his reputation on navigating the school through the most difficult chapter in its recent history. Now was the endgame. He had just received the NCAA report that would determine the obstacles that would shape the 2012 football season and beyond. Ohio State had already forced, though belatedly, the Memorial Day resignation of Jim Tressel, whose squeaky-clean image disintegrated with revelations that he had committed NCAA violations and lied about it. In July, Ohio State had imposed sanctions on itself, including scholarship reductions and vacating its 2010 Big Ten championship and Sugar Bowl victory, in hopes of warding off harsher penalties.

Now those penalties had been deemed inadequate by the NCAA. In his car, Smith seethed.

"I was just livid," Smith said.

Smith is a former member of the NCAA's Committee on Infractions, which levies penalties. He had studied the precedents of cases similar to Ohio State's. There were 32 of them, he had told reporters. None of those programs had received a bowl ban. Now the stark reality hit him as he read the NCAA ruling. He had been wrong. The NCAA had hammered Ohio State. Among other penalties, the Buckeyes would be banned from the postseason after the 2012 season.

Smith is a calm, even-tempered man, but he needed time to process the information before he went into Gee's residence, known as the Pizzuti House.

Inside, Smith, Gee, and other OSU officials had to decide whether to appeal the sanctions. Everyone else was as surprised and upset as Smith was.

"Everybody you talked to felt it didn't require a bowl ban," Smith said. "There was no precedent for it. None. Our association has for years operated on precedents. Even when I was on the infractions committee, it was very difficult to step outside of precedent."

But Ohio State had underestimated new NCAA president Mark Emmert's desire for a case to show that a new sheriff had arrived in town. The NCAA has long been criticized, with good reason, as secretive and unaccountable. In recent years, even before Emmert's arrival, it began taking steps to be more transparent. It holds an annual mock NCAA basketball tournament selection seminar for media so that reporters can then dispel common misconceptions about the process. In May 2011, before Tressel resigned, the NCAA held a similar mock seminar about its enforcement process. During a break, Emmert told reporters that he wanted to increase penalties for violators as a deterrent to others who might be tempted to break rules.

"Mark is taking a big risk because never before has the NCAA president stepped in to the infractions process," Smith said when told about Emmert's comment. "No, we did not see it coming."

Gee, as is his wont, caused a stir late in 2012 when he said that Ohio State's bowl ban was inevitable. Smith said that Ohio State only reached that conclusion with hindsight.

"No one in the business saw that coming. Nobody," Smith said. "That's when we realized we were test case No. 1. Everybody wanted us to appeal. I had colleagues who wanted us to appeal, to challenge it because it was way outside of precedent."

Because Ohio State had cooperated with the NCAA—going above and beyond, it believed—it thought it had political capital to use if needed. In the end, the school decided not to appeal. The process had dragged on for so long, since the initial tattoo-and-memorabilia violations story broke in December 2010. As unfair as they believed it to be, they just wanted it to be over.

In the midst of this, Smith knew he had another person to inform of the NCAA's decision before it became public knowledge—the coach he'd just hired after assuring him that a bowl ban was highly unlikely.

"I think Gene called and said, 'Do you have a minute? I'll be right over,'" Urban Meyer recalled.

He knew that was not a good sign. When Smith walked into his office minutes later, Meyer knew for sure.

"We got word from the NCAA," Smith said. "They took a bowl from us."

"What?" Meyer replied.

His reaction matched Smith's earlier.

"Shocked," Meyer said a year later. "Devastated. The first thing I thought was that we weren't going to a bowl game. The second was that the seniors could leave."

NCAA rules permit seniors at a program that has been hit with sanctions to transfer to another program without having to sit out a season. Under normal circumstances, a transfer must wait a year before competing for his new school. If even a few pivotal seniors left the Buckeyes, it could have had a huge effect, both in actual and psychological impact on the program.

"So I sat down and tried to gather my thoughts for a minute," Meyer said.

The tumultuous end to his coaching career at the University of Florida and his year away from the sidelines had taught him some perspective. He had learned, or tried to, that he should worry about only what he could control. The mysterious ways of the NCAA were beyond anyone's control. So after a couple minutes of processing the news, Meyer accepted it.

"Let's move forward," he told Smith. "'We'll get through this.' I looked him right in the eye and said, 'We're fine. Let's go.'"

Immediately, he began calling recruits so they'd find out from him rather than when the news broke in the afternoon. National Signing Day was six weeks away. Meyer wasn't coaching Ohio State in the Buckeyes' Gator Bowl game against his former team, Florida. Luke Fickell and his assistants were finishing out the season while Meyer concentrated on recruiting and settling into his new job. He and the staff he was still assembling had done a remarkable job turning a mediocre recruiting class into a top-ranked one, and he was determined not to let that work be undone because of the ruling.

It was the first time Smith had a chance to observe Meyer under difficult circumstances.

"He was livid for about 120 seconds," Smith said. "He didn't say a word, just walked around and then came back and sat down. Got out a piece of paper and then moved. That's what good leaders do. You face the reality and then you move. You have to say, 'This is it. We have to face it. How do we deal with it?' I was so impressed."

Players were summoned to a meeting in hopes they'd hear the news from Ohio State first. Smith spoke first.

"I had moved from pissed off to sad," he said. "I actually cried in front of the team, because I care for the kids, more than people realize. It hurt me a lot that I had to tell them that."

Many of them already had heard the news as they returned from a community-service visit at a local hospital. In the age of Twitter, nothing stays a secret for long.

"I think it was more of a shock thing," senior fullback Zach Boren said. "Guys were just sitting there kind of in disbelief and just had a lot of questions, and those were answered by Mr. Smith later on in the day."

These seniors enrolled at Ohio State after the Buckeyes had lost consecutive national championship games to Florida (coached by Meyer) and LSU. They came expecting to play for the national title themselves. Now they knew that dream was dead. There would be no chance for a Big Ten championship. There would be no January bowl game. No matter what lay ahead, this season would be like no other in the long and storied history of Ohio State football.

It would also be among the most special.

· 1 ·

THE HIRING

IN HIS PERFECT WORLD, Gene Smith would not have hired a new coach after the 2011 season. If all had gone well, he would have been happy to extend the one-year contract for Luke Fickell and have him be the head coach for the foreseeable future. Smith asked the former Buckeyes nose guard, who first made a name for himself as a three-time state wrestling champion at DeSales High School in Columbus, to take over for Jim Tressel on May 30. At 37, Fickell had never been a head coach. He'd never been more than a co–defensive coordinator. Longtime defensive coordinator Jim Heacock had the ultimate authority over the Ohio State defense.

At 11:00 PM on May 29, Smith asked Fickell to arrange a staff meeting for the next morning with the other assistant coaches. Smith didn't tell Fickell that he'd asked for Tressel's resignation. He gave him no clue as to what their meeting would cover. Fickell guessed that the topic would be to discuss an upcoming *Sports Illustrated* story that the school feared would be a bombshell. (The story fizzled, blowing over quickly.) When the notion of Tressel leaving flitted through his mind, he dismissed it as unlikely.

"The whole night, I thought, *Could it be? No. It couldn't be*," he said. "I had no idea."

He barely fell asleep and resisted the urge to awaken his wife, Amy. His meeting with Smith was at 8:00. The staff meeting was supposed to begin 15 minutes later. Fickell had little time to process or weigh the offer when it came. Then again, it wasn't that tough a decision. How do you turn down the chance to be Ohio State's head coach, even under these circumstances?

"All I could think about was those [players]," Fickell said. "Yes, it's my university, where I went. But all I could think about was those guys. What, are you going to hold those guys hostage?"

That night, Fickell visited Tressel at his house. They talked for a little more than a half-hour. It would be their last conversation for a long time.

"He said it's best for you, for the program, for the team, that we not talk," Fickell recalled. "That way, you don't ever have to answer questions about, 'Have you talked to Coach?'"

Fickell was pretty much on his own. The job proved to be a dream and a nightmare. The end of May is no time to try to hire a staff, even if he'd wanted to. He hired his friend and ex-teammate, former New England Patriots three-time Super Bowl champion Mike Vrabel, to take over his job coaching linebackers. But otherwise, the staff remained intact. Tressel had always run the offense. Offensive coordinator/offensive-line coach Jim Bollman would take over those duties and became the lightning rod for criticism that most coordinators of struggling offenses become.

The coaching staff issues paled in comparison to the looming suspensions. Quarterback Terrelle Pryor, running back Daniel "Boom" Herron, wide receiver DeVier Posey, left tackle Mike Adams, and backup defensive lineman Solomon Thomas were all suspended for the first five games of the 2011 season for their involvement in the tattoo-and-memorabilia scandal. The suspensions of Herron (one game) and Posey (five) were later extended when the NCAA ruled that they'd been overpaid for part-time work from longtime Cleveland booster Bobby DiGeronimo, who was later banned from associating with the program. Pryor, regarded as the fulcrum for the transgressions, saw the writing on the wall and declared himself eligible for the NFL's supplemental draft eight days after Tressel's departure. The Oakland Raiders selected him in the third round.

The departure of Pryor the person was not lamented. He was considered immature and a prima donna inside the walls of the Woody Hayes Athletic Center. But Pryor the quarterback was irreplaceable, in part because Ohio State had no appealing successor. Joe Bauserman, a former minor league pitcher, was a little-used fifth-year senior. Braxton Miller was a true freshman. Kenny Guiton was an afterthought as a recruit a year earlier and remained that way. Taylor Graham was also unproven.

Without Herron, Posey, and Adams for the first half of the season, the offense figured to struggle, and it did. Bauserman played well in the opener against overmatched Akron, then faded badly. Miller eventually was handed the reins and showed both amazing running ability and rawness in the passing game, hurt by wide receivers who were as unprepared as he was. No one caught more than 14 passes all season.

Still, the Buckeyes had a realistic chance for the Big Ten championship until the 10th game of the season. Despite their typical superiority in talent, the Buckeyes usually struggle when they play Purdue at Ross-Ade Stadium. That was the case again on November 12. But the Buckeyes appeared to have pulled off a dramatic victory when Miller somehow eluded pressure and lobbed a touchdown pass to running back Jordan Hall to tie the game with 55 seconds left. The glee was short-lived. The extra-point kick was blocked, and Purdue won in overtime. A home loss followed to Penn State, which was in the midst of the breaking Jerry Sandusky scandal. Ohio State's seven-game winning streak against Michigan then ended in a 40–34 loss that left the Buckeyes with a record of 6–6, its first non-winning season since 1999. Ohio State had a chance to pull out a last-minute victory, but Miller's deep pass to an open Posey landed just beyond the receiver's outstretched hands.

By then, Fickell's fate had been sealed. He won universal respect for handling a difficult job with dignity. He refused to indulge in self-pity and would not allow it for his players. But he needed a dream season to keep the job, and this was nobody's idea of a dream season for Ohio State, unless you were a Michigan Wolverines fan.

"It became clear after the 10th game, the Purdue game, that I needed to do something different," Smith said.

The week of the Penn State game, Smith started with what he called his "game plan." His wife, Sheila, the former associate athletics director at the University of Nevada, Las Vegas, was his sounding board.

"I would talk to her about my strategy because she's been with me before when I've done this at other places," said Smith, formerly the athletics director at Eastern Michigan, Iowa State, and Arizona State. "She challenges me on my process."

Smith had a list of four candidates and two backups. But one was clearly at the top of the list: Urban Meyer, who'd won two national championships at Florida before stepping down for health-related reasons after the 2010 season.

"Urban was our target from the start," Smith said.

Smith had played football at Notre Dame, and Meyer had coached there a generation later. They'd met at some functions over the years but had no real relationship. He didn't know for sure whether Meyer would even be interested. But he had a good hunch. Smith and Florida athletics director Jeremy Foley are close—as are Foley and Meyer—and they talked about the likelihood that Meyer would be receptive. Meyer was raised in Ashtabula in the far northeastern corner of Ohio. A lifelong Buckeyes fan, Meyer got his college coaching start as a graduate assistant at Ohio State in 1986–1987.

"It was pretty easy for me to figure out that if I called, he'd be interested," Smith said.

This was all happening in mid-November. In the spread-the-news-before-it-happens world of the Internet, Meyer's coaching Ohio State was declared a *fait accompli* in October. Websites breathlessly declared that Meyer had already agreed to a contract.

The conventional "wisdom" was that it was for six years and worth at least $40 million

"It was all wrong," Smith said. "That was all wrong. I don't know where that stuff was coming from. It was so far off it was ridiculous."

That Meyer would be the prime candidate for the Ohio State job was hardly a stretch. Even before Tressel resigned, Meyer said he was inundated with phone calls from ESPN, friends, and colleagues.

"Fifty a day," he said. "I quit answering my phone. It was chaos. I'm at home in Gainesville. I said I'm not coaching this year and wasn't going to. I told the truth. There was nothing going on, and I don't know anything about it."

After resigning at Florida, Meyer was hired by ESPN as a color analyst for college football games. His first game was the Ohio State–Akron opener, but he rebuffed reporters seeking comment about his availability for the OSU job.

"I just wanted to do a good job for ESPN," Meyer said. "That's not easy. It certainly wasn't easy for me. I wanted to focus on that and nothing else."

But not even he could totally ignore the pangs of his former school during the game, and it had nothing to do with anything any Buckeyes player did during the 42–0 rout.

"When the band came out—The Best Damn Band In The Land— I remember I teared up a little bit," he said. "It was the first time I'd been back since 1987, and I remember how beautiful the stadium looked that day. It's everybody's dream to come back to your home stadium."

Meyer said he did his best to repel any impulse to think about the possibility of coaching the Buckeyes.

"If [any] did, I pushed it out real fast," he said.

But Meyer's game-day duties took him to Big Ten sites. He could not help but hear the scuttlebutt that the Ohio State job was increasingly likely to open or the premature reports that he'd already agreed to it.

"They had a couple of losses, and people were saying, 'I think they're going to make a change,'" he said. "Everybody thinks they know, but no one knew. The speculation was every day. Nowadays with social media, if you push 'enter' on your computer, you're a reporter. It's silly. I learned down at Florida to just kind of keep walking straight ahead. Don't look left and don't look right, because it'll drive you nuts. I didn't think twice about it."

But late in the season, on a visit to Cincinnati to see his ailing father, Bud, the topic became unavoidable. His father was on oxygen treatment, and Meyer knew his time was probably short. They were watching ESPN when a graphic appeared of Ohio State, speculating about the coaching job, along with a picture of Meyer.

"I remember sitting right next to him, looking at him, and he looks at that and then to me and he said, 'Are you going to do it?' I said, 'I don't know. What do you think?' He was quiet for about 20 seconds and looks over and goes, 'Nah, I kind of like it the way it is. I don't care who wins or loses.'"

For Bud Meyer, that was completely out of character.

"That tells you the wear and tear that games put on your family," Urban said. "So it was a very difficult time."

Bud Meyer died November 11 at age 79. Unfortunately, Gene Smith would soon have something in common with the coach he would pursue. A week later, Smith's mother, Elizabeth, died unexpectedly in Cleveland. Smith got a text on the evening of November 17, drove the two hours north, and stayed up all night. His mother died the next day.

Smith did not give himself time to grieve right away. The day after his mother's death, while Ohio State was losing to Penn State, Smith sent a text to Meyer asking him if he could call on Sunday. The next day, they spoke for the first time. The conversation lasted more than two and a half hours. They discussed philosophy, management style, the impending NCAA ruling, their families.

"I had a list of questions, but it went from there," Smith said. "What are his values in life? What does he cherish? What was it like to sit out a year?"

Both men thought the conversation went well, and Smith told Meyer he wanted him to be the next Buckeyes coach. Given his résumé and general contentedness—regardless of his desire to coach again—Meyer wasn't willing to submit to the typical interview process that most coaches endure. Either Ohio State wanted him or it didn't. He wasn't going to put his wife Shelley or his three kids, Nicki, Gigi, and Nate, through a prolonged process. Ohio State hadn't been the only school to approach him in the previous month.

"Five or six on-the-table job offers," he said.

He declined all of them on the spot.

"If it wasn't for Ohio State, I wouldn't have coached," he said.

Smith and Meyer also discussed his ESPN contract, and whether that would be an obstacle. It wouldn't. His contract expired with the final game of the season. He was supposed to do the Ohio State–Michigan game but decided that might not be such a swell idea.

Smith arranged a meeting for Wednesday in Atlanta, where Meyer had a visit planned to see Nicki, a volleyball player at Georgia Tech. Smith was joined by Ohio State president E. Gordon Gee, chief OSU fundraiser Jeff Kaplan, and board of trustees members Robert Schottenstein and Alex Shumate. Meyer brought Shelley.

"We're a team," he said.

To ensure secrecy, Smith arranged to meet at the downtown Renaissance Hotel, partly because cars could pull into its underground garage and park just steps away from a meeting room. No chance for enterprising media to even get a sniff of anything.

"I didn't want to go someplace where they're taking pictures," Meyer said.

The conversation lasted about three hours.

"It was really a get-to-know-you," Meyer said. "Obviously, Ohio State has gone through a very difficult time in the program. I wanted to know what the future held. I had a lot of concerns."

So did Ohio State officials. They asked Meyer about his health and requested that his doctors send OSU his records vouching for his well-being. Meyer had no problem with that.

"It was a very productive, great meeting," Meyer said.

Shelley Meyer, still quite skeptical about her husband's ability to handle a high-stress coaching job, was mostly assuaged.

"It was a formal meeting, but after five minutes it didn't feel like a formal meeting," she said. "Nobody was stuffy or prim and proper. Gordon said, first of all, that this is not an interview. We're just talking. We're just getting to know each other. He kind of set the tone that way. And Gordon's always joking around. We laughed. It ended up being very relaxed."

By the end of the meeting, she knew, whatever her misgivings, that a deal would be consummated. Over the next day or two, the two sides worked out contract terms, which went smoothly. Meyer agreed to a six-year, $24 million contract. So much for the $40 million bandied about on the Internet.

"They offered me something, and I said sure, and that was it," Meyer said. "It's never been about that."

Smith's business wasn't done that Wednesday. He had to tell Fickell that he would not be retained as head coach. When Fickell took the job, he asked Smith to inform him right away if the athletics director decided not to keep him as head coach beyond the 2011 season. Smith had promised him he would. So he flew back to Columbus right after the meeting with Meyer ended. While the men's basketball team was hammering Virginia Military Institute at the Schottenstein Center, Smith met with Fickell in the women's locker room to tell him that the Michigan game and bowl game would be his last as OSU's head coach.

"It was an awkward meeting," Fickell said. "But I respected Gene for what he had to do and what he was going to do. All I wanted was what was best for the program."

But that didn't remove the sting. If Smith planned to tell him who was likely to become the coach, Fickell wasn't in the mood to hear it.

"He had told me a few weeks prior that was he was looking at two guys—three, including me," Fickell said. "I don't know if he wanted to talk to me about it, and I really didn't want to talk about it."

It wasn't until Fickell did his weekly radio show the next day at the on-campus Fawcett Center that he saw ESPN discussing the possibility of Meyer that he learned the identity of his likely successor. The whole world may have known, but little permeates the coaching bubble, especially during Michigan week.

"[My assistants] were coming up to me hearing rumors, and I said, 'Guys, quit listening to rumors.' I was like Tress. 'Who cares?' But that was the first time I thought, *Well, maybe it is the case* [that Meyer will take over]. I didn't care. I didn't worry about it. I wouldn't allow myself to think about it because it had no bearing on the outcome of that game, and that was the only thing that was important."

Smith could identify with Fickell's feelings. Many years earlier, Smith served as interim athletics director at Eastern Michigan, where he had to give tours to each of the six candidates interviewing for the permanent AD job. That Smith got the job didn't cause him to forget the stress of would-be replacements interviewing for the job.

"I know how hard that is—the emotions," he said. "Luke was masterful."

Fickell didn't tell anyone, not even Amy, that his time as OSU's head coach was ending. Asked about his job status in the postgame press conference in Ann Arbor, Fickell got choked up. But he declined to address his situation out of respect for the rivalry. Even on the bus ride back to Columbus with Amy, Fickell kept mum. He hadn't told her beforehand because he didn't want to burden her with the truth, knowing she'd have to make the trip to Michigan and have to keep the news to herself. Both Fickells pride themselves on honesty, and Luke had told people he'd let them know as soon as he knew. But it became impossible to keep that pledge, even to his wife.

"I didn't want to keep it inside, but I felt it was the best for the situation," Fickell said. "She never asked. She didn't look at TV. She didn't worry about the rumors. That's kind of what we said: 'We're not going to get caught up in outside things and things we have no control over.'"

So all ride home, he stewed, upset at losing the game and worrying about how he was going to tell Amy that he wouldn't keep the job.

"I knew it would be emotional, and I didn't want her to be too emotional on the bus ride home," he said.

He finally told Amy when they arrived back in Columbus. As for his own future with Ohio State, Fickell had no idea. He didn't know that Smith had gone to bat for Fickell in his conversations with Meyer. Smith didn't try to insist that Meyer retain Fickell—that would have been unfair—but he did vouch for Fickell's character and coaching ability.

"I said it would be to our advantage, his advantage, and Buckeye Nation's advantage if when he went to the [introductory] press conference, he had an answer about Luke," Smith said.

In truth, Meyer was leaning against keeping Fickell. But a meeting between the men and their wives would change that.

· 2 ·

ASHTABULA

URBAN FRANK MEYER III is the son of parents who on the surface couldn't have been more different. His mom was born Gisela Gumpert in eastern Germany in December 1936. According to Meyer's older sister, Gigi Meyer Escoe, the Gumpert family owned a flour mill in Thuringia. Gisela's father was the town mayor. But their comfortable lives were destroyed by World War II and then the Communist takeover of East Germany when the country was divided after the war. The East German regime removed all remnants of capitalism. Gisela's father, Horst, was sent to a Russian prison camp where he was essentially starved. When he was released a few years later, Horst showed up at the family home weighing 80 pounds on his 6'-plus frame. He died three weeks later, leaving a widow and four children.

"My mother endured things like Communist youth camps and hiding in bomb shelters," Gigi said.

Gisela was the second-youngest of four children. Gisela's mom, Julianna, was desperate to escape to democratic West Germany, a few miles south. Her eldest child, Anna Marie, was already there studying to become a nurse. One night, a sympathetic East German prison guard told Gisela's mom that she and her children would be deported toward Prussia before dawn. If they were to escape into West Germany, it would have to be that night. So Julianna packed a bag of silver and other valuables and took Gisela and her brother Walter and escaped through a riverbed into West Germany.

Julianna's youngest child, Peter, was already in West Germany with a nanny. In her haste to cross the riverbed with her two children, she dropped the valuables.

"So she got to West Germany with very little material belongings," Gigi said.

Gisela enrolled in hotel school to become a chef. She trained in London, Paris, Switzerland, and Italy before making her way to the United States. She visited Anna Marie, who'd married a German-born American soldier and was working at the famous five-star Maisonette restaurant in Cincinnati. The owners of the Maisonette liked having servers with foreign accents and offered her a job. One of the regulars was a man named Urban Meyer, who found Gisela adorable and thought his namesake son, nicknamed Bud, would, too. Bud did. Bud and Gisela were married only a few months later.

Raised in the Western Hills section of Cincinnati, Bud's life had taken detours as well. According to Gigi, he went to seminary school with the intention of being a priest.

"After four years in the seminary, he decided he needed to be a married man," Gigi said.

Exceptionally bright, Bud went to the University of Cincinnati and studied to be a chemical engineer while also going through the Reserve Officers Training Corps program. He became a First Lieutenant in the Army between World War II and Korea, so he never saw combat. Gigi said he was in charge of the unit that taught Elvis Presley to drive a tank.

Bud and Gisela had had three children in a three-year span—Gigi, Urban, and Erika. Urban was born in Toledo on July 10, 1964, but grew up in Ashtabula in the far northeastern corner of Ohio. His father was an executive at Detrex, a chemical company. Gisela became executive luncheon chef at a high-end restaurant in Mentor. Later, she worked as a chef at the local country club and had a catering business on the side.

"She was an amazing cook," Gigi said. "Did it all by memory and taste. Nothing was written down, and she never looked at a cookbook."

Bud and Gisela's primary job, however, was raising their children—but with vastly different styles and personalities.

"A saint," Urban said of his mom. "I never heard her say a bad word about anybody. Just an incredible woman."

Gigi described her as "perfect and warm and loving, supportive and nonjudgmental. She was different than other people's moms because she had a different background."

Descriptions of Bud tend to portray him as almost a cardboard figure, as someone who was unreasonably demanding and harsh. Urban and Gigi dispute that. Oh, sure, he swore like a sailor. He was opinionated. He was blunt.

"But he wasn't the Christopher Plummer character in *The Sound of Music*," Gigi said. "That was not him. Somehow, the press has made him out to be hard and cold and unemotional."

At Christmastime, Bud would leave elf footprints around the house and put reindeer marks around the front yard. He attended all of his kids' games and events and kept a file with all of their report cards.

The oft-told reports that he insisted that his children be high achievers were absolutely true.

"That's the way we were raised as far as back as I can remember," Meyer said. "There are only two things that can happen. You can either win or lose. There's no gray area."

As Meyer points out, the results speak for themselves. Gigi is vice provost for undergraduate affairs at the University of Cincinnati. Erika served in the U.S. Air Force and now also lives in Cincinnati, where she works at Dunnhumby, which creates loyalty cards for businesses such as Kroger.

"I had a C one time—once," Meyer said. "It was made very clear that that was unacceptable. Average is not acceptable. There were consequences. His whole mindset of us growing up was, 'Average is not acceptable.' You don't have to be the most talented, but it was kind of like the Woody Hayes mentality—just outwork people."

The Meyers would much rather their children be active than sit around watching television. If that meant playing ball in the house and something broke, well, it wasn't the worst thing in the world.

"Our living room was like a great room," Gigi said. "That room had a few nicks and a few broken vases."

Care to guess the culprit? Urban was a good kid, though a bit mischievous, Gigi said. The Meyers lived on Lake Road, just a football field's length from Lake Erie. Though sailing was a big part of his life, Urban spent even more time on more traditional sports. He was a standout athlete, though it wasn't until high school that he really grew. What he had most was drive, prodded on by his father.

"We had a motto when we worked out: 100 percent, 100 percent of the time," said Greg "Mac" McCullough, a close friend of his at St. John High School. "That's what we lived by. We believe in that. We believe if you do that every day, you can sleep with ease and wake up the next day ready to do it again."

McCullough and Meyer were safeties on the football team under Paul Kopko and double-play partners on the baseball team. Bud Meyer was deeply involved in making sure they reached their potential.

"After football games on Friday nights, everybody went to McDonald's," McCullough said. "[We] were at his dad's watching film. That's what his father would make us do. His dad used to tape the games on a recorder and he would announce what we were doing and point it out on film. He'd ask, 'What the hell are you doing here? I don't understand. Explain it to me.'"

Bud Meyer helped conduct some of their drills. One for football consisted of having the boys stand 10 feet apart and throw at each other as hard as they could.

"And you had to catch with your hands," McCullough said. "He'd make us do that for a half-hour. Then we'd go to the beach and we'd have to wrestle in the water for a half-hour, which was one of the hardest things I've ever done in my life."

McCullough came to love Bud, but it took some time to get to understand him.

"His dad was very intense, a no-nonsense guy, very sarcastic," he said. "Until you got to know him, you wouldn't know he was joking around, but he was joking around."

Urban's competitiveness may have been stoked by his father, but it came naturally. Though several inches shorter than Meyer, McCullough was the superior basketball player. He can't recall Meyer ever beating him in one-on-one games at a neighbor's court, but it wasn't from lack of effort.

"He'd throw elbows, anything he could to try to beat me," McCullough said. "He was so relentless and so not willing to lose, especially to me. He was six inches taller, but he couldn't shoot. I used to call him, 'The Bricklayer.' We would come off that court and we'd have blood coming off our knees and elbows from falling down. That was his intensity of, 'I'm not going to lose to you.' We would fight about it and scream at each other. Then when it was all over, we'd sit down and have fun again. We would play for hours. His dad would laugh at us."

No matter the score, Meyer demanded the best out of himself and others. One game, Meyer's St. John baseball team was in the middle of a 39–0 victory—yes, 39–0. It was oppressively hot, and as the score got out of hand, the umpire's strike zone expanded. Most batters would have grudgingly accepted that. Not Meyer. He was so upset at a called strike that he got ejected. The funny thing—not to Meyer—was that the pitch was only strike two, not three.

"It was a terrible call," Meyer recalled with a wry smile. "I didn't say the F-bomb, but I said some bad things."

St. John coach Bill Schmidt was more amused than angry.

"At least wait until the umpire calls you out, you know?" Schmidt said.

As he matured physically late in his high school career, Meyer developed into a shortstop with power potential.

"He was a tremendous shortstop," Schmidt said. "He had an unbelievable arm. If you watch a baseball game and watch the shortstop go into the hole and make the throw, that was Urban's signature play."

Major League teams took notice, and the Atlanta Braves selected him in the 13th round of the 1982 draft. Meyer wasn't yet 18 when he was drafted, and he said he was the youngest player taken that year.

Meyer was a straight arrow when he joined the Braves' Gulf Coast League (Rookie) team in the summer of '82. "[I was] from a small town, kind of sheltered, [from] a small Catholic school," he said. "I saw some things I'd never seen before." While he was dutifully going to bed at 9:00 or 10:00 PM after doing his 300 push-ups a night, his roommate was living the stereotypically carousing professional jock life.

"I smelled it coming out of his pores," Meyer said of his room-mate's drinking. "He hits a home run and could barely open his eyes."

The tightly wound Meyer had trouble dealing with failure for the first time. Baseball requires equilibrium. Coping with going 0-for-4 is essential. Too often with Meyer, such nights—and they were frequent—would result in shattered bats. He hit .170 in 53 at-bats in the Gulf Coast League his first season. Discouraged, he wanted to give up and return to Ashtabula. His father would have none of it, saying that he wouldn't tolerate a quitter. Meyer did better the next year, hitting .250 for Pulaski in the Appalachian League and hitting his only professional home run. But he injured ligaments in his throwing elbow, and that ended his baseball career.

He enrolled at the University of Cincinnati, where he became a walk-on backup defensive back. It was there, in May 1984 at his Sigma Chi fraternity Derby Day party, that he met Shelley Mather, a freshman nursing student.

"He wanted to talk to me, and he made a gesture to one of his fraternity brothers to get my attention so that I would go talk to him," Shelley said. "We spoke for just a few minutes that day. I was already in a relationship with a boy back home. We talked, and he said, 'Well, if you ever get rid of that boyfriend, you know where I am.'"

Shelley had grown up about 50 miles south of Columbus on a farm in tiny Lattaville, which she guessed had a population of 200. She was a three-sport athlete at Frankfort High School and had won Miss Ross County Junior Fair Queen after her senior year, but she had never been any place bigger than Cincinnati.

"He grew up in a different place and had a lot different experiences than me," she said. "He was way more worldly than me."

She liked Meyer but had that boyfriend back home. In any case, she almost sabotaged any chance for a future relationship with a flippant comment after Meyer told her about his ambitions.

"When I knew him for three weeks, at the end of my freshman year, he told me that he aspired to be a coach," Shelley said. "I said, 'I don't think I want to be married to a coach.' Again, I'd known him for three weeks. He said, 'Marriage?! Who's talking about marriage?'"

"I didn't know what a coach did. When I think about that now, now that I'm 48, I think, *Where did that come from?* I'm surprised he didn't run."

Meyer didn't run. He was already smitten.

"Immediately," he said. "You hear stories about that. I realized she was different. She was tough and strong and didn't go for the nonsense that college guys give to college girls."

Shelley broke up with her boyfriend, and she and Urban quickly became a couple. Meyer never did become a starter at UC and switched majors several times. He started as a math major until freshman calculus made him reconsider that idea. He switched to architecture and then broadcasting before settling on a major that he describes as being "priceless" in his coaching career—psychology.

"I fell in love with it," he said. "It blew me out of the water. As the classes get smaller when you're a junior and senior, it becomes real."

His favorite class was Theory of Motivation. The class would break into small groups and discuss the most powerful forms of motivation.

"We came up with love, fear, hate, and survival," Meyer said. "It was love, fear, and hate at first. I later added survival. That's when you see moms pick up cars [to save their child]. You do things your body really can't do. But love, fear, and hate, that's how you motivate."

That has been a foundation of Meyer's coaching philosophy.

"I want that kid to love me or hate me or fear me," he said. "You use them all. Each kid is different."

· 3 ·

CLIMBING THE COACHING LADDER

TOM LICHTENBERG WALKED into St. Xavier High School in Cincinnati to visit a coaching friend. It was 1986, and Lichtenberg was the Ohio State quarterbacks and wide receivers coach under Earle Bruce. Lichtenberg, who'd coached at nearby Purcell High School, was buddies with St. X coach Steve Rasso. At OSU, Lichtenberg was responsible for recruiting the fertile Cincinnati area. He'd recently signed St. X quarterback Greg Frey to play for the Buckeyes. Lichtenberg also was in charge of Ohio State's graduate assistant program, so his ears perked up when Rasso asked him a question.

"He just said out of the clear blue sky, 'You're not looking for any graduate assistants, are you?'" Lichtenberg said.

As a matter of fact, he was. He asked whom Rasso had in mind. He mentioned a volunteer assistant coach and University of Cincinnati grad named Urban Meyer.

Rasso quickly located Meyer, who made an immediate impression on Lichtenberg. He told Lichtenberg that he wanted to become a coach and was looking for an opportunity to get a foot in the door.

"He felt he was the right guy for the job," said Lichtenberg, who died of cancer in May 2013 at age 72. "He left you with a feeling of self-confidence. 'If you hire me, you've hired the right guy.'"

Lichtenberg needed someone to assist him coaching wide receivers, so he asked Meyer about his expertise with them.

"I don't know if he knew anything about coaching receivers, but he made me feel he did," Lichtenberg said.

Meyer went to Columbus that weekend to meet with the coaches. Some were more enthusiastic about learning about the potential GAs—the low men on the coaching totem pole—than others. Bruce would count among the others.

"I went to Earle," Lichtenberg said with a laugh, "and said, 'Coach, I've got a graduate assistant I really like.' He looked at me and—this is exactly what he said—'Hey, I don't have time for that shit. You take care of it.'"

And so Urban Meyer's college coaching career was born.

*　　*　　*　　*

FROM THE START, Meyer tried to set himself apart. He found a willing mentor in second-year GA Tim Hinton, now Ohio State's fullbacks/tight ends coach.

"He's a guy who was full of energy and wanted to learn and be good and would take the time to do a little extra," Hinton said. "He was a really good guy to have on the staff. He coached tight ends in '86, and in '87 he ended up taking wide receivers from me and doing a great job. He was very self-assured and knew what to do. For some guys, it's kind of intimidating when you get there. I don't know whether it was because he'd been in minor league baseball and had been around the block a little bit and was a little bit older [that he wasn't intimidated]."

Pictures from the time show Meyer as a young, serious coach— and sporting quite the mustache.

"It was the look, man," Hinton said, laughing.

Hinton had one, too, proudly. "Absolutely," he said. "There were a bunch of us who had them. And we looked good, too."

Lichtenberg was stretched thin with his duties, so he was happy to give someone as eager as Meyer more responsibility. "He was way more than a GA," Lichtenberg said. "My title was offensive coordinator, and I coached quarterbacks and receivers. You can't coach that many guys. He was basically my assistant, coaching receivers. He did a lot of the drills with them. We'd sit down and break down film on coverages we'd see."

Back then, putting together tape wasn't the simple process of pressing of a few buttons to sync footage that it is now in the digital age. Film had to be physically spliced. "It was a hard job," Lichtenberg said. "He did a great job. I had a lot of confidence in him. I'd bring kids in for recruits, and he'd take them on college visits. One of them was [future OSU quarterback and ESPN college football analyst] Kirk Herbstreit."

In 1987, Shelley graduated from UC and moved to Columbus to begin her career as a psychiatric nurse. "Finally, we were in the same city—it was hard being in separate cities—but we didn't see that much of each other," said Shelley, who lived with a nursing friend. "He was always working, and I worked a lot of double shifts because I really loved my job and was trying to make money."

Finances were an issue for Meyer, too. To make ends meet, Meyer took a graveyard shift at Consolidated Freightways. Shelley called it his "Archie Bunker job," referring to the blue-collar lead character of the sitcom *All in the Family*. He went out and bought steel-toed boots for his job and operated a forklift and loaded trucks for $16 an hour. That was good pay back then.

"Three days a week, just to pay my rent," Meyer said. "I'd go to work at 6:00 PM and work until 6:00 AM, take a shower, and come in here to work."

He became an expert at stretching a dollar. He quickly learned which local dives had cheap happy hours. Though Urban and Shelley didn't see that much of each other, he was able to get her a ticket to Ohio State games as one of the few perks of his job. Shelley had gone to UC games at Nippert Stadium, but there was no comparison with games at Ohio Stadium.

"Amazing. Unbelievable," she said. "That's when I fell in love with college football. I learned a lot about the game and tradition of college football, especially Ohio State's tradition."

But never did she imagine that one day she'd return as the wife of Ohio State's head coach. Still, a football wife she'd become. Shelley and Urban got engaged in 1988 and married in 1989.

"She's awesome," Gigi Meyer Escoe said of her sister-in-law. "Shelley and Urban have the real deal. They're perfect for each other. She's fun as hell. She loves to dance. She gets football. She's completely confident on her own. I think that's why she's good at this. She's a very accomplished woman all on her own."

But it took some time for her to realize all the sacrifices required for a young coach—and his wife. When they got married, Meyer was in the second year of his first full-time coaching job under, coincidentally, Jim Heacock at Illinois State. The Redbirds were a dismal team, and Meyer made only $6,000. He was so strapped for money that first year that he slept on a friend's couch and kept his clothes in his car.

"When he got his first job and I saw how little money he got for working 18 hours, I thought, *This is really crazy*," Shelley said.

Meyer moved on to Colorado State in 1990 when Bruce, who'd been fired by Ohio State in 1987, offered him a job. The Meyers loved it there. Their two daughters, Nicki and Gigi, were born in Fort Collins. Shelley never wanted to leave. She loved the climate and had formed deep friendships. Meyer began to blossom as a coach.

"He was very intent on being successful in whatever he did," Bruce said. "That's what made him a good recruiter, a good coach, a good leader of young men."

Bruce recalled having a star player—he didn't want to name him—who was having personal problems. Bruce made him Meyer's personal project.

"I said, 'You've got to save him because he's in trouble,'" Bruce said. "I said that you've got to stay with him and make him part of your family for a while. He and Shelley did that. They turned the kid around and made it possible for him to graduate. It was a real work of art. He's a very successful person now, all to the credit of Urban."

To Meyer, that was just part of being a coach.

"I didn't have to have him tell me to do that," Meyer said. "My wife and I, that's the way we saw Earle and Jean Bruce do it. I learned it from him. Shelley is so gifted. She gets it. She gets what these kids need. She as much as anybody saved that kid and has saved many kids."

Bruce was fired after a 5–7 season in 1992, but Meyer developed a deep affection for his successor, Sonny Lubick, who kept him on the staff. Lubick had a gentler style than Bruce, and some of that—some—rubbed off on Meyer. He learned he could dial down the volume, if not the intensity, and still get results.

Lubick wasn't the only influential person he met while at Colorado State. Meyer's recruiting territory included Southern California. A former CSU player who lived there named Hiram de Fries became a highly successful Shell Oil Company executive and attorney. He was an efficiency expert who, among other achievements, led a team in a joint project with the Mars candy company in creating the pay-at-the-pump credit-card machine. De Fries also served as a volunteer assistant high school football coach at Mission Viejo High School near Los Angeles. He became an important recruiting contact, and then much more to Meyer. The young coach and the man 23 years his elder clicked from the start. Meyer was impressed with de Fries' intellect, generosity of spirit, and wisdom. De Fries discerned Meyer's potential from the start.

"He had a mind like a sponge," de Fries said. "He just sucked things up, and he always wanted to know, 'Why?' He could absorb and process information better than most people I've ever met in my life. But then he's [also] performance-driven. He has a way of taking all that in and getting it focused and going."

De Fries became so close with Meyer that he followed him to Utah, Florida, and then Ohio State as an under-the-radar but trusted advisor. De Fries was among the first people Meyer invited to join him with the Buckeyes.

"He's my alignment coach," Meyer said. "I just always want to make sure there are no hidden agendas in our program. He understands how organizations and businesses work. He understands the power of one is much better than a bunch of independent contractors. He's my eyes and ears of the program and the players."

De Fries and his wife also became close to Bud Meyer. Hiram was impressed with the elder Meyer's intelligence and amused by his bluntness. He recalled an agitated Bud getting in de Fries' car for a ride to the Salt Lake City airport after a Utah game years later when Urban was the Utes' head coach. Apparently, there'd been a decision Urban had made that didn't meet Bud's approval.

"He gets in the car, doesn't say 'hi' or anything, and says, 'Who called that play?' de Fries recalled, laughing. "My response was, 'Well, you can start with your son.'

"You could see where Urban's performance-driven [philosophy] comes from. He was a really good guy. I miss him."

Meyer's mom, Gisela, died in 2000 after a long bout with cancer.

"They had an absolutely beautiful marriage," Gigi Escoe said. "He sponge-bathed my mother when she was dying."

Even at the beginning of Meyer's climb up the ladder as an assistant coach, his mom had always predicted success for her son.

"She was my biggest fan," Meyer said. "'You're going to be a great head coach. I can't wait for you to be a head coach'—just when I started on the journey. I guess it was a realistic expectation, but at the time, I'm like, 'What are you talking about? I'm not going to be the head coach at Notre Dame or Ohio State.'"

He said he thinks about his mother every day.

"I'm always saying a prayer," he said. "But I know she's paying attention."

*   *   *   *

AS COMFORTABLE AS Colorado State was for the Meyers, it was still a second-tier program. When Notre Dame coach Lou Holtz asked Meyer to become his wide receivers coach in 1996, Shelley knew they'd be packing for South Bend. Early in their relationship, Urban and Shelley came to an agreement that she could have a say in any potential coaching move unless the call came from one of three schools—Ohio State, Michigan, or Notre Dame. Meyer, who's Catholic, grew up loving the Fighting Irish as well as the Buckeyes. The Michigan part came from Meyer's deep respect for former coach Bo Schembechler, though he is loath to even mention that school by name now.

"When he went to interview with Lou, I was just so scared," Shelley said. "I didn't want to go. [I thought], *Maybe he won't get it, maybe he won't get it.*"

He did get it. When Holtz called to offer Meyer the job, Shelley answered the phone, handed it to her husband, and burst into tears. "I knew there was nothing I could do or say," she said. "He was taking that job, and we were moving."

Soon enough, Shelley wouldn't be the only one who wished Holtz hadn't made that call to offer Urban Meyer a job.

Bobby Brown was a redshirt freshman at Notre Dame when his new wide receivers coach arrived. His previous position coach, former Fighting Irish quarterback Tom Clements, had a laid-back style. The new guy, uh, didn't. Asked about his first day of practice under Meyer, Brown laughed.

"I try and forget it," said Brown, now a lawyer with an MBA who's in the sports entertainment business. "It was very intense. I was still trying to get my confidence to the level it needed to be to play on the college level. It wasn't there yet. And he has a very passionate way of finding that lack of confidence and exploiting it. That's what happened."

Meyer told his players that he wasn't there to be friends with them. He was there to make them better. Period.

"He was very transparent about how intense he was going to be," Brown said. "He was very transparent that he was going to give seniors every chance to play and succeed, and that he believed in that as a coach. He expected us to be the best receivers in the country as a group, and that was his job."

Wide receivers are often regarded as prima donnas, players more interested in making highlight plays than reveling in grunt work like blocking. Meyer made it a point to disabuse his players of any notion he'd accept that.

"Before you become a good wide receiver, you've got to be tough," Meyer said. "And some of them aren't real tough. We did a lot of stuff without the ball. We said, 'Keep the balls in the bag. You've got to earn getting the balls out of the bag.'"

Brown recalls a drill the players referred to as "butt 'em ups" in which players collided against each other, often leading with their helmets. (This was in the 1990s, before widespread awareness of concussions stemming from repetitive head contact.)

"There were some times when I think the football managers wanted to give us a hug because they felt so sorry for us," Brown said. "It was his way. He let you know from the very beginning. You couldn't say, 'I had no idea it was coming.' It's what he said from the very first meeting. It was how he coached in every practice, in every game. It was all about intensity."

Even Shelley Meyer felt bad for her husband's players because of his relentless coaching.

"I thought he was a lunatic at times, a raving lunatic," she said. "He was crazy. That's where I saw the Earle Bruce in him. I love Earle and have the utmost respect [for him], but he was a hard guy. He was a rough coach and a hard-nosed coach, like Woody. Urban idolized Woody and Earle."

When Shelley would suggest to her husband that he ease up a little, he answered that he had his methods and had been successful doing things his way.

Mickey Marotti, then a Notre Dame strength coach and one of Meyer's closest confidants, admired Meyer's intensity but worried about its possible consequences. "He's pretty close with his wife," Marotti said, "and we both told him back in 1998 that you're not going to make it to 40. You need to calm down. I knew at some point he was going to have to take a chill pill, to use a layman's term."

Meyer's body would make that point clear. He began having major headaches, which was later diagnosed as coming from an arachnoid cyst on his brain. It was a minor condition, but displays of temper can cause the pain to flare.

"He calmed down after he found out about the arachnoid cyst," Shelley said. "He learned he didn't have to scream all the time."

By then, Meyer's roughest edges had been softened by his experience with Lubick. But turning down the volume didn't mean reducing the intensity. It would have been hard to convince Brown that his coach could have been much tougher. At times, Brown admits, he wanted to slug Meyer. He resisted the temptation because he'd grown up with disciplinarian parents who taught him better. Besides, the players may not have loved Meyer's methods, but they could see that it produced results. They did learn how to block. They did learn to be tough. They learned that the pressure he put on them in practice prepared them to handle playing in front of 80,000 fans.

Brown said he was as headstrong as Meyer, so they had an uneasy relationship during the player's career at Notre Dame. That came to a head when Brown got an unsportsmanlike conduct penalty late in a game at Michigan in 1999 that contributed to the Irish's last-minute loss. Brown was flagged for taunting after scoring a touchdown. A gesture he said was meant to honor the national fraternity he belonged to was misconstrued by officials as taunting. On the sideline, Brown, by his own admission, used disrespectful words with Meyer. The next week, Meyer wouldn't let Brown start. After Notre Dame's 5–7 season ended in a loss to Stanford, Brown was unsure how he'd leave his relationship with Meyer. But as Brown walked to the bus to go to the airport and passed by Meyer, he got a surprise. Meyer stopped him and told him that he was proud of him, that he'd improved dramatically and that he'd be happy to help him any way he could.

"I don't know if he remembers those two minutes, but for me it was something I'll never forget."

All these years later, Brown said he's thankful for the experience he had, playing for Meyer. "He was instrumental in making me the man that I am," he said. "I think that's the power college coaches have. They're taking someone from young manhood to manhood. That's a very powerful time to be in someone's life."

Meyer's reputation grew during his Notre Dame years, and he was formulating a philosophy in preparation for becoming a head coach. He had seen a new type of offense run at Kansas State under Bill Snyder and at the University of Louisville under John L. Smith and offensive coordinator Scott Linehan. Intrigued, he asked Holtz successor Bob Davie if he could take graduate assistant Dan Mullen and drive to Louisville for a one-day trip. One day became four as Meyer learned the ins and outs of this new offense called the spread. He became an instant devotee. When Bowling Green was looking for a head coach after the 2000 season and called Earle Bruce, asking for candidates, Bruce suggested Meyer.

Meyer had turned down a couple of previous head-coaching opportunities because he wasn't sure he was ready. He felt ready now, but he still resisted. Bowling Green was hardly anyone's idea of a dream job. The Falcons hadn't had a winning season since 1994.

He called Holtz and told him he intended to turn it down.

"It's a bad job," Meyer said.

"Of course, it is," Holtz replied. "If it was a good job, why would they call you?"

That convinced Meyer, who took the plunge, eager to implement the spread and see how far he could ride it.

On December 4, 2000, Meyer, 36, was announced as the Bowling Green head coach. Thus began a decade of phenomenal success as a head coach. But it was also one that looked like it was destined to end with a crash landing.

· 4 ·

RISE AND FALL

URBAN MEYER'S ASCENT to the top of his profession was rapid. At Bowling Green, he and his ambitious young staff would meet in the bowels of Doyt Perry Stadium for countless hours, figuring out how to fully exploit this new toy they'd developed called the spread.

"We all sat in that nasty meeting room at Bowling Green, Ohio, where every time it rained the water would drip down on the table," Meyer recalled. "It was incredible. The months of February and March, we'd come in for 10 hours, [analyzing everything] from the huddle to the snap count, because there was no other model."

Meyer and his staff, which included Greg Studrawa, Gregg Brandon, and Dan Mullen, did take elements from several other programs using the spread. They watched tape of Northwestern, who, under the late Randy Walker, used a version of the offense. They studied Purdue's basketball-on-grass spread, looking for things to poach. They saw what Rich Rodriguez, long before his ill-fated stint at Michigan, was doing at West Virginia. But Bowling Green, a lower-echelon MAC program, couldn't get enough of the caliber of athletes a Big Ten or Big East team could. Meyer and his staff would have to improvise.

They relished the challenge.

"It was one of the greatest experiences I've ever had," Meyer said. "There was no model. Go build something. But there was no book to build it. I really enjoyed it."

In his very first game, Meyer's hopes were validated. Seemingly outmanned Bowling Green upset Missouri 20–13. The next year, the Tigers traveled to northwest Ohio, expecting revenge. The Falcons drilled them 51–28. Meyer attributed it to the scheme, executed by a talented quarterback from Columbus named Josh Harris.

This spread thing had a future.

"People had no idea how to stop it," Meyer said. "Defenses weren't near as sophisticated as they are now, and we had a really good player at quarterback, Josh Harris. We had a distinct schematic advantage."

Meyer resurrected Bowling Green's down-and-out program, taking the Falcons to a 17–6 record in two seasons before leaving for Utah. In two seasons with the Utes, he finished 10–2 in 2003 and 12–0 in 2004, his only undefeated season until 2012. At Florida, he reached the pinnacle. In his second season, the Gators were only on the periphery of the national championship picture until upsets of higher-ranked teams gave them a shot at No. 1 Ohio State in the BCS title game.

For Meyer, coaching against the team he'd grown up following was surreal.

"It was the national championship game," he said. "You want them to be a faceless opponent, and they really are for a while."

That changed after practice moved from Gainesville to Glendale, Arizona, a week before the game. As is customary, Meyer had director of football video/software operations Brian Voltolini pump in the music associated with the opponent to simulate what the game-day experience will be.

"We're at practice," Meyer said, "and I tell him to raise the music, and it's 'Hang on Sloopy,' my favorite song of all time, and I remember thinking, *Oh my God, it's really happening.*"

Ohio State was a one-touchdown favorite, and the Buckeyes' Ted Ginn Jr. returned the opening kickoff for a touchdown [before sustaining a game-ending injury in the celebration]. But after that, Florida dominated. The Buckeyes were no match for the speed of Florida's linemen and had no answer to the spread as the Gators moved the chains at will in a stunning 41–14 upset.

It could have been more lopsided.

"We kind of knelt on the ball or ran the ball a bunch of times," Meyer said. "I have a lot of respect for Jim Tressel and a lot of respect for Ohio State."

For the rest of the Meyer family, it was as much relief as joy.

"It was a nightmare," Shelley said of playing the Buckeyes. "It couldn't have been worse. All our family was Ohio State fans. We loved Ohio State. Urban loved Ohio State. Of all the teams, we had to play them? It was hard, but at the end of the day we had to win. I've rooted for Ohio State every day except January whatever-that-was in 2007."

Two years later, behind quarterback Tim Tebow, who'd won the Heisman Trophy the year before, Florida won another national championship by beating Oklahoma 24–14 in Miami.

Meyer was king of the college football world. But fissures had begun to form in the Gators program, and the toll hit Meyer hard and fast. He had always been hard-driving. Now that strength was turning into a weakness. He skipped meals. He skipped workouts. Many of Meyer's cadre of trusted assistant coaches had earned promotions elsewhere, so he didn't have them to fall back on.

"He lost a ton of weight in 2009 because the pressure was so immense," Shelley Meyer said. "You can't just win a national championship or two. You don't get a free pass. You really don't. You think you should, but you don't because then everyone wants more and more. The media want more, and the fans want more. It's really hard to keep it going in that direction all the time—up, up, up."

The week of the 2009 SEC Championship Game against Alabama, star defensive end Carlos Dunlap was arrested for driving under the influence and suspended. A few days later, the Gators lost to the Crimson Tide. Earle Bruce attended the game and was alarmed by what he saw from Meyer.

"He was not right," Bruce said. "I said, 'What the hell's the matter with you?' He was talking nonsense, and he doesn't normally talk nonsense."

That night, Meyer awoke in the middle of the night yelling about severe chest pains. For 30 seconds, Shelley thought he was having a heart attack. She frantically called 9-1-1. As a nurse, she soon realized after taking his vital signs that it wasn't his heart, but that only diminished her fear slightly. It was later determined that Meyer had been stricken by esophageal spasms, which can mimic the symptoms of a heart attack.

But there was no denying that Meyer's health wasn't good, physically or emotionally. Dunlap was hardly the first Florida player who'd been arrested, but that one, particularly its timing, may have been the last straw.

"That player getting arrested, it messed up our whole mojo, and Urban took it so hard," Shelley said. "Urban took it personally that that kid did that. That kid did not do that to Urban. He did it because he was a kid who made a stupid decision. But Urban just put so much of himself into them that anytime there was a problem, he took it personally. It just crushed his spirit."

When things went wrong with the football team, Meyer thought he could solve it by working harder. He'd dissect film endlessly, probing for problems and solutions. He'd draw up different punt formations. He called and texted assistant coaches in the middle of the night. He'd sleep for only a couple hours at a time.

"[I drove] everybody nuts—players, coaches," Meyer said.

Compounding it was the physical pain from the esophageal spasms. He said that for three years—on and off—he felt as if somebody was hitting him with a shovel in the chest. He would stand on the sideline and pound his own chest trying to relieve the shooting pain.

When his older daughter, Nicki, arrived home for winter break after her first semester at Georgia Tech, she was stunned by how gaunt her father looked. She was so taken aback that she just looked at him and stared.

"I went from August to December without seeing him at all," Nicki said. "When I finally did see him and hugged him, I thought, *Oh my gosh*. He'd gone through a lot of changes. One second he was fine and healthy, and he lost a lot of weight and was exhausted. It hit me really hard because I had no idea what was going on. It was just a huge shock. I swear if that ever happens again, I will go nuts because that was one of the scariest things I'd ever seen. It was really sad because I could tell he wasn't happy. He looked skinny and he looked tired."

However unrelentingly serious Meyer had always seemed to the outside world, at home he was relaxed and, in Nicki's words, "a goofball."

"It's funny because on TV you see this crazy, intense, straight-faced coach," she said. "When he comes home, he's not that way at all. He's the funny one, the one who pulls the pranks and jokes. You'd never believe that because of the way he presents himself when he's coaching. It's funny. He's actually the complete opposite."

Told of his daughter's characterization of him, Meyer gave a sheepish laugh.

"Yeah, she's right," he said. "Absolutely. I take great pride in that, too."

Once, he found old photographs in a photo album of Shelley in a bathing suit, took them out, and plastered them all over the house. "So when she woke up that day, she's like, 'Where the heck did you find those?'" Nicki said.

Shelley said that when they're at the airport together, he'll sometimes sneak away and stay just out of her range of vision while reporting things she's doing until she spots him.

That's the father Nicki had been used to. Seeing him so subdued when she came home from college made the difference that much starker.

"He's one of the most lively, funny people I've ever met," Nicki said. "To see someone like that not joking around after not seeing you in three months, you knew something had gone wrong."

Meyer could see the fear in her face.

"You get in your cocoon and you don't realize it," he said. "Then I kind of evaluated it. 'Whoa, we've got a problem here.'"

On Christmas, Meyer told Shelley and their three kids that he would step down as Florida's coach to focus on them and his health. Relieved as they were, there was also the sense that the decision was too impulsive.

"I know when you're in crisis, you don't make big, life-changing decisions," Shelley said, drawing on her psychiatric training. "I kept telling him that."

The next day, Meyer did reconsider. He rescinded his resignation and took a leave of absence instead. He didn't travel during the final phase of recruiting and reduced his overall workload. But the 2010 season served to confirm that Meyer did need a prolonged break. Without Tebow, the Gators went only 7–5 in the regular season, Meyer's worst record as a head coach.

Florida running backs coach Stan Drayton had been with Meyer on and off throughout their coaching careers. He was a graduate assistant at Bowling Green when Meyer was hired there. He was at Florida with Meyer from 2005 to 2007 and returned there for the ill-fated 2010 season.

"Yeah, it was a rocky year," Drayton said. "They had a coach who was initially going to retire and then came back. I'm sure that played on the mindset of that team to some degree. You had a bunch of coaches coming and going. They were getting opportunities elsewhere. You had so much going on that year. You had a huge transition of some of your key players and your key leadership leaving because of graduation or leaving early—Tim Tebow and [linebacker] Brandon Spikes. So you've got a lot going on."

To Drayton, the fire in Meyer that produced two national championships had flickered. He wasn't as aggressive. Drayton could see how concerned Shelley and the kids were about his well-being. That couldn't help but trickle down to the coaching staff.

"If things are not okay at home, how can you come to work and pretend that things are okay?" Drayton said. "You can't operate like that, especially in this business."

Drayton understood that Meyer felt the need to dial down his hard-driving ways to preserve his health. But at what cost? "At the end of the day, if Urban Meyer can't wear his emotion on his sleeve and reveal a little bit of urgency for the sake of the team and the sake of the coaching staff and be intense and be who he is," Drayton said, "is that really the Urban Meyer that you want?"

By the end of the regular season, Meyer was spent. On December 8, 2010, he resigned again, this time for good.

"I didn't feel right," Meyer said. "I felt like something was severely wrong. I felt I was cheating my kids. I was in a bad place. It's hard to explain why. But the more I talked to people and people reached out to me, a lot of people are going through it, where they're consumed by their work. I thought there was something with my health and it turned out to be very manageable—esophageal spasms.

"I actually had a bad day the year before and just didn't feel right and didn't give it time to get away from it. [After the 2010 season], I just felt it was time. My two girls were playing volleyball in college, and I wanted to watch them play, never dreaming that Ohio State, my home state, would be looking for a coach. I really thought it was over."

It was at younger daughter Gigi's signing announcement that she would play at Florida Gulf Coast University that it hit home to Meyer how out of whack he'd become. Gigi thanked Shelley for being at all her high school matches and activities. She then pointed out that her father hadn't. That cut to the bone. Shelley said that Gigi didn't intend for the words to bite so hard. Shelley and the three Meyer children understood that coaching a program like Florida's had demands that most fathers' jobs don't. But Meyer took the message to heart.

"That was a tough day," he said. "The emotional tugging and drama, that wears on you. What matters most to me are those kids."

Meyer was always aware of the dangers of coaches becoming so consumed with their jobs that they lost sight of family. He didn't want to grow into old age becoming, as he put it, "that guy"—who sits around the table with his buddies, reminiscing about this championship or that one, only to realize how hollow they were because he'd missed important events in his family's life.

"I felt I was becoming that guy," Meyer said.

Drayton saw the change in Meyer and in society that contributed to his difficulties.

"He is a man who's completely invested into these young men," he said. "Anytime you're invested to young men like that, both feet in, you're going to deal with the decisions they make and the immaturity that they bring. With social media, these kids compare themselves to the president of the United States at times. They really think they're the best thing since sliced bread.

"When you get those kids, at that point it's your job to raise them and try to change their mindset. To sit there and say it's an easy task, it's a lie. It's not easy. It takes a toll on you. It takes time. It forces a coach to take time away from his family because you're raising these young men, in some respects, as much as your own family and sometimes more than that. If it gets out of control, you can, as a coach, lose personal balance in your life. It's the nature of what we do. We sign up for it. But at the same time, maintaining balance is going to allow you to reach your full potential as a coach."

Meyer coached the Gators in the Outback Bowl. He went out on a high note, leading Florida to a 37–24 victory over Penn State in what turned out to be Joe Paterno's final bowl game as Nittany Lions coach. At the time, Meyer figured it might be his last game as coach, too. His family hoped so, as well.

"As great as it is when you win, when you don't win and things are just not going well and fans aren't happy and your family isn't happy, it's like the worst ever," Shelley said. "You're just in the tank. It's so silly when I think about it. I have perspective. I know losing football games isn't the worst thing in the world. I know that. Sometimes I question whether other people know that. I was ready to move on with my life and not let that continue to get me down. But when your husband is in the house and totally in the tank and can't pull out of it, it affects your life in every way, every moment. I'm thinking, *Jeez, I don't have time for this. I want to get on with life here.*"

Shelley was ready for her husband to pursue something else, something less stressful.

But it wouldn't take long for the pangs of coaching to return. Shortly after taking the ESPN job, Meyer went on a walk with Shelley. He turned to her with words he knew she wouldn't like.

"I think I made a mistake," he said.

"What are you talking about?" Shelley said.

"I don't know if I can do this," Urban replied, referring to abandoning coaching.

"That was the first time we'd had that conversation," Meyer recalled. "She looked at me like I was nuts and said, 'Well, you need to give it some time.' And I did."

Just as she'd done when Meyer resigned abruptly after the 2009 SEC Championship Game, Shelley counseled patience.

"I was like, 'Oh no, we're not even talking about this, can't even talk about this. You haven't even been debriefed yet,'" she said. "That's what I kept telling him. You're not giving this enough time.

It's a term we use in the psych world. After you go through something traumatic, you have to have a processing period where you come down from that trauma. I'm dramatizing it a little bit, but it was traumatic. You have to step away and look at it and process it and see exactly what happened and deal with it. I told him he hadn't even grieved yet. He lost his profession for a little bit there, and you have to go through a grieving process."

Meyer's first steps toward reengagement with college football came when he went on a series of visits for ESPN—pilgrimages of sorts—to study college programs and coaches he admired and wanted to examine. He'd done that as a young coach, and it'd been invaluable to his development. But as he got settled at Florida, he stopped because a common coaching malady—paranoia that someone might beat him with his own ideas—had set in. Now he had the freedom to pursue it again.

So on the road he went for spring practices—to Michigan, Notre Dame, Texas, Oregon. He later went to see coaching friends such as Bob Stoops at Oklahoma and Paterno at Penn State, obviously unaware of the latter's impending demise.

"I did it for ESPN, but in my own soul, I wanted to learn some more football and just be around the game," Meyer said.

That itch he'd mentioned to Shelley was getting stronger.

"I'm out there at spring practice and I wanted to get out there and coach," he said. "I found myself getting closer and closer to the huddle."

* * * *

MEANWHILE, in Columbus, Jim Tressel's once-ironclad security as Ohio State's coach was growing tenuous. In March, Yahoo! Sports revealed that Tressel had been informed that a few Buckeyes players had sold memorabilia eight months before the school claimed it found out about it. At a hastily arranged news conference, Tressel was contrite. But the tone of unqualified support that President Gee and AD Gene Smith used in defense of Tressel struck many as wrong, particularly when *Dispatch* OSU beat reporter Tim May asked Gee if he'd ever considered firing Tressel.

"I'm just hoping the coach doesn't dismiss me," Gee replied flippantly, a comment he'd come to regret.

As much as Ohio State officials may have wanted to deny it, the ground around Tressel was sinking. The revelation that he hadn't passed along to his OSU superiors an email from a local lawyer alleging misdeeds among his players tightened the noose, as did the news that Tressel had signed a standard NCAA form the previous September saying he had no knowledge of any possible violation. By the end of May, Tressel staying had become untenable. Smith asked for his resignation.

Meyer said he didn't follow the Tressel saga closely. He figured at the beginning that it would blow over. "We had a kid sell a jersey at Florida," he said. "He had to miss four games. A bunch of kids had issues. I just thought it was minor."

But Shelley knew what Tressel's resignation meant. She was watching TV when the news broke. She instantly felt the way she did when they were in Fort Collins and she burst into tears after answering the phone call from Lou Holtz with the Notre Dame job offer.

"I was like, 'Oh no, oh no, oh no,'" Shelley said. "I knew. It was Ohio State. If he was going to go back, that would be the one. And I knew he'd get a phone call about it."

The phone call wouldn't come anytime soon. Meyer settled into his ESPN job, and that was going well. His stress level decreased. He looked good. He felt good. But something was missing.

"His heart wasn't in it," Shelley said. "His spirit was not to be an analyst yet. It's a great job. ESPN is a great employer. But it's not coaching."

As much as Meyer missed coaching, he knew he'd have to have the support of his family if he was to return to it. At one point in the summer or early fall, Meyer broached the idea of coaching again to his 13-year-old son Nate. He told Nate that if he did get back into coaching, he'd love to have him on the sideline with him. Another day, Urban was in the car with his son when out of the blue, Nate said, "Dad, if you want to coach again, I'm with you."

Meyer got choked up.

"You're my guy," he told Nate.

One down, three to go. Shelley suspects that Meyer raised the idea of returning to coaching with their kids before he dared pursue it with her. But all of the Meyers knew that coaching was in his blood and, along with family, was what made him whole. As the rumors, albeit premature, of Meyer coming to Ohio State became impossible to escape, Nicki Meyer decided to put pen to paper. Bored while sitting in her management science class at Georgia Tech, she began writing a list of do's and don'ts into her pink notebook.

"I'm the pink queen of my family," she said. "Everything I have is pink. I take all my notes on pink paper, so that's what I had."

The color may have hinted at frivolity, but the underlying message was absolutely serious. Things would not be as they were at the end at Florida. The bulk of the 10 points in the contract came to Nicki during classes. She added and subtracted a couple in the next couple of days after consulting with Shelley and Gigi. Then she mailed it home.

"I was real serious about this," Nicki said. "On the back of the envelope, I even wrote, 'Important Document Enclosed.' Just like in a real contract, with the stuff at the top saying, 'I, Urban Meyer, promise to abide by the rules. Failure to comply would result in no more coaching.'"

The contract stipulated the following:

1. My family will always come first.
2. I will take care of myself and maintain good health.
3. I will go on a trip once a year with Nicki—MINIMUM.
4. I will not go more than nine hours a day at the office.
5. I will sleep with my cell phone on silent.
6. I will continue to communicate daily with my kids.
7. I will trust God's plan and not be overanxious.
8. I will keep the lake house.
9. I will find a way to watch Nicki and Gigi play volleyball.
10. I will eat three meals a day.

Nicki knew that Rule No. 4 wouldn't fly. No Division I football coach can work as little as nine hours. A mere bargaining chip, she explained. But the other ones had to be followed. The night before Urban and Shelley's interview in Atlanta with Ohio State, the Meyer family met in Nicki's apartment and made Urban commit to the terms of the Pink Contract.

"They saw what happened to me down there near the end," he said. "They were concerned about my health. No. 2, they wanted me around. Even if I couldn't be there physically, be there with them."

He signed the contract. The next day, the Meyers were relieved that the Ohio State officials understood and supported the need for him to maintain balance in his life.

"I have to give them credit," Meyer said. "In this world of dog eat dog, win at all costs, that was very important. Because they could tell it was important to me."

The following Monday, during his introductory news conference, Meyer was asked about how he planned to avoid the pitfalls that had ensnarled him at Florida. That's when he reached into his pocket and pulled out Nicki's contract. Nicki was watching the news conference on TV with a friend who'd been sitting next to her in that management science class that day. The Pink Contract had become famous.

"Literally, both of our jaws dropped," Nicki said. "It meant a lot to me. I knew he was going to take it seriously."

Intentions were one thing. Whether he could live up to the contract, whether he could change and still be an effective coach, well, nobody knew the answer to that.

. 5 .

BUILDING A STAFF

BEFORE ACCEPTING THE Ohio State job, Urban Meyer made a call to a guy he'd known for 25 years, someone he deemed practically essential.

"Mick was the first phone call," recalled Meyer. "I said, 'If I do this, I'm not doing this without you.'"

These days, head coaches consider strength coaches to be their most important hire. Unlike position coaches, strength coaches are allowed to work with players throughout the year. But Meyer and Mickey Marotti had developed a bond deeper than most head coaches have with their strength coaches. They had grown into kindred spirits. Marotti is from the Pittsburgh area, with a blue-collar ethic similar to the one Meyer developed in Ashtabula. Marotti and Meyer met while both were graduate assistants at Ohio State. While Meyer was on the football side, Marotti was a GA on the strength and conditioning side. They were only acquaintances then. They didn't work in the same building, and Marotti lived in Grove City, just south of Columbus. Their working relationship and friendship began to sprout after Marotti took a job at the University of Cincinnati. Meyer was then at Colorado State, but would visit Cincinnati to visit his sister Gigi, then a professor at the school. Meyer would stop by the Bearcats' weight room and hang out with Marotti. They began exchanging information about weight training and coaching. When Meyer moved to Notre Dame and the strength-coach position opened there, he helped Marotti get the job. Marotti, like most strength coaches, naturally gravitates toward linemen while watching practice. Yet he was so enthralled by Meyer's intensity coaching wide receivers that he spent much of his time watching Meyer drill them. When Meyer became head coach at Florida, he lured Marotti away from South Bend.

"I think we're cut out of the same mold," Meyer said. "Our families mean the world to us. We cherish our wives. We cherish our children. We're from the same part of the world—very similar work ethic. Tough. We love our players, but we show them love in different ways. When you love someone, it means you maximize them."

Ohio State maximized Marotti's title. He was not hired as merely the strength-and-conditioning coach. He was designated the Assistant Athletic Director for Football Sports Performance.

Like it was for the Meyers, it wasn't easy for Marotti to leave Gainesville for Columbus.

"It was a hard decision," Marotti said. "I was settled there. I loved everybody there. I had a great relationship with the AD, Jeremy Foley, and a real good relationship with [Meyer's successor] Will Muschamp. My daughter was a junior in high school at the time. My son was graduated. My wife was comfortable."

But other factors swayed Marotti toward coming. His parents still live in Pittsburgh.

"They're getting older, and you never know," Marotti said.

Meyer also had familiarity with two coaches on the existing Buckeyes staff—Stan Drayton and Taver Johnson—and wanted to keep them. Johnson was a graduate assistant at Notre Dame in 1999 when Meyer was there. But Johnson left for Arkansas when the Razorbacks offered him the assistant head coach/linebackers job. Drayton agreed to stay and switch from coaching wide receivers to his more familiar role as running backs coach.

As Meyer interviewed for his staff, one potential issue had already been addressed. Salaries for assistant coaches had soared in recent years nationally, but Ohio State, like most of their Big Ten brethren, had been reluctant to get into that arms race. Gene Smith realized that had to change. If he hadn't, Meyer would have prodded him.

"One thing I have really learned over the years is an appreciation of a great staff, and you have to pay great people," he said. "You have to be competitive. When I talked to Gene about this job, I said, 'We're trying to be the best program in America, right?'"

That didn't mean paying exorbitant salaries, but Ohio State didn't want money to be a reason to lose coaching candidates. The Buckeyes would end up paying their nine assistant coaches about $3.25 million in 2012, almost $1 million more than in 2011.

Meyer knew he would have to move quickly but carefully to construct a staff. The recruiting season was entering the home stretch, and he needed help. But he also knew how important it was to hire the right people. By the end of his time at Florida, most of his most trusted assistant coaches had moved on to become head coaches or coordinators elsewhere. The lack of familiarity and comfort with their replacements had contributed to Meyer's problems in his final years. He knew he needed to have the right chemistry on his staff. That's why, at first, he leaned against retaining Luke Fickell. It had nothing to do with Fickell's ability as a coach. Meyer had done his homework about that and was impressed. But he worried that it might be too awkward to have a guy who'd been the head coach—albeit under unique circumstances—be back in a supporting role. When on the night before his official hiring, Meyer met with Fickell at trustee Robert Schottenstein's house, he still was skeptical, despite Gene Smith's endorsement.

"At first, I wasn't going to keep him," Meyer said. "That had 'agenda' written all over it. So in my mind, it wasn't going to happen."

The meeting changed his mind, starting with the fact that Amy Fickell joined her husband at the Schottensteins'.

"I didn't ask him to bring his wife," Meyer said. "When that happened, I said, 'This is a real guy. This is a family.'"

The meeting lasted two and a half hours. Meyer and Fickell had met only once before. In the spring of 2006, months before the Buckeyes and Gators would play for the national championship, Fickell and some OSU defensive coaches went to Gainesville to meet with Florida's defensive coaches. Now, neither man knew whether they would join forces or part ways.

"Probably the first thing I told him was, 'You know, you don't need me,'" Fickell said. "'This place is in fine shape. It'll be in fine shape. You've got to do what's best for the program, and that's what's best for me, too.'

"We talked about philosophy, nothing about Xs and Os," Fickell said. "Just football things in general and what our goals were and what kind of match it would be. It was a true, honest meeting. We had nothing holding either one of us back."

Meyer grew comfortable with Fickell. Their wives, who chatted in a separate room, also hit it off. "I loved Amy right away," Shelley said. "We spent a long time talking."

They bonded over their strong religious faith. They talked about Bible studies. They talked about their kids. Amy suggested the Catholic school that Nate would end up attending.

"She's a great mom," Shelley said. "She spends all of her time being a mom. After everything she'd been through [with the difficult season], she was very strong and positive, very friendly. Amy could have had an attitude like, 'Well, we should have had this job.' You just don't know. Some women would have been totally different. But they were both so gracious.

"I knew she was someone I would love to be friends with. You just know good people when you meet them."

Meyer was reassured, but he wanted to sleep on it.

"The next morning, after some prayer and some conversation with Shelley, I offered him the job," Meyer said.

Told more than a year later that Amy was instrumental in making the Meyers feel comfortable about keeping him on board, Fickell replied, "My wife has helped me get a lot of things. If that's what impressed him the most, then I'm lucky."

Fickell would become the defensive coordinator, though that wasn't hashed out right away. For a brief time, it looked like he might leave, after all. Fickell interviewed for the University of Pittsburgh head coach job, but that went to Wisconsin offensive coordinator Paul Chryst.

"Obviously, there were some other opportunities," Fickell said. "If I had to move, then that would have been the next step. But I've always wanted to be here. People often ask, 'How can you go backwards [in job title]?' If you have a really, really big ego, I think it is hard to go backwards, if you look at it that way. For me, it wasn't much of a decision because I love the place and would love to be a part of it."

While Meyer's decision to retain Fickell came quickly, that wasn't the case with Fickell's former OSU teammate and close friend, Mike Vrabel. He'd just finished his first year of coaching after his long, successful NFL career, primarily with the New England Patriots. Vrabel wanted to stay and asked Meyer about his status. Meyer wasn't ready to commit.

"I wanted to evaluate him because I didn't have time," Meyer said.

The truth is, Meyer didn't plan to keep Vrabel, for the same reason he was initially skeptical about Fickell.

"Former players want one of their guys and not me," Meyer said. "I'm not going to deal with that. I told him to go out and sign a guy. He'd never recruited. You want a job? Go get a couple players. I'll meet you in a week."

When Vrabel returned, Meyer kept putting him off. Then Meyer called Patriots coach Bill Belichick, a friend, and asked him about Vrabel. Belichick vouched for him. But Meyer wasn't totally convinced. So Meyer put Vrabel through an interview in which Vrabel had to stand up and demonstrate teaching techniques while Meyer grilled him.

It did not go well.

"I felt worse than I ever felt on the first day of training camp getting whipped by an offensive lineman," Vrabel said. "I'd never interviewed. I'd never done that. I just didn't know what the hell I was doing. He simply asked that I go back and collect my thoughts and show up at 6:00 in the morning and redo it. I stayed up most of the night just trying to practice. I thanked him for the second chance and went in there and obviously did much better."

That won over Meyer.

"Here's a guy who's one of the most famous players in Ohio State history, has three Super Bowl rings," Meyer said, "and here I am saying it's not good enough. For a lot of reasons I did that. But I wanted to see what would happen when he was critiqued. And he was awesome."

Meyer put Tom Herman through a similar test when he interviewed him for the offensive coordinator/quarterbacks coach job. Unlike Vrabel, whose first coaching job was with the Buckeyes, Herman started his career at the very bottom. In the mid-1990s, Herman was a Division III wide receiver at that noted football power, California Lutheran. The first career he pursued was broadcasting. He hosted a campus radio show and interned at a local television station. Then, the summer before his final year of college, he took a trip to Lake Tahoe. There, he had an epiphany.

"I was like, 'What are you going to do with yourself?'" he recalled. "I just kept talking to myself. I said that I wanted to live a life less ordinary and be passionate about what I want to do."

He liked broadcasting, but he thought he might love coaching. If it didn't pan out by the time he was 30, he told himself, he'd switch to a more conventional career. Herman called every Division I and I-AA school, looking for a job. He sent his résumé everywhere. He mailed Florida State coach Bobby Bowden's secretary a pack of gum so that she might remember him when he called. "Hey, remember that guy who sent you gum?" He even bought shoes at Goodwill and mailed them to schools, explaining that he just wanted to get his foot in the door.

"I did all sorts of crazy stuff," Herman said. "None of it worked."

But eventually he caught a break. The Cal Lutheran defensive coordinator, Bryan Marmion, got a job at tiny Texas Lutheran University. He offered Herman a job as wide receivers coach and recruiting coordinator for $5,000 and a campus meal ticket.

"So I packed my Civic and got on I-10 and went to Texas Lutheran without ever seeing the school," Herman said.

The University of Texas was only 45 minutes away. Every chance he got, Herman would drive to Austin in hopes of eventually getting a graduate assistant job, which he did. From there, he moved to Sam Houston State, making a whopping $10,000 as receivers coach. Herman became an offensive coordinator in 2005 when David Bailiff hired him at Texas State in San Marcos.

"I was actually about to hire somebody else, but I had a coach, Craig Naivar, who would come in to my office every day and stand on the table for Tom Herman," Bailiff said. "He would tell me that he was brilliant and that I should at least talk to him."

Naivar, who coached with Herman at Sam Houston State, wasn't exaggerating when he described Herman as brilliant. Herman really is a card-carrying member of MENSA, which is reserved for most intelligent 2 percent of the population. When Bailiff's leading candidate dragged his feet, he interviewed Herman and offered him the job.

He followed Bailiff to Rice University and then after two years was hired at Iowa State. Rice and Iowa State are hardly traditional powers, and Herman knew he couldn't just have an offense where his players lined up and went up and down the field because of superior ability.

"We needed an underdog offense, where you could take your less-skilled players lining up and find a way to beat a maybe more skilled, stronger, faster, more athletic team," Herman said.

That scheme was the spread, and to Herman, the oracle was Meyer. Herman tried every year to wrangle an invitation to Gainesville to study the offense with Florida's coaches but was always rebuffed. So by hook or crook, Herman got his hands on every single snap Meyer ran at Utah and Florida and studied them.

But the addition that Herman would bring to Meyer's spread at Ohio State came by accident. Bailiff's predecessor at Rice, Todd Graham, used a no-huddle offense with much success. But Herman's offense still used the huddle, and that's what he stuck with during training camp, with some resistance by his players. In Rice's opener that year, the Owls got beat 16–14 by Division I-AA Nicholls State and also lost their next three games. After that, quarterback Chase Clement and wide receiver Jarett Dillard went to Herman's office and pleaded to use the no-huddle.

"They felt the no-huddle had given them so much of a level playing field and that to take that away from them really hurt them," Herman said.

The no-huddle had allowed Rice to push the tempo, tiring out the opponent and prevented defenses from substituting as easily. Combined with the spread that stretched the field both horizontally and vertically, opponents were run ragged. So Herman relented. For the next week, he took a crash course in the no-huddle.

"We had to change everything," Herman said.

He quickly became a convert.

"I saw the advantage that it gave," Herman said. "My issue was out of ignorance. I didn't know how to call a play. I didn't know the procedure. For me, it was like trying to think about the size of the universe. When those two kids came in, they said, 'This is what we believe in, please consider it.' It was a no-brainer. I dove into it and just fell in love with it."

Rice won three of their final eight games and really took off the next year. The Owls ranked fifth nationally in passing offense, eighth in scoring offense, and 10th in total offense, and won 10 games.

Bailiff knew he wouldn't be able to keep Herman for long.

"He was a great young coach, and a lot of the reason I am where I am is because of Tom Herman's efforts," he said. "He's brilliant, but he brings an enthusiasm with him. He's really able at his age to still relate one-on-one with the college athlete. I think it's rare you find somebody at his age that has that much retention of the game. He's got old-man wisdom with teenager energy. That's a hard combination to find."

Sure enough, that's when Iowa State lured Herman away. Like Rice, the Cyclones were usually doormats in their league, the rugged Big 12. Herman's offense didn't light up the stat sheet there, but Iowa State had its moments. The highlight was a 37-point, double-overtime upset of No. 2 Oklahoma State in 2011. Herman's reputation as one of the game's bright young coaches caught the attention of Meyer, who had mutual friends with Herman. At Florida, Meyer hadn't used a no-huddle offense. He was intrigued by its possibilities and called Herman for an interview.

"I honestly didn't believe it when I got that phone call," Herman said. "I thought it was one of my buddies playing a prank on me. He said, 'Tom, this is Urban Meyer.' I almost said, 'Yeah, right.' I was almost like, 'C'mon, who is this really?' I'd never met the man, never talked to him. To get that phone call saying he wanted to interview me, I damn near said, 'Coach, I'll start walking. You just send a bus or plane ticket and it'll pick me up wherever I am.'"

Given that Herman had thoroughly dissected Meyer's plays, it wasn't a shock that he mastered the clinic part of the interview with Meyer. He got the job.

"There was no, 'Let me check with my wife. Hey, what's the salary?'" Herman said. "It was yes all the way. It was a no-brainer."

Part of that was because of his Ohio ties. Though he grew up in California, Herman was born in Cincinnati, and almost all of his relatives still live there. His grandmother is a seamstress, and Herman said she custom-tailored the suits of Pete Rose, Johnny Bench, and others from the Big Red Machine–era Cincinnati Reds.

"I've got autographs out the wazoo of that generation of Cincinnati Reds," he said. "They're probably among my most cherished possessions."

Meyer wanted another offensive coach with play-calling experience and targeted Notre Dame offensive line coach Ed Warinner. A Strasburg, Ohio, native, Warinner played at perennial Division III power Mount Union. Warinner had been offensive coordinator at Army and Kansas. One of Meyer's closest coaching friends is former Kansas coach Mark Mangino, who highly recommended Warinner. It would prove to be one of Meyer's best hires.

"I think this is the only place he would have left Notre Dame for," said Meyer, who gave Warinner the additional title and responsibility of co–offensive coordinator.

The same went for Tim Hinton, Meyer's former mentor when he was at Ohio State as a graduate assistant. Meyer hired Hinton to coach tight ends and fullbacks. (In Meyer's spread, those positions are largely interchangeable.)

"One of the hardest-working guys I've ever been around," Meyer said. "Very well-respected. There was a group of GAs at the time, I think six before [rules changes] knocked it down to two. There were guys there who didn't work very hard but were always on the phone trying to get a job and not getting their job done. Tim was just a worker, a grinder. He was the one who taught me."

Hinton was a longtime high school coach in Ohio before coaching at the University of Cincinnati and then Notre Dame. His family has owned Ohio State season tickets since 1950, the year of the Snow Bowl game against Michigan. He jumped at the chance to return to Ohio and coach under Meyer.

"It took me about 30 seconds—actually not even that long," Hinton said.

For his wide receivers coach, Meyer tabbed a young coach with an unimpeachable Buckeyes pedigree. Zach Smith, then just 27, is the grandson of Earle Bruce and grew up in suburban Dublin, Ohio. At the urging of his grandfather, Smith walked on at Bowling Green so he could learn from Meyer. He later became a quality-control assistant and graduate assistant at Florida under Meyer before becoming an assistant coach at Marshall and then Temple. The job offer to come to Ohio State came at a poignant time. His grandmother, Jean Bruce—Earle's wife—died the day before Temple played in the New Mexico bowl. Zach talked to his grandparents every day and was closer to them than most people are with their own parents. Smith relied on his grandmother's judgment.

"She had an unbelievable sense to say whatever you needed to hear," he said. "You may not like it or agree with it, but hindsight being 20/20, she was unbelievable."

It crushed him that he couldn't get back to Columbus for one last visit before she died because he had a pretty good idea that Meyer was going to offer him the wide receivers job. He debated whether to tell his grandma, afraid of being premature but also worried that she might pass away without knowing he was likely to coach for Ohio State. He decided not to tell her.

"She didn't tell me, but she told my wife [Courtney], 'I don't know how long I'll make it, but I promise you this, if he coaches in the Horseshoe. I'll be there for the first game,'" Smith said, his voice cracking at the memory. "It was tough for me because I didn't want to tell her that—and that'd be the last thing I told her—and then all of a sudden I don't get hired. But at the same time, I wanted her to know. In hindsight, I wish I'd told her I was going to get the job, but I just didn't know, and I didn't want it to be the last thing I told her."

Smith still felt that remorse as he prepared to deliver his grandma's eulogy, which he said was probably the hardest thing he'd ever had to do. Then, during breaks between sessions of visitation hours, Meyer decided to make the job offer official.

"He didn't make an ordeal of it, but he talked to my grandfather and saw me in the setting," Smith said. "He just said, 'So you want to coach at Ohio State?' It's one of those things I'll never forget. It was a really, really hard time for me, for my grandfather, and for everyone else in my family. When he offered me the job, it was like I felt she was there and she knew."

*   *   *   *

THE ONLY COACH Meyer hired with no ties to Ohio was Everett Withers, hired as co–defensive coordinator and safeties coach.

"He's a guy who was strongly recommended and a very high character guy," Meyer said. "I wanted two coordinators in the room. He had southern ties in recruiting. I thought it'd be a good mix. When I got to spend some time with him, he was great."

Like Fickell, Withers had spent the 2011 season in a high-profile but thankless position. Withers served as North Carolina's interim coach after Butch Davis was forced out because of a scandal involving improper benefits and other violations. If anything, Withers' task may have been harder in Chapel Hill than Fickell's was in Columbus. In the summer of 2011, Withers detected a negative vibe about the situation at North Carolina. Certain annual events, such as dinner with the university chancellor, were mysteriously canceled.

"You're going, 'What's going on?'" Withers said.

On July 27, Davis was fired. Withers was one of three assistants who interviewed to become interim coach. Two days before camp started, Withers got the job.

"I have aspirations of one day being a head football coach," Withers said. "So I felt like, if nothing else, it'll give me training. The neat thing about it was I felt all the players respected me… and the other assistants, [and] I just kept hearing from our leaders, 'What's changed, guys? Yes, we lost Coach Davis, and we didn't want that to happen, but the other coaches were there.'"

Much like Ohio State did under Fickell, North Carolina's season started decently but fell apart at the end. The Tar Heels finished 7–6 after a 41–24 Independence Bowl loss to Missouri, and Larry Fedora was hired as head coach. Withers interviewed with Meyer for the OSU job. They have the same agent, Trace Armstrong. Withers also interviewed with Arkansas coach Bobby Petrino to be the Razorbacks' defensive coordinator. Withers said Petrino offered him the job.

"I was pretty close to taking it and then thought, *No, this is a better fit*," Withers said.

Smart move. Petrino would soon be fired for not disclosing an "inappropriate relationship" with a female employee in the athletics department that came to light after the two were involved in a motorcycle accident.

The final piece to the coaching puzzle was hiring Kerry Coombs to coach cornerbacks. Meyer had originally hired NFL coach Bill Sheridan, but two weeks after he joined the Buckeyes, he left to become defensive coordinator for the Tampa Bay Buccaneers. Meyer had known Coombs as a highly popular and successful high school coach at Colerain High School in Cincinnati before becoming an assistant coach at the University of Cincinnati.

Other than his college days at the University of Dayton, Coombs had lived his entire life in Cincinnati, as had his wife, Holly. The youngest of his three children, Dylan, had committed to playing football for UC. Kerry had made a pact with Dylan that they would be together as Bearcats. Then the job offer from Meyer came.

"We had a long conversation about it," Coombs said. "His first comment was, 'Really, Dad? Really?'"

But Dylan realized that coaching at Ohio State was an opportunity his father couldn't turn down.

"He said, 'I would never want to be the reason you didn't,' which was very mature of him," Coombs said. "My wife said, 'Go.' I didn't find anybody other than [UC coach] Butch Jones, of course, who didn't say, 'Go.'"

It took until March 1, when Coombs' hiring became official, for the staff to be finalized. Meyer liked what he had assembled. He believed all of his assistants were good family men and all of high character. That was essential to Meyer. But any new staff is a mystery, and Meyer had some trepidation about how it would all work out.

"I felt good," he said, "but there was—I don't want to say 'buyer's remorse'—but I was a little skeptical because I didn't know many of them, and we had a lot of work to do," Meyer said.

· 6 ·

DIVINE INTERVENTION

ABOUT 3:00 AM on November 29, 2011, Helen Spence awoke in her Harrisburg, Pennsylvania, home with a strange vision in her head. She had fallen asleep to ESPN in the bedroom she shared with her husband, Greg. In what she thought was a dream, she pictured Urban Meyer at a podium with her son Noah's name underneath. This was more than a bit odd because, for one thing, she had no idea who Urban Meyer was. In fact, when retelling this story, she called him Urban Meyers. When her husband awoke three hours later, she told him about this Urban Meyers fellow and asked who he was. Greg, a former linebacker at North Carolina State, laughed and informed her: he's only one of the best football coaches around.

"Why would he have Noah's name underneath?" Helen asked Greg.

"You must be imagining it," Greg responded.

Later that day, Greg Spence got a phone call. It was Urban Meyer. The night before, Meyer had been introduced as Ohio State's head coach. Perhaps Helen had drifted off to sleep with the reports about the news conference on the TV and it seeped into her dream by osmosis. Who knows? In any case, Meyer wanted to meet with the Spences about Noah, rated as perhaps the best pass-rushing defensive end prospect in the country. Greg called Helen.

"Wow, you'll never guess what happened," he said. "That guy you thought you saw on TV with Noah's name? He called."

The Spences have a deep religious faith, and they took this as a form of divine intervention. Spence, who had 35½ sacks as a junior and senior at Bishop McDevitt High School, was coveted by almost every elite program in the country. Florida, LSU, and Notre Dame all made home visits, the first two on the same day. But throughout the process, Penn State was the clear leader. Ohio State had been in the picture in the spring. After Luke Fickell laid some of the groundwork, Jim Tressel had in fact called the Spences in late May. Tressel impressed them. But just days later, Tressel was forced to resign. His departure seemed to eliminate the Buckeyes from consideration.

"They really weren't on the radar," Greg said. "We didn't get a chance to form a relationship."

Spence hadn't formally committed to Penn State, but that looked to be only a matter of time. Then the Sandusky scandal broke. Greg Spence remembers reading the Sunday Harrisburg *Patriot-News*, whose work uncovering Sandusky's crimes and Penn State's inattention to them won a Pulitzer Prize. As he read the horrific details of the victims' suffering, he broke down in tears. For the Spences, the fate of at-risk children at the heart of the Sandusky abuse hit home. In addition to their four biological sons—Noah was the youngest—they had adopted five more as young boys. Joe Paterno was soon fired, Penn State faced an uncertain future, and the Spences knew they had to reassess Noah's recruiting. The Spences hadn't eliminated the Nittany Lions from consideration, but they were no longer the clear front-runner.

"We were just flapping in the wind," Greg said. "We had no real direction of a school being in the lead."

In that sense, the timing of Meyer's hiring was fortuitous.

"I know that Noah was one of the first young people that Coach Meyer reached out to," Greg said. "They had a wonderful conversation. Noah came downstairs and said, 'Dad, you'll never guess who I just spoke with.'"

Ohio State wasted little time getting to Harrisburg. Right after Mike Vrabel was challenged to reel in some prized recruits, here was the premier one open to persuasion. With Meyer concentrating on hiring assistants and settling in, Fickell and Vrabel hit the road. The two have been best friends since their days as defensive linemen for the Buckeyes in the 1990s. Fickell may have been a three-time state wrestling champion, but that didn't mean Vrabel didn't challenge him, even at 2:00 AM.

"He doesn't lack confidence in anything he does," Fickell said with a laugh. "There's been many a time [we wrestled], but it would last too long because neither of us would stop."

It didn't matter to Vrabel that he couldn't beat Fickell. It meant more to never concede.

"Just a couple of knuckleheads," Vrabel said. "He would get me in some damn choke hold or something, and I was like, 'Okay, bud. We can sit here and do this all day,' and I think he realized that, too. So after about 10 minutes of that damn hold, we'd say, 'Okay, 1-2-3, and we'll stop.' I never knew how to wrestle, but I wasn't going to give in."

Now Fickell and Vrabel would be a team, one the Spences wouldn't forget.

"For a week, we pretty much had the private plane and we were going from Boston to Pittsburgh to Harrisburg," Fickell said. "There were only about four of us recruiting. It was pretty good for us."

Fickell and Vrabel arrived at the Spence house and started their pitch. Fickell spoke to Helen in the kitchen about how Ohio State could help Noah reach his potential as a player, student, and young man. As they talked, Helen could see Vrabel and Noah in the adjoining dining room. Except they weren't just talking. They began simulating pass-rush drills. Then it became more than simulating.

"We cleared the tables out and we started working drills," Vrabel said. "Next thing you know, we're throwing stuff around. We were having a good time. It was a hands-on approach, and I think they appreciated it. I was just trying to show Noah how I'd coach him when he'd come to Ohio State."

In the kitchen, Helen stopped what she was doing to see her son and Vrabel going at it.

"He was showing him hand moves, how to position his hands," Helen said. "Something happened, and the next thing I knew, they were all tangled up together. I said, 'Hey, what is going on?' He was grabbing Noah, and Noah was grabbing him."

Vrabel emerged from the dining room with a bump on his lip and scrapes on his face, and newfound respect for and from the prized recruit and his family.

"He made quite the impression, a very good impression," Greg said. "He's about 36 or 37 years old, and this is a gentleman who still has that fire in his heart and his head—and apparently in his hands, too."

In mid-December, Meyer made his visit to Harrisburg to meet the Spences. This time, there were no pass-rush drills in the dining room. In fact, there was little talk of football at all. They talked mainly, Helen said, about family and faith. Meyer told the Spences about his family, about the Pink Contract, about his wife and daughters and son.

"All of that is very important to me because that's what my life is," Helen said. "We related right away. It was unlike any other coaches. They talked to us—nobody [from other schools] was mean or disrespectful—but they talked over my head because they were talking about [football-specific] things I didn't know about."

The Spences then drove to Columbus for their official visit. They met with Mickey Marotti, with academic guidance representatives and even the team chaplain, who took them to a service. Noah had intended to announce his choice of schools at the Under Armour All-Star Game in January. Now he saw no reason to wait.

"He said, 'I want to commit now,'" Greg recalled. "That's what he shared with Coach Meyer."

Meyer's reaction?

"He jumped up, hugged him, and hugged us," Greg said with a laugh.

Spence may have been the biggest recruiting prize for the Buckeyes, but it would take much more than him to salvage a class that some analysts ranked outside the top 20. He began the process as soon as he was hired. Meyer, along with OSU director of football operations Greg Gillum and other staffers, settled into a room at the Woody Hayes Center. Gillum had compiled a list from the Internet of the top players at different position. For hours, they all basically made cold calls to see if any of them might have interest in Ohio State.

"It was rapid fire," Meyer said. "We had phones blazing. I love that kind of stuff. It was chaos. I was sitting at the desk in the staff room. I said, 'Give me the top five linebackers, the top 10 linebackers.'"

It seemed like a scene out of *Glengarry Glen Ross*. If someone got an interested recruit, they'd rush the phone to Meyer, who'd scan the notes and begin his selling job.

"I'd say, 'Hey, I'm the new head football coach at Ohio State,'" Meyer said. "'We have the No. 1 alumni base in America. We're going to win a championship.' I would throw out Florida a lot because they knew my name from Florida. 'We're going to do what we did at Florida.'"

Meyer made remarkable progress, but the announcement on December 20 by the NCAA of the bowl ban threatened to derail that. Right away, he took preemptive action. As soon as he got word from athletics director Gene Smith in his office in that early-morning meeting, he called recruits to inform them before they heard it on the news.

"Noah Spence was the big one," Meyer said. "He was our marquee guy at that time. [Fellow defensive linemen] Tommy Schutt, Adolphus Washington said, 'We're all in. Don't worry about it, coach.'"

Meyer acknowledged that the sanctions did cause them to lose some potential recruits. For a few weeks, he said, the Buckeyes had to play defense in recruiting. But for Meyer and the staff he was assembling, the best defense, not surprisingly, was offense.

In suburban Boston, the Buckeyes would have a chance to reel in two recruits at once. Linebacker Camren Williams and cornerback Armani Reeves were as close as brothers. Though they weren't a package deal, they did prefer to go to the same school. Williams' father, Brent, grew up in Michigan [as a Wolverines fan], played at the University of Toledo, and was teammates with Vrabel with the Patriots. The Williamses lived in the same Massachusetts town, West Roxbury, as Vrabel did when he was with the team. The Williams' older son, Brennan, played offensive line for North Carolina after being recruited by Butch Davis and Everett Withers. Meyer tried to lure Brennan to Florida late in the recruiting process and made a favorable, if not quite persuasive enough, impression.

"We've been exposed to so many recruiters and recruiting styles," Brent Williams said. "Butch Davis had an air about him. Butch could talk to you for four hours, and it could seem like a half-hour conversation. Good recruiters have an air about them. Urban definitely does. But Urban also has the ability to be very personable. He can communicate with me, who's had football experience, to my wife who's been around football around the perimeter, to Armani's mom, and the players. I'm speaking to them at the same time, but I'm speaking to them in their language. I think that is a unique ability to do that."

Williams said Meyer does his homework as well as any coach he's been around.

"There's no fumbling through a conversation," he said. "He's able to recall things about you as a player, things you'd done well, things he thinks you can improve on."

Camren Williams had committed to Penn State, with Ohio State a distant second place, long before the Sandusky scandal broke.

Early in the high school season, Vrabel called Williams' coach to gauge how firm his commitment was. Camren said it was firm. Vrabel backed off. When the Sandusky story exploded, the Williamses called Vrabel.

"They never called back until we reached out to them," Brent Williams said.

As it did with the Spences, the home visit in West Roxbury at times bordered on the comical, but for a different reason. Like Vrabel had done at the Spence home, the Williamses' living room had become a de facto football field. Withers was on this trip, and he showed Reeves various footwork drills. In another room, Meyer spoke of how important it was for Williams and Reeves to play behind the big defensive linemen from whom the Buckeyes had gotten commitments. Meyer knew he had to broach it delicately.

"He said, 'There's no other way to say this,'" Brent Williams said with a chuckle. "So he apologizes to my wife and Armani's mother. 'But understand this: I've got this kid coming in. His name is Adolphus Washington, who's got a really wide ass. Then I've got this other kid coming in, Tommy Schutt, who's got another really wide ass. I've got another kid coming in—he doesn't have as wide an ass, but he's really fast.' He's talking about Noah. He's talking about them and said, 'My goal for Camren is to put three really big asses in front of you to protect you to make plays.'"

With Camren, who understood what a Cover 2 defense was in the second grade, the Ohio State coaches could give detailed explanations of what schemes the Buckeyes would be using. When Reeves' mother, Victoria, said she needed more of an explanation about the benefits of wide-bodied linemen, Meyer gave a Football 101 talk explaining it.

"He was able to speak at Camren's level, my level, my wife's, Armani's mom's," Brent Williams said. "The thing great recruiters do is they're visionaries. They're great at giving a kid the vision of who they're going to fit in with—the school and the football team. If that kid can see himself behind Adolphus Washington and Tommy Schutt and Noah Spence, you start to see, 'Hey, I can fit.'

"Then when Coach Fickell can say, 'Hey, our defense is not this simple, but here are three reads every linebacker has to know,' all of a sudden he really gets the vision of how he's going to fit in this program. They did that better than anyone involved in their recruitment."

That vision also includes conveying what Meyer's goal is for the whole program. Ohio State's intention, he told recruits, wasn't merely to win Big Ten championships or a national title, but national championships—plural.

"He doesn't shy away from saying there's other things we expect out of you, too," Fickell said. "You're going to be treated like a professional football player. But you're also expected to be a professional student. He doesn't have a problem saying, 'Yeah, we're going to win national [championships], multiple. That's our expectation.'

"Coach Tress was much more laid back. Urban is an emotional guy. He's much more direct and outwardly emotional. At times gets very aggressive. He gets up close up in your face. He wants to see and talk to you. People love that. They like the energy."

Like Spence, Williams and Reeves—and their families—were sold. They committed to the Buckeyes. Ohio State's once-mediocre recruiting class finished a consensus top-five one. Meyer would say a year later that his brand-new staff had acted like cowboys, rounding up the best players they could without having the time to devise a master strategy. That would be in place next year when the Class of 2013 would challenge for the mythical prize of top recruiting class in the country. But under the circumstances, assembling the Class of 2012 might have been an even more impressive achievement. Another part of the foundation had been put in place.

· 7 ·

THE WORK BEGINS

THE PLANE RIDE on January 2, 2012, back to Columbus from the Gator Bowl was a quiet one. Ohio State had played listlessly in the 24–17 loss to Florida, giving the Buckeyes seven losses in a season for the first time since 1897. That wasn't the only reason for the somber mood. While assistants Luke Fickell, Mike Vrabel, and Stan Drayton were retained by Meyer, the other assistant coaches knew they would not be. Longtime defensive coordinator Jim Heacock, who'd hired Meyer for his first full-time assistant coach job at Illinois State two decades earlier, was among the departing. He'd indicated to Meyer, who'd been interested in retaining him, that he was leaning toward retirement. Also leaving was offensive coordinator/offensive line coach Jim Bollman, who was often criticized by fans but deeply respected by his players. Running backs/special teams coach Dick "Doc" Tressel, who'd stayed on despite the forced resignation of his younger brother, was another casualty. While preparing for the Gator Bowl, they'd also been trying to line up their next jobs or deciding whether even to leave coaching. In postgame interviews, the coaches dismissed any bitterness they may have felt about their fate and preferred to remember happier moments as Buckeyes. But players had to board the team plane realizing that their collapse down the stretch had contributed to the dismissal of the coaches they'd grown to respect and love.

"It was hard because you knew a lot of those coaches who'd meant so much to you were leaving," fullback Zach Boren said. "That was the hard part. We wanted to get a win for those coaches, for everything they'd done for us and what they'd gone through. It was hard knowing it was going to be a whole new coaching staff. Football is a lot about respect. The previous coaches had earned your respect because you'd spent, in my case, three years with them."

Compounding their sadness about one era concluding was anxiety about what they faced in the next.

"The plane ride was terrible," cornerback Travis Howard said. "Just to go out with a season like that, everything possibly that could go wrong went wrong. The whole plane ride back, I don't think anybody said a word. Everybody was in deep thought because of how that year ended and what the next year might bring."

The plane landed late at night. Meyer, who had vowed to hit like a hurricane, had already scheduled a 7:00 AM meeting for the next morning. Meyer was mostly a stranger to them. He'd stayed away from the Gator Bowl, not wanting to add anything more to the Old Meyer School vs. New Meyer School storyline that dominated what was otherwise a forgettable matchup of underachieving 6–6 teams.

If Meyer thought he was taking over a nationally elite program that happened to be coming off an aberrational season, he was about to find out how deep the problems ran. When he entered the team room at the Woody Hayes Athletic Center to give his first address as the clear man in charge, he was stunned to see that several players weren't there.

"All I remember was when they were calling roll," Howard said, "and they were checking to see if everyone was there. His reaction was like, 'Are you fucking kidding me?!' He was amazed and shocked at how a team could possibly go out in this type of fashion and then have guys not show up.

"He was yelling at the top of his lungs, and you could see his veins were popping out of his arms and neck because he was so angry."

Orhian Johnson was one of the players who missed the start of the meeting. He awoke at 6:00 AM, intending to arrive early. But his car, which hadn't been driven since Johnson left for bowl practice after Christmas, wouldn't start. He called backup quarterback Kenny Guiton for a ride. They arrived about five minutes late. Among the missing were four offensive linemen, including starting left guard Andrew Norwell. Offensive linemen form the unit that's supposed to be the foundation of a team. They're expected to be the most conscientious of any group.

"I was kind of devastated and extremely upset," Meyer said. "And I let them know it. I was very clear about the style of program we were going to have and the work ethic."

The next morning, and for the rest of the week, the tardy and absent players were punished with what Mickey Marotti called "dawn patrol." Johnson said the players were assigned to scrub clean the entire weight room—every bar, every weight, every inch of every piece of equipment. Newly hired associate strength coach Rick Court enforced a code of absolute silence on the offenders while they toiled.

Johnson said it could have been worse. Marotti was still new. Ensuing offenders would get even more severe punishment.

"We didn't have to do the physical training part," Johnson said.

Details about how tough the new "enhanced" dawn patrol was remain sketchy, but it was severe enough that John Simon said his emotions changed from anger at the no-shows to compassion when he learned of the consequences required from subsequent violators.

"You take those two words—dawn patrol—and try to analyze and you can probably figure something out," running backs coach Stan Drayton said. "I guarantee you it is nothing nice. We try to make it as awful as we possibly can. We try to deter a negative decision-making process."

Told that it conjured an image of cleaning latrines with toothbrushes common in movies about the military, Drayton laughed.

"It's not too far from that."

But the message about accountability didn't sink in to everybody on the team. A couple days later, Meyer had another team meeting. Again, there were stragglers and no-shows.

Now Meyer was beyond livid. The Buckeyes were supposed to start their off-season conditioning program in a week. Meyer and Marotti saw no need to wait. Meyer ordered his players to assemble at 4:45 the next morning for what Marotti euphemistically called "attention training."

As disappointed as Meyer was at some of his players' attitudes, he also saw an opportunity. It gave him ammunition to impose his form of shock treatment.

In my own mind, I was happy it happened," Meyer said. "You only get a chance to make a first impression one time. So in my own mind, when I saw a little bit of dysfunction, it was actually what I wanted to see."

Meyer was also disturbed when he learned about the football team's academic performance in the fall.

"Not good at all," he said.

What happened the next week would be something the players would never want to repeat. The next day many players showed up wearing shorts and T-shirts, expecting to work out in the heated indoor facility. They were wrong. The workouts would be held outside on the practice field. That the temperature was in the 20s didn't matter one bit to Marotti.

"I remember walking into first workout, it was so cold," said Howard, who's from Miami. "I remember guys had socks on their head. We couldn't use our stuff from football, so guys had to use their own stuff. Once the whistle blew, that's when it got real. He was going to see who was a part of the program and who wasn't. It was like, make or break you. It was crazy. A couple guys quit the team because of that. It just showed who really wanted to be there. I think it was his way of bringing in a new attitude with the new year."

One of the strength coaches in players' faces was Anthony Schlegel, who played linebacker for Ohio State in 2004–2005 after transferring from the Air Force Academy. After a brief NFL career, Schlegel returned to his alma mater in January 2011 as an assistant strength coach. He and fellow holdover Jeff Uhlenhake were joined by Court and Kenny Parker as Marotti's full-time assistants. As a former OSU player like Uhlenhake, it pained Schlegel to watch the 2011 season disintegrate. So if that meant the new regime had to break down players to build them back stronger, so be it.

"I know they were shocked and stunned at what we were doing and how they were being coached and what they were doing in the cold," Schlegel said. "I remember there was some shock, some 'What's going on here?' They got trained really hard."

Players were forced to do drills named bear crawls, lunges, and one-legged scalded dogs.

A one-legged scalded dog?

"It's almost like a bear crawl," senior linebacker Etienne Sabino said, "but you can only use one leg. You're kind of hopping down the field on one leg and your hands."

For 400 yards.

"It's really hard," Marotti said. "Really, really, really hard."

Adjacent to the practice field is a sand pit where players do pull-ups and dips, a triceps exercise. For the Buckeyes, it became almost a torture chamber. Strength coaches ordered the Buckeyes to do pull-ups and dips with no end in sight. In the frigid temperatures, their hands became raw as they rubbed on the bar. Players took turns spotting each other for pull-ups, and they did so many that players were on each other's shoulders to keep them from falling.

"Your hands are sticking to the dip bars and pull-up bars, and your skin is getting all torn up," offensive lineman Jack Mewhort said. "It's freezing cold and your nose is running. They have no sympathy for you. You're doing pull-ups and dips until they say so, and they were just not giving in. It was like a scene out of a bad movie. I remember looking around thinking, *This is what it's going to be like.*"

Marotti said most of the players were too stunned to say much of anything.

"They were scared to death," he said.

But one player spoke up. Standing in the middle of the front row, Boren kept yelling, "You can't break us! You can't break us!"

Meyer was incredulous.

"I'm looking at Mickey, saying, 'Who is this guy?'" Meyer said. "He's supposed to be a leader. He just kept saying that. Finally, I look at Mick and grab the kid and say, 'Can't break you? We could break you like a twig right now if we wanted to. Be positive. Encourage guys. 'You can't break us'? We can break you in a second. The purpose of this isn't to break you. Just do what we ask you to do. It's not us against you. We're trying to build a team here.'"

In the broad spectrum of Ohio State's season, Boren might be the player who showed the greatest difference between "before" and "after." This was Boren at the dawn of the Meyer era.

Not that Meyer or Marotti cared about his opinion or any of the players'.

"We were going to do it, anyway," Marotti said.

The idea was to test the players' commitment. If they didn't have the drive to stick it out, better to find out right away. The ones who persevered would have to learn that the bar had been raised significantly.

"It was definitely grueling," Sabino said. "Being out there in the cold, 5:00 in the morning, snow on the ground, your hands freezing, it was tough. That kind of laid the foundation for everyone. Everyone knew it was about to get real serious. After going through that, we all had a wakeup call that this was going to be a serious year."

Those 5:00 AM outdoor workouts lasted a week. And the regular conditioning workouts that followed that Hell Week were not much easier. The Meyer/Marotti formula was in some ways simple: Everything would be a competition. Everything would have to be earned, not given.

During that first week of 5:00 AM workouts, players were even barred from the weight room, which was soon to be upgraded. They also were deemed to be unworthy to enter their own locker room. They couldn't wear anything with Ohio State logos on their workout gear, so they had to show up wearing their own clothes. Until a player had earned the privilege of dressing in the locker room, he would grab his clothes from a hook adjacent to it and find a place to dress, whether in the cafeteria, racquetball court, or multipurpose room.

"It was really a sight to see the Ohio State Buckeyes looking as ragtag as we did, getting dressed in the hallways," Mewhort said. "It certainly made you appreciate it when we got our stuff back."

As much as players understood the need for a culture shift, that a 6–7 season and no-shows at meetings required consequences, there was grumbling that things had gone too far.

"A lot of guys looked around like, 'This is stupid. I didn't accept a scholarship to Ohio State to be doing this,'" senior punter Ben Buchanan said. "The attitude was, 'I should have the best. I'm here at Ohio State.'

"There were a lot of whispers in the locker room of guys doing this, guys doing this. This guy's going to transfer. Forget this. I'm done with this. There were definitely those whispers in January and February before we got in the midst of spring ball."

Buchanan said he and place-kicker Drew Basil were among the last to earn locker-room rights.

"Drew and I are two of the hardest workers, but they had a little knock against the specialists because they know you have to be mentally tough," Buchanan said. "For a while we bought into it, but then we were like, 'This is ridiculous. We're established guys. Why are we not in there with the other guys?'"

Mewhort said Marotti wouldn't even refer to the kickers by name. "Coach Mick is real funny about that," he said. "He just calls them 'kickers.' I think they were the last guys in there. I think it was just a little mental game he was playing with them."

Everything in the Buckeyes' workouts was designed to pit players in competition. Standings of who won and lost one-on-one sprints and other drills were posted throughout the weight room. If players were deemed not to have given maximum effort, they were given demerits on a "loaf chart."

"You don't want to be on the loaf chart, especially because they post it right there in the weight room," fifth-year senior Zach Domicone said. "Your position coach sees it. The [NFL] scouts who come in see it. In the spring, families would be walking in and see the loaf chart, looking to see if you've got a loaf."

Meyer even ordered that a continuous loop video from the long history of the Ohio State–Michigan rivalry play in the facility, a never-ending reminder of the ultimate challenge in the Buckeyes' season and yet another reason to push on beyond what they believed were their limits. Everything was designed as part of Meyer and Marotti's philosophy of motivation and transparency. If you were doing well, it was no secret. If you weren't, you couldn't hide.

"We were monitored in everything we did, whether it was academics, or the weight room, or the film room," Domicone said.

In the past, Domicone said, it was possible to skate by, by doing the minimum. If you wanted to be great, that would certainly be encouraged and rewarded. But those along for the ride weren't necessarily pushed overboard.

"Now, you're challenged every day to be better than you were the day before. Every day, you have to improve in the weight room, you have to improve in the classroom, you have to be smarter in the film room."

Some competitions were unorthodox. Biceps-measurement contests were held after upper-body workouts. One staple was the mat drill, in which two players faced off on a wrestling mat. One player had eight seconds to try to reach a line eight yards away while another player did everything in his power to stop him.

"They just said, 'Go,' and whatever happened, happened," Simon said. "Things got nasty pretty often. I enjoyed those things. I think a lot of guys enjoyed those. You learned who you could rely on and, when the pressure was on, who could step up and perform."

Early on, the strength coaches could see who the leaders would be and who would have to get with the program. Simon was an obvious leader, in fact *the* leader.

"Some of it was just folklore," Marotti said. "The Vrabels and Fickells and Schlegels and Uhlenhakes, they said that you're going to love John Simon. They were like, 'You're going to see it pretty quick,' and you did see it pretty quick."

When the weight room was closed to the players during that first week of 5:00 AM "attention training," it was like denying Simon sustenance. Picture John Belushi in *Animal House* when he's standing outside the Delta house as the authorities haul out the booze. That's Simon standing outside the weight room unable to lift.

"I remember talking to John and asking him, 'Dude, what are you going to do without the weight room?'" Mewhort said. "He just kind of shrugged. He's the top of the Christmas tree. He's *the* guy. If he's not allowed in the weight room, it's like, wow, these guys mean business."

Even without being allowed in the weight room that first week, Simon made a strong impression on Meyer.

"An animal," Meyer recalled. "That week he was like Tebow was. Win everything and go as hard as he can."

That's the way Simon has always been since he was a tyke in Youngstown. His father, John Jr., was a devotee of weight-training long before it was in vogue. Little Johnny tagged along. Even in preschool, he was doing push-ups, sit-ups, and chin-ups every night. By the time John was in fourth grade, his father began allowing him to start a formal workout regimen. His youth league coach, Ken Kollar, recalls that during warmup drills his team would do push-ups. There would be John, doing two pushups for each one his teammates were doing.

"He was so intense with his work ethic that he made the other kids around him better," Kollar said.

When Simon was in elementary school, he met Meyer at Bowling Green. Simon's dad had a friend whose son was a walk-on when Meyer coached there. They drove across the state to attend the spring game. While John was playing on the field after the game ended, the friend introduced Meyer to the older Simon, pointed to John, and said, "You'll be looking at his son one day." Meyer smiled and said that he'd file that away in his memory.

A Pittsburgh Steelers fan—in Youngstown, loyalties are mostly divided between the Steelers and Cleveland Browns—Simon would go out on the street outside his home and chalk out a makeshift field and play an imaginary game by himself. He'd throw passes and try to catch them. He'd elude pretend tacklers and fall to the street, skinning his knees.

He was a star at Cardinal Mooney High School but was rated only a three-star recruit when he committed to Ohio State.

"Sometimes they get it right," Simon said of recruiting analysts' rankings. "Sometimes they don't. You can't judge character or passion or work ethic or heart. You only see how people react when other people are around. You don't know what they're like when no one's around. You can't judge by the stats. You have to judge by the player's character."

Nobody would outwork John Simon. Players talked of seeing Simon's car at the complex at midnight. He got up before dawn some days to start his workouts. As Marotti noticed Simon's relentlessness, he hit upon an idea. He told Simon that he loved his work ethic, that he was everything a strength coach would want. But putting in extra workouts by himself wasn't going to make the team better. So Marotti told him that on light team workout days, he wouldn't be allowed in the weight room unless he brought a teammate with him.

"By the end of the summer," Marotti said, "he's got like a cult of eight or nine guys doing his routine. That's leadership."

Marotti quickly identified other leaders, guys such as Boren, Mewhort, running back Jordan Hall, cornerback Bradley Roby, safety C.J. Barnett, and defensive tackle Garrett Goebel.

Though there were still stragglers, the foundation was slowly being put in place.

· 8 ·

SPRING QUESTIONS

BY THE TIME Ohio State's first spring practice under Urban Meyer started on March 28, the shock of the new demands on players by Mickey Marotti had passed. Almost all of them had survived it and were adapting to the new culture, however grudgingly. But as they took the field that spring day, no one really knew what type of team they'd become in 2012. There was no assurance they'd be better than the sub-.500 team they'd been in 2011, and they'd have to adapt from a pro-style offense to Meyer's spread. At almost every position, even the most important one, there were questions. At quarterback, the Buckeyes had a gifted athlete who'd earned respect with his humility under difficult circumstances as a freshman. During Meyer's introductory news conference, he gushed about the prospect of coaching Braxton Miller.

"With all due respect [to] everybody in this room, that was the highlight of my day, not this, sitting there, shaking hands with that good-looking quarterback with a nice smile, and a very humble player," Meyer said. "I watched him play throughout the year. I've watched him compete in the big game. And to tell you I'm excited to coach him, I'm not using the correct adjectives. And because there's mixed company around, I'm not going to use the correct adjectives, [that's] how excited I am."

Miller and Meyer bonded quickly. Kevin Miller, Braxton's father, drove from his family's home in the Dayton suburb of Huber Heights to the Woody Hayes Athletic Center just a couple of days after Meyer's hiring. He and Meyer talked for an hour while Braxton was in class. When Braxton got to the football facility, Kevin was stunned by the way coach and quarterback greeted each other. Instead of a nod or a handshake, the 19-year-old Miller and 47-year-old Meyer chest-bumped.

"That was the first time I'd seen them interact together," Kevin Miller said.

But it wasn't the first time they'd been in contact. When Miller was a highly prized prospect at Wayne High School, Ohio State had always been considered the front-runner to sign him. But Meyer pursued him for Florida, recognizing that his skills were ideal for the spread offense.

"It's unfortunate he stepped down," Miller said, "so I just chose Ohio State."

If Meyer had stayed with the Gators, Miller said, "it would have probably been 50-50" that he'd have gone to Gainesville.

"I guess it finally worked out that he came up here," Miller said.

On the surface, Meyer and his quarterback couldn't be more different in temperament. Meyer is blunt, often quotable, and invariably described as intense. Miller's personality is so reserved that he often seems to have just awoken from a nap. Though always polite, Miller's answers during interviews were often so short and bland that writers found them close to unusable. But beneath that placid exterior is a competitiveness that rivals anyone's, including Meyer. When he was four years old and his family had just moved into a new neighborhood in Springfield, Ohio, some older kids were playing basketball. They looked at the new kid and said he was too young to play. Miller wouldn't accept that. He plunked himself down right in the middle of the action.

"He got kicked off the court," Kevin Miller said. "That's one we laugh about a lot."

Another time, Braxton and his sister Bailey, who's three years older, were playing kickball in the Millers' backyard. Braxton kicked the ball, and Bailey threw him out at first by hitting him with the ball.

"He got so mad that he chased her around the yard for five or 10 minutes," Kevin said. "He didn't think it was fair. We've got it on video somewhere.

"I knew right then he was competitive," Miller said, before adding with a laugh, "but I was hoping he didn't have an anger-management problem."

To Kevin's relief, that competitiveness only manifested itself between the lines. Mickey Marotti learned quickly during off-season conditioning that Miller had a tendency to coast unless prodded with some sort of competition.

"He's a lights-on guy," Marotti said. "If you tell him, 'You're going to race, one's a winner and one's a loser,' he's going now. He's a lights-on guy, so I try to put lights on as much I can."

For a quarterback in Meyer's spread, that light can illuminate or it can burn. The spread's foundation is based on making the quarterback such a threat on every play that the offense has a numerical schematic advantage against the defense. Because the skill-position players in the spread are deployed in a way to force the defense to defend the full 53-yard width of the field, its options are limited. During Meyer's pilgrimage to Louisville as a Notre Dame assistant to learn Scott Linehan's spread, he thought he'd found a vulnerability in the scheme. Thinking that there wouldn't be enough blockers to counter a free-safety blitz, Meyer asked Linehan how he combatted that threat. Linehan said opponents hadn't seen a free safety blitz in four years because defensive coordinators realized that doing so would leave their defenses so exposed. That was the "aha" moment for Meyer.

"The tighter the formation, the more pressures," Meyer explained. "It's really numbers. In here [in a conventional offense], you have to worry about 11 guys. Out here [in a spread], it's six because [they] have to cover all these guys."

A quarterback who's an effective runner can maximize the math advantage. Because the quarterback in Meyer's spread always gets the snap from the shotgun, he's able to read and react to what the defense is doing. In a pro-style offense, the defense usually doesn't have to scheme to defend a quarterback run. In the spread, there's rarely a snap when that's not an option, depending on what the quarterback sees.

"Defenses have to account for the quarterback nine out of 10 times," running backs coach Stan Drayton said. "We're going to try to get their best players, be it defensive ends or linebackers, to have something to think about before the snap. They have to account for the quarterback, account for all the gaps in the run game and still be able to cover those displaced receivers we have."

It's not essential for a quarterback to be a major threat as a runner in Meyer's offense, but it helps. Alex Smith became the No. 1 pick in the NFL draft after playing in Meyer's offense at Utah, and he's not a gifted runner. Neither was Chris Leak, the starter on the 2006 national championship team at Florida. But Josh Harris was dangerous as a runner at Bowling Green, as, of course, was Tim Tebow. Having that dimension essentially gives the offense an extra player. Miller's speed and innate ability to elude tacklers makes him the prototype for the spread.

But Meyer also had questions about Miller. The first concerned his leadership. Meyer wanted to see more urgency in his sophomore, a feeling that he could be a vocal leader if necessary. Then there was the major question of how quickly he could adapt to the spread's demands. Being a physical fit for an offense doesn't matter if a quarterback doesn't understand its nuances and get his teammates on board with it. In Meyer's spread, the quarterback hardly ever gets a play call and knows for sure that he'll hand to a running back. He has to read the defense, usually a defensive end, and react accordingly. This would take time.

There also would be the issue of his throwing mechanics. Like Meyer, offensive coordinator Tom Herman did not watch much tape of the 2011 Buckeyes because he wanted to step on the field without preconceived notions about their strengths and weaknesses. But Herman had heard mixed things about Miller's arm strength. That concern was allayed right away.

"When we got him out there day one of spring ball and watched the ball come out of his hands, it was a welcome relief," Herman said. "I was very relieved he could throw the football."

But Miller's footwork was a mess, which led to major issues with accuracy and touch. Ohio State had the 115th-ranked (out of 120) passing offense in 2011, and at times it seemed worse than that. In a 24–6 loss to the Miami Hurricanes, when Miller and Joe Bauserman split time, the Buckeyes completed only 4-of-18 passes, all to running backs. Against Illinois, Ohio State won 17–7 despite Miller attempting only four passes and completing just one, a touchdown to Jake Stoneburner.

"To say there was one particular thing with his feet would probably be doing that an injustice," Herman said. "He was so inconsistent with his footwork that we really had to develop a lot of muscle memory."

Herman, like Meyer, also had to get used to Miller's placid demeanor and prod him to be more vocal when necessary.

"He's a quiet, laid-back kind of guy, and I'm used to quarterbacks being the type-A, fiery kind of guy," he said. "He wasn't that, and that's okay. That can be a negative to a certain degree. But when the lights came on, he'd perform. It wasn't like he was a lazy guy or disrespectful or anything like that. There [just] was an adjustment period, at least for myself, as far as getting used to his demeanor, but yet also try to teach him, 'Hey, maybe you should be a little more like this or that.'"

If Miller was under the spotlight, so were his passing targets. When DeVier Posey was out because of suspension for all but the final three games of the 2011 season, the Buckeyes desperately needed other receivers to emerge. None did consistently, and the pressure was on them to emerge quickly. In what was otherwise a strong recruiting class, especially under the circumstances, Meyer had failed to land a home run threat at wide receiver. Improvement among the receivers group would have to come from internal development and maturity. Devin Smith showed game-breaking ability as a freshman. His last-minute touchdown catch of a bomb thrown by Miller to beat Wisconsin was probably the biggest highlight of the Buckeyes' 2011 season. But too often, Smith was a non-factor. Junior Corey "Philly" Brown also showed glimpses of potential, but like Smith, was prone to drops. (Brown was from Upper Darby, Pennsylvania, near Philadelphia, and was given his nickname to differentiate him from cornerback Corey "Pittsburgh" Brown, who was from Monroeville on the western side of the state.) Sophomore Evan Spencer, son of former OSU running back and NFL assistant coach Tim Spencer, was another receiver hoping to emerge.

"You look at the roster and the guys I was going to coach, they were babies," wide receivers coach Zach Smith said. "Philly Brown was going to be a junior, but the others were sophomores. And honestly, they shouldn't have played the year before but because of the depth and the [Posey] situation, they were on the field."

The receivers had come to Ohio State knowing the expectation Buckeyes fans have for the position. Since 1995, the Buckeyes have had seven wide receivers taken in the first round of the NFL Draft. To have no one catch as many as 15 passes in 2011 with that kind of standard for the position left the receivers feeling "shell-shocked," Smith said.

Now they had to learn a whole new system under a new coach with a head coach who had no hesitation in making their failings public knowledge. When Meyer's Florida team played Ohio State in the 2007 national championship game, the Buckeyes' starting receivers were Ted Ginn Jr. and Anthony Gonzalez, both of whom became two of those first-round NFL Draft picks. Meyer didn't see anything comparable with the current Buckeyes receivers, or what he called a "wow factor." Things were so bad early in the spring that Meyer would refer to the team's feeble attempts at a passing game as a "clown show."

"There was a time in the spring when it was one of the worst offenses I'd ever seen," Meyer said. "I knew we couldn't put that on the field. The receiver position I was really disappointed with."

There was no escaping it, either. Smith would post newspaper stories critical of the receivers in their meeting room as motivation.

"It was tough," Devin Smith said of the public criticism. "It really lingered on our minds a lot. For some of us it was annoying, but I felt it was something we needed."

For the spread to work to its potential, receivers have to be able to consistently beat single coverage and have reliable hands. Like Miller, they had to adapt to the demands of the spread. Instead of running predesigned routes, as they would in a pro-style offense, receivers in Meyer's scheme must adjust instantaneously to the defense's coverage.

"Our offense is all about choice routes," Brown said, "being able to see a coverage and run a route off of every coverage they have."

Brown said he wasn't discouraged at the early struggles.

"We knew what we had to do," he said. "We had a new offense. We knew it wasn't going to cook just like that."

Brown had already experienced plenty of change in his Ohio State career. He was a running back in high school and expected to play that position or cornerback for the Buckeyes. But OSU coaches looked at his lean 186-pound frame when he arrived as a freshman and assigned him to play wide receiver, which he'd never played. It took some time, but he came to embrace the position. When Meyer was hired, he was excited about the prospect of playing in such a receiver-friendly offense. But the negativity of 2011 took a while to subside.

"He had a very bad reputation, and it was all earned," Meyer said. "He was not productive in the classroom. Every time you brought up his name, it was something negative. And then I witnessed it."

In their first meeting, Brown said, he and Meyer got into an argument.

"[I thought], 'This guy doesn't know what he's talking about,'" Brown said. "I was a whole different person in January. I was a negative person in January. When I walked out of there, I wasn't listening to anybody. I've had three different position coaches and three head coaches in three years. I guess it was a lack of trust. It was hard for me to be able to trust someone like I did with Coach Tress and Coach Fick."

But coaches could see a competitive fire in Brown. Despite his lack of girth, he did well in mat drills.

"I don't lose in mat drills," he said. "I can't lose a mat drill, and if I lose, I'll keep going until I win. Then when I win, I stop," he said with a laugh, "so I don't lose again."

Brown has a natural charisma, and receivers coach Zach Smith said other players naturally gravitate toward him.

"He is the guy that, when you jog on the practice field, he controls the tempo of my group, for sure—and maybe other groups," Smith said. "That's a little uncomfortable for him, having that power, but he slowly embraced it as time went on."

Brown's hopes of making a big splash in the spring took a hit when he tore the meniscus in his right knee on the first day of practice. Later, Evan Spencer's spring was cut short by a shoulder injury. By the end of the spring, whatever progress the receivers had made was modest.

"I knew there was a lot of work to be done, but I also knew spring served a purpose," Zach Smith said. "It showed them they weren't near where they needed to be."

If Meyer was worried whether anyone would ever become a consistent threat as a pass-catcher, he at least was somewhat reassured as spring wore on that the offensive line might not be a disaster. That would be crucial. Despite the common perception that the spread is a finesse offense, Meyer's scheme is one based on a power run game.

"We're different," he said. "We're a power offense that runs from spread sets. We're not a chuck-and-duck, throw-it-70-times-a-game offense. We want to lead the country in rushing and be very balanced. It all starts with being a tough, physical outfit. You can see on our great teams, we weren't very good throwing, but we could pound the ball at you. We did it from outnumbering people."

Of all the units on recent Ohio State teams, the failure of its offensive line to dominate consistently was a constant source of complaint among Buckeyes fans. For the previous several years, the line had been anchored by a trio of blue-chip recruits whose promise didn't yield the expected production. Center Michael Brewster was a productive player, but the burden of trying to be a leader on the team as a senior seemed to affect his play. Left tackle Mike Adams was among the players involved in the tattoo scandal and had an up-and-down career. Right tackle J.B. Shugarts was known more for his numerous false-start penalties than for his blocking. But their departures still left a void, and there was no assurance that the holdovers could fill it. Left guard Andrew Norwell was a solid player, as was Jack Mewhort, whom coaches decided to move to left tackle from right guard.

The other spots, who knew? Marcus Hall was a part-time starter at right guard and was the favorite to keep his spot. Brian Bobek was once considered the heir apparent to Brewster at center, but Meyer considered him overmatched. Corey Linsley was given first crack at the spot. Linsley had done little to distinguish himself to that point, even getting suspended for the first two games of the 2011 season for violating a team rule. Before Meyer took over, Linsley did some soul-searching and committed to change his ways. He had a bit of advance warning how things would be under Meyer. His high school coach at Youngstown Boardman High School was D.J. Ogilvie, who played at Bowling Green in the 1980s and remained connected to the Falcons' program. After Meyer's hiring, Ogilvie shot Linsley a text.

"All it said was, 'Buckle your chinstrap,'" Linsley recalled.

Linsley was prepared to do just that.

Right tackle was a bit of a black hole. The two contenders were senior Reid Fragel and freshman Taylor Decker. Once committed to Notre Dame, Decker switched to Ohio State after Warinner and Tim Hinton left South Bend for Columbus. At 6'7" and 313 pounds, Decker had good size. He also impressed with his football intellect.

"I remember the first day he came to the meeting room," Linsley said. "He knew the whole offense. That was a little bit of a shocker, in a good way."

But he was still a freshman. Fragel had been a backup blocking tight end his previous three seasons. With the change to the spread, Fragel knew he didn't have much of a future at tight end, so he volunteered to switch to tackle. It's a tough transition to make, and no one knew if he could. Meyer was particularly dubious.

"I didn't want him to be our right tackle," Meyer said. "I was hoping Taylor Decker would beat him out. I couldn't trust him, for a variety of reasons—his whole lifestyle from academics to practice habits to his weight. He couldn't keep his weight on."

In January, Fragel's first impression on Meyer was so unfavorable that Meyer essentially gave him an ultimatum.

"'Reid Fragel, really you have no value to this team,'" Meyer said he told him. "'You don't give anything to this team. You do nothing but take from us and Ohio State, and that's not fair. So it's time to start giving back, or you're going to have to find another place to go to school.' He was really struggling in school and was nothing but a pain in the butt."

It wasn't as if Fragel wasn't bright or tough. Warinner said he might have been the smartest linemen in his room. As for the toughness, well, this story from his visit as a recruit ought to answer that. He was with his father, Mark, standing outside the Blackwell Hotel on campus when a man tried to grab Mark's laptop and started running. Reid chased after him and caught him. The thief had picked the wrong target. Mark Fragel was taken aback when he saw what Reid had done to the assailant.

"He thought I used a knife on the guy's face," Fragel said. "He said, 'Where'd you get a knife?' because the guy's face was all bloody."

Linsley laughed when retelling that story. "That's the epitome of Reid," he said. "He's the nicest, friendliest guy in the world, and you'd never expect him to do that. But screw with him or his family and friends, and you'll see another side of Reid."

But Ohio State coaches were looking for another side of Fragel to emerge—the serious football player—and they weren't sure it would.

It was Warinner's job to turn this assortment of questions into a cohesive line. Remember, this was the unit that had four of its members skip Meyer's first meeting.

When spring practice began, the linemen felt like they'd entered boot camp.

"To be honest, it was scary at first," Mewhort said. "Coach Bollman was such a laid-back guy. Coach Warinner is up-tempo and intense."

It was that way everywhere. Coombs acted like some kind of overcaffeinated maniac with his cornerbacks. He chirped nonstop, barking criticism and screaming praise, sometimes in the same sentence.

"Do you know how good and how bad that was, all at once?!" Coombs yelled at Bradley Roby after the sophomore made a nice break on a ball but couldn't catch it.

When Adam Griffin didn't crouch low enough on a footwork drill, Coombs screamed, "Am I the only one seeing this? We've got a lady in the third row who can see this!"

Compared to the offense, the defense was relatively settled. The Buckeyes' defensive line, led by Simon and mammoth-but-nimble Johnathan Hankins, was expected to be the strength of the team. If defensive end Nathan Williams could make the difficult recovery from microfracture knee surgery, it would be an added bonus, but no one was sure whether that was realistic, not even Williams himself. The secondary looked to be in decent shape, as well, with senior Travis Howard trying to fend off sophomore Doran Grant at cornerback opposite Roby as the key position battle. It was a measure of the cornerbacks' confidence—and their coach's—that they put a sign "BIA" (Best in America) on the door of their meeting room.

"That was Coach Coombs," Roby said. "He said he came to Ohio State and wanted to coach a first-round pick and win the national championship. That was his goal. From that, we just came up with BIA—Best in America. That's what we wanted it to be."

The biggest question on defense was at linebacker, specifically in the middle, and whether Curtis Grant could seize control of that crucial position. Grant was considered the crown jewel of the 2011 recruiting class, rated even higher than Braxton Miller. But he was slow to pick up the defense as a freshman and was relegated to special teams. The Buckeyes were underwhelmed by the play of Storm Klein in the middle in 2011. Klein was slowed by a knee injury in the spring and would battle a chronic back issue during the season. In Meyer's mind, Grant's rapid development was essential.

"We have no choice," Meyer said early during spring practice. "He has to be a player for us. If not, we've got problems."

But Grant's progress was slowed by a pinched nerve in his shoulder. Grant wasn't alone. Toward the end of the 15 practices, as many as 20 players were out with nagging injuries. The injuries combined with the expected growing pains learning the spread often made spring practice painful to watch for Meyer and the coaches. As was the case with off-season conditioning, Meyer tried to speed the development along by making everything a competition. Winners got Gatorade. Losers drank water from a hose. Those on the victorious team in designated scrimmages would be treated to a fancy Champions Dinner that might feature steak or lobster. Those on the losing team settled for hamburgers and hot dogs. Meyer even got regular students involved in the process. After rain forced a scheduled open outdoors practice at Ohio Stadium to be moved to the Woody Hayes Center, Meyer concluded the workout by having students encircle Basil as he kicked field goals.

Most Buckeyes fans got their first glimpse of this new era of Ohio State football at the spring game on April 21. Under Tressel, the spring game was a low-key affair. Sure, young players tried to seize the opportunity to make a splash in front of fans desperate to see any glimpse of next season's team. But Tressel would sometimes spend the latter part of the game chatting it up with reporters behind the end zone. Anyone wondering whether the Meyer era would bring a different vibe didn't have to wait long. Before the game, he had players square off one-on-one in what the Buckeyes call the circle drill. Players lined up against each other and collided like battering rams until someone took the upper hand. Whoever won got mobbed by his teammates, while losers got hang-in-there taps. Even Miller and backup Kenny Guiton, who were deemed off-limits for contact in the actual spring game, went at it as the crowd roared.

"I just wanted some energy," Meyer explained. "I think it was fun for fans, and I know the players came out of their shoes when we did that."

Despite temperatures in the 40s and rain, a crowd announced as 81,112, the largest in the nation for a spring game in 2012, watched the Buckeyes' passing game show signs of life. Miller and

Guiton combined to complete 40 of 55 passes for 443 yards. It was encouraging, but hardly definitive. Wanting to keep things simple and ensure that quarterbacks didn't get injured, the Buckeyes didn't blitz. It's a lot easier to complete passes when the quarterback knows he won't be hit.

Miller said afterward that the Buckeyes used only 30 percent of their playbook. The real work lay ahead.

"We identified our issues," Meyer said after the game. "We also identified our strengths. I told them it has to be the best off-season in the history of college football."

Before he relinquished hands-on control of his players for the summer, Meyer had them come in for individual meetings in which he gave them detailed report cards exhaustively listing their strengths and weaknesses. The message didn't come just on paper. He was brutally frank with his players about what he expected.

Because of NCAA rules, Meyer and the position coaches couldn't have on-field instruction with the Buckeyes until preseason camp. But the development, and the challenges, would continue.

NOT A LAZY SUMMER

AFTER SPRING PRACTICE, players were on their own. Sort of. They still had workouts under Marotti as the process of changing their bodies and their mindsets continued. Their physiques had already begun transforming, and needed to. In the Urban Meyer–Tom Herman, no-huddle, spread offense, a fast tempo would be essential. Blubbery linemen wouldn't cut it. Just as Meyer made hiring Marotti his first priority, Marotti knew what he needed to add right away. It's astonishing that an elite program like Ohio State lacked someone to oversee the team's diet, but that was the case. So one of the first things Marotti did after his hiring was approach athletics director Gene Smith about hiring a team dietitian. Smith was receptive.

"He said, 'I've got the perfect person for you,'" Marotti said.

Sarah Wick, a 49-year-old mother of two teenage boys, had worked with athletes in other sports at OSU since 2003. She and other dietitians in the athletics department had wanted to become involved with football, but were always rebuffed, for reasons never really explained. Now she was brought on board to help players learn to eat right. Too many of them ate like typical college students. That might be fine for a business major, but Meyer wasn't coaching Football 101.

"They didn't have a plan," Wick said. "Many of them skipped breakfast and didn't eat all day until they finished training or got back from their studying late at night. There was no rhyme or reason [to their diet], no preparation. My goal going in was to give these guys a plan and really stress breakfast."

She brought a holistic approach. Every player was given a nutrition plan that would help them get into optimal condition. For some, like Johnathan Hankins, that meant losing weight by eating more often but with smaller portions heavy on vegetables. For others, like slender linebacker Ryan Shazier, it meant eating foods that would add bulk.

Because of NCAA regulations that limit how often a school can feed its athletes, most of what Wick did was educate. She didn't ban foods—even French fries were okay occasionally—but she preached the importance of balance and moderation. She set up a snack station where fruits, vegetables, and protein bars were readily available. She explained the necessity of proper hydration. Players were instructed to drink 75 percent of their body weight in fluid ounces each day. For someone like Hankins, that meant drinking at least a gallon and a half. Wick told players they'd know if they consumed enough fluid if their urine was clear at night. Wick held cooking classes for players, showing healthier ways to prepare foods. She took players to the grocery store and advised them about which foods to get and which to avoid.

A cancer survivor, Wick could speak from first-hand experience about the importance of proper nutrition.

"Nutrition was huge in my recovery," she said.

Wick believed the cancer battle empowered her.

"It's pretty obvious that to come back from something like that, with all the chemo, you go to the deepest, darkest place and have to build back," she said.

The players were drawn to her immediately. In an OSU football culture bursting with testosterone, Wick provided a nurturing female presence. They called her "Miss Sarah." They'd confide in her things far removed from proper diet.

"Literally, she was like our mom," Zach Boren said. "She was the team mom."

The results from Wick's program were impressive. In the first few months, Buckeyes players lost a total of 457 pounds of fat and gained 520 pounds of muscle.

"It was crazy the fat percentages that everyone went down," Boren said. "I lost 25 pounds in three and a half months. I went from 14½ percent body fat to 8 percent. I felt 100 times better. Going to class, walking up stairs was so much easier than it was in the past."

The players were increasingly more equipped to handle the load Marotti was putting on them, but it still wasn't easy. The competition was neverending. Marotti believes one pivotal moment came during the summer. He split the players into teams for an interval training competition in which they had to run across the field and get back under a certain time. Offensive lineman Marcus Hall, whose body was one of the most in need of reshaping, was dragging. He had the misfortune of having John Simon on his team.

"He wasn't hitting it hard, and John was trying to help him, be a leader," Marotti said. "Marcus was tired and didn't want to have anybody in his face."

Simon was definitely in his face.

"You get into that breaking point, that 'fight-or-flight,'" Marotti said, "and he wanted to fight John. Probably not a good thing to do."

Pushing, shoving, and yelling ensued, if not actual punches. The next day, Marotti said, Hall was a completely different guy.

"That's kind of when it changed," Marotti said. "That was the thing we needed. The way I look at things, in the summer, you need conflict, you need confrontation, you need confusion. Because in the game of football, that's what's going to happen."

If a player tried to cut corners, even the smallest one, Marotti made sure they paid the price.

"We're teaching you to help you and be accountable, to teach you what it means to be responsible and teach chemistry and team leadership and togetherness and all the things we talk about. That [incident] kind of helped."

But there would be others that were unwanted and tested the Buckeyes in other ways. The first came in early June. Suburban Dublin's Muirfield Village Golf Club hosts the annual Memorial Tournament run by Jack Nicklaus. Meyer's house is on the course, as is the family of Buckeyes senior tight end Jake Stoneburner. Late one night of the tournament, Stoneburner and Jack Mewhort went to the nearby Bogey Inn restaurant and bar. Both players were of legal drinking age, and they did what many young adults do. When nature called on the short walk back to the Stoneburners' home, they chose to relieve themselves on a building instead of finding a restroom. When they were approached by some men, they ran. It turned out that they were police officers.

"At the time, nobody had identified themselves as a police officer," Mewhort said. "Someone approaches you, and it was just instinct. You were doing what you were doing and you take off. I had no indication at the time [they were police]. Resisting the police is not in my DNA."

The police caught Stoneburner quickly. Mewhort ran until he stepped into a ditch and fell, with his face paying a stiff price.

"It was real steep and was dark, and I fell into this ravine and was just lying there, and that's when the cops got me," Mewhort said.

They were taken to the Shawnee Hills police station. Mewhort said they sat handcuffed in a folding chair for 11 hours. They worried how they would tell their parents. They were petrified how they would inform Meyer. When they were released after being charged with misdemeanors and posting $2,000 bonds, they headed to see their coach.

"It was probably the single hardest thing I've ever had to do in my life because I have such respect for Coach Meyer," Mewhort said. "I was already starting to see where we were headed as a program. He really had this program going on the right track. I was supposed to be a leader. For me to throw a monkey wrench into that, it was so embarrassing. I just couldn't believe that happened to me. I was so selfish to do that to the team. I couldn't believe all the people I let down. I was supposed to be the guy who could be counted on."

This would prove to be a test for Meyer as well as the players. At Florida, Meyer would take each of his player's arrests personally, and it would rip a hole in him. When the arrests mounted and media scrutiny began to portray the Gators program in a negative light, Meyer chafed at what he considered to be inaccurate or misleading coverage.

"It drove me insane and drove people insane," Meyer said. "We had some issues, like most programs have issues. It almost became like that was the lead story. Everybody was waiting around like, 'What's next? What's next?' They made it out to be like we were a bunch of bad guys, and that wasn't the case at all."

Now two of his key players at his new school had gotten into trouble. This time, he said, he handled it differently. He had come to appreciate the power of free will—his and others. He knew he couldn't take responsibility for every action by everyone he coached.

"I don't want to get overdramatic, but I had a little bit of a spiritual rebirth, as well," Meyer said. "It's not our job to change. You can't control people. It's our job to set the table, but they have to eat. Human beings live by a set of rules. Without rules, it's chaos. If you break the rules, there's punishment.

"But I'm not going to lose sleep over it. That's night-and-day different. [Before] I would stay up all night and be in their dorm room. I'd have them over to the house for 12 hours trying to get them right and change their thinking. [Now] I make it real clear. I get very close with these players, but I go home at night. When I go home, I go home. If you do something wrong, I'll deal with it when I get back. It's much different."

Meyer suspended Mewhort and Stoneburner, took them off scholarship for the summer quarter, and made them do community service. He met with both families. Jack Mewhort's dad, Don, wrote a contract for his son to follow about how Jack would repay him for the several thousand dollars in tuition he'd have to pay in lieu of scholarship funds.

"It's exactly the way I would have handled it," Meyer said. "You can tell why Jack Mewhort is the way he is. His dad doesn't play [around]."

To Meyer, what Mewhort and Stoneburner had done was stupid, but it fell more in the venal sin than mortal sin category. Later in the summer, linebacker Storm Klein was arrested and charged with domestic violence after an alleged altercation with his ex-girlfriend, with whom he'd had a baby.

"Devastating," Meyer said. "That was bad."

Meyer has no tolerance for disrespect toward women. It was one of what he calls his "Core Values" that his players must follow, along with honesty, not stealing, and not using drugs and weapons.

"My dad made it very clear to me when I was six years old," Meyer said. "You can break windows. You can get speeding tickets, whatever. But don't you ever lie to me. Don't you ever touch a woman or do anything that would disrespect a female."

Meyer dismissed Klein from the team and was not inclined to reconsider. But as the case proceeded through the legal system, Meyer talked with Klein, his family, the alleged victim's family, and directly to her. He became convinced that Klein was innocent of the charges. Klein eventually pleaded guilty to a lesser charge of misdemeanor disorderly conduct. His attorney said the plea "was the equivalent of making excessive noise."

Klein asked to be reinstated, and Meyer granted it, though he suspended him for the first two games of the season.

"If I believed that he hit her, I wouldn't have cared what the law said," Meyer said. "I would never have brought him back. Storm handled it like a grown man. I give him credit. I give both families a lot of credit. He handled it. He did everything I asked him to do. I think he's a better man because of it."

Legal issues weren't the only problems the Buckeyes encountered in the summer. The one that potentially had the greatest impact on Ohio State's fortunes was a freak injury suffered by running back Jordan Hall.

He had taken his dog outside of his residence to do its business. Hall was barefoot and he stepped on a piece of glass and sliced his foot in two places. He went to the emergency room and got nine stitches to close one wound and five in the other. The next day, he saw OSU team doctor Chris Kaeding.

"He said he thought we should get an MRI because I couldn't really bend my big toe," Hall said. "He said he was scared that it might have hit a tendon."

Kaeding's suspicions were correct. The injury required surgery. Hall was told he'd miss 10 weeks, which meant he would miss the start of the season. It looked like a devastating loss. Hall, a high school teammate of Terrelle Pryor in Jeannette, Pennsylvania, was the closest thing to a prototype running back for Meyer's spread offense that the Buckeyes had. He was shifty and had good hands and a high football IQ. Hall had shown glimpses of his ability in his first three seasons, but as the 2011 season ended, coaches had begun to sour on him.

"When Urban first took the job, Jordan Hall was in a bad place mentally," running backs coach Stan Drayton said. "He wasn't living right. He was making some bad decisions socially in his life. I don't know how serious he took his academics—late for classes, things of that sort."

But Hall also had aspirations of having a big season for the Buckeyes and then making the NFL. Drayton set him straight. "It doesn't work that way," he said. "Urban Meyer's system is about developing the whole man."

Once Hall realized that Drayton was serious, he changed his ways. Hall earned a grade-point average of 3.0 for two consecutive quarters.

"Mentally, I wasn't worried about school," Hall said. "I was just worried about football. I talked with Coach Meyer and Coach Drayton, and they said that football can't last forever. They've coached a lot of guys who've played in the NFL, and now they're successful in other ways. Why not listen to them?"

During spring practice, he was one of the few skill-position players who impressed.

"Anytime you have a kid who is almost dysfunctional off the football field and becomes not only functional but a leader, that's good," Drayton said. "He was able to pull some other guys who were kind of off the beaten path along with him and got them straight."

All that progress was now temporarily derailed by a stray piece of glass.

"It was tough at first," Hall said. "It was during the summer, and I couldn't really do anything. I was in a cast. Then I had to miss the whole camp."

But it wasn't all trouble for the Buckeyes over the summer. The players had taken seriously Meyer's challenge to make the months on their own productive. Miller and Guiton worked out most days with the receivers, improving their familiarity with the offense and chemistry with each other.

"The wideouts as a whole, I don't think there was any position group that worked harder than us in the summer," Philly Brown said.

The offensive linemen were out to show they were no slouches themselves. It might seem hard for offensive linemen to be able to show demonstrable improvement without going toe-to-toe with

Urban Meyer leads the Buckeyes onto the field for the first time as Ohio State head coach.

Travis Howard (7) and Orhian Johnson (19) flank Coach Meyer as they give the "O" sign at a spring game practice open to OSU students.

Buckeyes defensive end John Simon was regarded as the team's heart and soul for his relentless work ethic.

Devin Smith's acrobatic, one-handed touchdown catch ignited the Buckeyes after a sluggish start in their 56–10 season-opening victory over Miami University.

Shelley Meyer (left) has been invaluable to her husband's career, sharing the joy of his success and helping him navigate through the difficult times. For cornerbacks coach Kerry Coombs (right), this qualifies as a subdued, reflective moment.

Johnathan Hankins closes in on Central Florida quarterback Blake Bortles in the Buckeyes' 31–16 victory.

Etienne Sabino, here intercepting a pass against Central Florida, became a leader and crucial player as a senior.

Defensive line coach Mike Vrabel celebrates with Joel Hale during Ohio State's 29–15 victory over Alabama-Birmingham.

Ohio State wide receiver Devin Smith catches a long touchdown pass from Braxton Miller in the third quarter to provide the winning touchdown in the Buckeyes' 17–16 victory over Michigan State.

Safety Christian Bryant loves to deliver knockout blows, as Michigan State's Keith Mumphery can attest.

The victory over Michigan State marked the turning point for the season. Urban Meyer and Braxton Miller look as if they know this is the start of something special.

Cornerback Bradley Roby's interception return for a touchdown sparked the Buckeyes in their 63–38 victory over Nebraska.

Corey "Philly" Brown's punt return against Nebraska broke the game open.

Kenny Guiton had to wait longer than expected for Jeff Heuerman to break free on the two-point conversion against Purdue, but he stayed calm in the pocket.

Center Corey Linsley (71) and another teammate congratulate Jeff Heuerman after the tight end caught the two-point conversion to tie the game against Purdue.

defensive linemen, but that didn't deter them. An hour before their scheduled 6:00 AM workouts with the strength staff, the offensive linemen would get together to walk through blocking schemes and fundamentals.

Despite their lack of experience playing together, the linemen had developed a bond. Mewhort may have been off scholarship, but he remained a leader in the unit's eyes. Besides, all of the linemen had dealt with their own adversity. None of them had walked a straight line to success. Linsley had been an underachiever his first three years in the program. After playing in nine games as a freshman, right guard Marcus Hall redshirted as a sophomore for academic reasons. Norwell started off on the wrong foot when he was late to Meyer's first team meeting. Fragel was still battling to change Meyer's poor opinion of him. In the heat of summer, with no coaches allowed to watch, they did their work quietly, determined to dominate.

For Meyer, summer was a time to make sure that he spent time with his family and was properly balanced for the season. As enthused as he was to be coaching his home-state school, he knew his family was still adjusting to the move. Even though she was an Ohioan, Shelley hadn't lived in the state since the late 1980s. She hadn't wanted to leave Fort Collins when Meyer took the Notre Dame job. She'd become even more immersed in Gainesville. She'd lived there seven years, longer than in any place except the farm on which she was raised. Her friends were there. Her life was there. She loved the warm weather. Her daughters were in college, but both she and Urban worried deeply about uprooting Nate. Seventh grade is tough time for a kid to start over. Ohio was Urban and Shelley's native state. Nate was born when Meyer was at Bowling Green, but he had no memory of that. To him, Ohio might as well have been Iowa.

Shelley and Nate flew to Columbus on March 28, which happened to be the first day of Ohio State's spring practice. Nate had his last day at his Florida school while Shelley spent a few final hours with her friends. The friends got a van and took Shelley and Nate to the airport.

"Nate was very upset when he left his school," Shelley said. "He'd been there six years. Those were all the friends we knew."

The next morning, Nate started at his new school in Dublin, the one Amy Fickell had suggested. Shelley could see the trepidation in her son.

"When I dropped him off at that school, that look on his face worried me all day long," she said. "But at end of the day he was actually smiling. He had a bunch of new phone numbers and invitations to hang out with this kid and that kid. And he had his first baseball practice that night. Nate's a really social young man. He said, 'Mom, don't worry about me, I make friends really easily.' He did much better than I did."

Urban made sure that he had bonding time with Nate. In May, they went fishing off the Florida Keys, which was recorded for the *Gridiron Outdoors* show on the Outdoor Channel.

"A dream come true," Meyer said. "I try to do that as much as I can."

In June, they went to both Cincinnati and Cleveland for Reds-Indians interleague games, where each threw out ceremonial first pitches at Great American Ball Park and Progressive Field. The Cincinnati trip was a particular thrill for Meyer because he got to meet boyhood idol Pete Rose. Nate joined a travel baseball team. They played one game near the Youngstown area. John Simon and Corey Linsley were home visiting and went to watch him play.

"He's a pretty good baseball player, I'll say that," Linsley said. "He played shortstop and did well. He was whipping the ball over there."

He and Simon got a glimpse of Meyer, the father.

"It was a different side of him, but he still was motivating Nate," Linsley said. "He gave him that look like, 'C'mon, man.' It was kind of cool, seeing him being a dad."

They would see him as a coach again soon enough.

· 10 ·

CAMP MEYER

ON AUGUST 2, Mickey Marotti gave a present to Urban Meyer: the 2012 Ohio State football team. It's a ritual the two had shared since their days at Florida. Marotti had been in charge of molding the team since the end of spring practice. The next day, the start of training camp, the coaches get their paws back on the players. So the night before, Meyer has a ceremony in which Marotti formally presents the team back to him. Marotti had had his ups and downs with the players. It had taken time for all of them to get with the program. But their last workouts had been excellent, and he believed the team he was giving Meyer was far more sound of mind and body than the one he'd inherited in January.

"I don't know if they were tired of training and conditioning and were ready for football, or they were really starting to really come together as a team," Marotti said. "I thought they were ready for that next chapter."

But Marotti knows that players can meet benchmarks for physical readiness and still not be capable football players. That would be the test. Under Tressel and Fickell, recent training camps hadn't been easy, but they were a vacation compared to the wringer Meyer would put them through. In the past, players got a break in the afternoon. They could return to their hotel and take a nap during the three-hour break between practices. Not anymore. Meyer had air mattresses brought in that filled the facility. There would be no time to catch a bus back to the hotel for a rest. If they wanted a quick doze, they'd have to plop on an air mattress.

"We started that at Florida," Meyer said. "I think it's a great idea because time is of the essence. To take a 20-minute bus ride to your hotel and back, that's 40 minutes of sleeping you can have here. So players love it—some of them."

For 11 days, from sunup to sundown, it was complete football immersion. Meyer had warned his players that camp would be tough, and they'd learned enough about their coach to heed those words. That's why they worked out so hard on their own and with Marotti. Not everyone was willing to make such a deep commitment. Adam Bellamy, a key member of the defensive line rotation in 2011, quit the team. "When Adam quit, he basically just said it's too much, it's too serious, I'm not ready to go all in for that much," punter Ben Buchanan said. "He was a good friend of a lot of guys. Coach Meyer said you're not a bad guy for doing that. But you can't play for this football team if you feel that way."

Meyer's camp would test how deeply all of his players loved the game.

"Treacherous," Zach Boren said. "It was the hardest thing we've ever done as a team. It was a nonstop, 24/7, complete grind. It was by far the hardest thing I've ever done as an athlete or...ever been put through. As a team it made us closer. When times got hard, the ranks kind of closed and we got closer. We leaned on each other for support and help. I think that's what really made our team—fall camp. How hard that was and how much we were put through really brought us closer as a team."

Practices went at a breakneck speed. Players ran from one drill to the next, with every move subject to coaches' criticism. Meyer preached constantly that he wanted four to six seconds—the typical duration of a play—of relentless effort. There was also the plus-two rule. If a drill was designed to make players run 10 yards, they had to run 12. Everything was two steps beyond the standard.

Much of this was captured on camera. ESPN did a series of week-long programs showing the inner workings of college training camps, their version of HBO's *Hard Knocks* series chronicling NFL training camps. Meyer, despite his previous employment with the network, was skeptical at first about participating when ESPN asked.

"I normally wouldn't do things like that, but I felt there was so much negativity around our program," he explained. "People were just bashing us during recruiting. I'd talk to a kid, and he'd say, 'You guys aren't going to go to a bowl game for five years,' and, 'Jim Tressel did this' and 'the tattoos that.' I said, 'Wait a minute, stop. That's over.' So I talked with [football sports information director] Jerry [Emig] and Gene Smith. I said that we need some positive [exposure], and that's why we did that. It was a home run."

Even in the heat of August, the prospect of a certain chilly day in late November was never far from Meyer's mind. One day, a delivery guy came to drop off some equipment. He stood by the door outside the Woody Hayes Center and watched a few minutes of practice. No harm there, Meyer thought, except that he had the audacity to be wearing a blue shirt. That was Michigan's color. That could not be tolerated. Meyer ordered one of the equipment guys to get the guy a red shirt.

"We all thought it was a joke," Boren said. "But he was definitely serious about that. There is nothing blue around the facility at all. No one really wears blue. I guess it's just the motto of the program."

It wasn't just some poor delivery guy. A New York Giants scout came to watch practice one day. The Giants' dominant color is also blue.

"We all as coaches saw him," co–defensive coordinator Everett Withers said, "and thought the same thing: this guy right here ain't gonna make it long in practice with that blue jacket."

Sure enough, Meyer noticed.

"I started screaming, 'Stop practice! Stop practice!' and made him put on a red jacket," Meyer said. "Then I went over and shook his hand."

Asked if he had any blue in his wardrobe—after all, Florida's colors are orange and blue—Meyer replied, "I've still got them. I just don't wear them."

The avoidance of all things blue even extends to writing utensils. Blue pens are banned from the football facility. Really.

Occasional moments of levity aside, camp was serious business. The season was approaching, and many of the questions Meyer had in the spring had yet to be answered. Meyer had said during spring practice that starting jobs were to be won in March and April, that training camp was designed to prepare the Buckeyes for the opener against Miami University. But some positions remained open. Curtis Grant, the ballyhooed recruit from 2011, was still struggling at middle linebacker. Storm Klein hadn't yet been reinstated, so options were limited. The defensive line was also unsettled because of the uncertainty of end Nathan Williams. He was on the field, but only participating in individual drills as he built up strength in his knee. Travis Howard and Doran Grant were still battling at the cornerback spot opposite Bradley Roby. Though cornerbacks coach Kerry Coombs was increasingly comfortable with either Howard or Grant as a starter, he was deeply concerned about the depth behind them.

On offense, more questions lingered. With Jordan Hall out, running backs were a major concern. But one player was starting to erase the doubts coaches had about him. Carlos Hyde had been an enigma since his arrival in Columbus. At 235 pounds and with pure speed as fast as any of the running backs, Hyde had the physical tools to be a star. But he hadn't exactly won over coaches with his attitude or work ethic. Marotti, in fact, said coaches had a nickname for Hyde: "Carloaf."

"He is lazy by nature," running backs coach Stan Drayton said with a laugh. "He is a lazy dude. But I will say this about Carlos. He doesn't have an ego. Carlos knows he is lazy by nature. Because he knows that, he can self-reflect and he can fight and try to change that."

That's what he did. Hyde has always had enough self-awareness to avert serious trouble. Growing up in Cincinnati, he was a self-proclaimed mama's boy as a young kid. But as he became a teenager, he began hanging around with the wrong crowd.

"Guys I was growing up with started getting killed, and some were going to jail for long periods of time," Hyde said. "I was thinking to myself, *The path I'm on, I've got two options: I'm either going to die, or I'm going to jail.*"

Hyde didn't get into trouble for anything more serious than violating curfew, but he and his mother, Dermidra, decided it'd be best to have him move to Florida to live with his grandmother, Irma Butler, for high school.

"My mother knew it was best for me," Carlos said. "I knew it was best for me."

In Naples, Florida, Hyde became a star. He committed to Ohio State but had to spend a year at Fork Union Military School in Virginia because his ACT score didn't allow him to qualify. He came to Ohio State the next year and bided his time. He thought it arrived in 2011 when he had a couple of 100-yard rushing games. But he was frustrated and confused when he got only three and four carries, respectively, after those big games.

"It was really hard for me because I thought I was doing everything right," Hyde said.

But his reputation worked against him.

"Carlos' history around here wasn't so positive," Meyer said.

With the prodding of Drayton and Marotti, Hyde got with the program. By summer, he had transformed himself.

"He was one of our most improved guys," Marotti said. "By the summer, he was lights-out. I think it takes time for people to buy in. Sometimes, when somebody's not as gung-ho about weights and training, it takes him longer. Sometimes they struggle until they're in shape."

Similar progress was being made by the offensive line, building on its improvement during the spring.

"I thought Reid Fragel was terrible, but I thought we had four other guys who were going to be okay," Meyer said. "I didn't think 'good,' but I thought 'okay.'"

Center Corey Linsley was showing on a daily basis that his vow to turn his life and football career around hadn't proven hollow. A good thing, because there really was no viable alternative to Linsley. Brian Bobek had decided to transfer to Minnesota. Jacoby Boren, Zach's freshman brother, had impressed coaches early in the spring. The Buckeyes knew he needed major shoulder surgery eventually and encouraged him to do it as soon as possible so he might be ready at some point in the season. As of August, he was clearly not ready.

A year earlier, Linsley might have shirked the responsibility now on his shoulders. Now he embraced it. He spent hours working on his shotgun snap. That did not go well at first. The act of snapping isn't necessarily that difficult, until you factor in the responsibility of making the right blocking calls while knowing that a 300-pound defensive lineman is waiting to knock you into tomorrow as soon as you release the ball.

Because he's tasked with making the blocking calls at the line of scrimmage, the center is the quarterback of the line. Meyer calls it the apex of the offense. Given Linsley's lack of experience and previous problems, that could have been problematic. So Linsley broached the topic with his linemates.

He told them that he understood that they were veterans and he was the new starter. But he also said that it was his job as center to be the leader of the unit. Meyer described the center's role as being the center of a belt. Whichever way he goes, the other four must flow the same way. Sometimes, that would require Linsley to chastise his linemates or order them around. It would be nothing personal, he said. Just his job.

The other linemen assured him that it was a non-issue, that they understood it was a center's job to lead the way and that he had earned their respect. Besides, they were all getting enough tough coaching from Ed Warinner that they'd develop a strong bond.

"He'll push guys to the edge of the table," Meyer said. "That's what I like. I don't want to compare all our guys to Ed, but he wakes up in the morning coaching and he goes to bed at night coaching. When the doors open, he's the first one out there."

Players told of receiving multiple texts a day from Warinner with instructions on what they needed to do. On the field, he was relentless. Pity the player who made the same mistake twice.

"Sometimes, the way he'd get after guys, everybody on the team would know," Mewhort said. "To be honest, it was scary at first."

If he was this intense at practice, the players wondered, how crazy would he get in the heat of the game? They'd be nervous enough without having a lunatic coach making it worse.

As for the wide receivers, they hadn't shown enough progress to assuage the concerns of Zach Smith. "I was a little nervous about it," he said. "I didn't think we were where we needed to be. I knew the ability was there. It wasn't like I was coaching a room that was incapable of doing what we needed them to do. But I knew I hadn't gotten it out of them yet."

The season was fast approaching, ready or not. Thirteen days before the opener, Buckeyes players selected their five captains. John Simon became only the seventh Ohio State player ever voted to be a captain for a second time. Boren, Etienne Sabino, and Jordan Hall also were selected. The surprise pick, at least among outsiders, was Garrett Goebel.

"It was one of the greatest feelings you can get, knowing that your teammates think that highly of you and want you to help represent them," Goebel said. "It was just unbelievable."

The nose guard was not a star. He was more of a plugger, a guy who just day in and day out did his job quietly and gave everything he had. Goebel would only make 17 unassisted tackles all season, 12th on the team. After the season, Meyer couldn't name a signature play that Goebel had made. But he was the kind of player who would occupy blockers so that others could make the plays.

"Playing nose guard, you don't really get a bunch of glory or a bunch of stats," Goebel said. "You don't really play nose guard for yourself. You play for the guys beside you and behind you."

His unassuming, aw-shucks personality added to his appeal.

"Oh, my gosh, I love Garrett Goebel," Meyer said. "Give me 100 Garrett Goebels. I'm a big fan of selfless people. When he got voted captain, people were amazed. Amazed. Being elected by your peers is arguably the greatest gift that can happen to you as a teammate. And he had a lot of votes. The great thing about Mickey's program is that it identifies people. The phonies disappear. The Goebels go like this [he lifts his arm like an airplane taking off]. In our weight program, Garrett Goebel surfaced, and everybody sees it."

Goebel came by his work ethic honestly. His dad, Greg, owns a residential construction business in Chicago. When he was a young boy, Garrett would beg him to let him work during the summers. His father acquiesced when Garrett was nine or 10. He worked 12-hour days for $4 an hour, doing such tasks as lifting chunks of cement.

"I thought it was a lot of money," Goebel said. "I loved doing it, but you start realizing how hard it is."

As a high school junior, Goebel was surprised when Ohio State offered him a scholarship.

"They were the first big-time school who offered me," he said. "I was like, 'Wow, holy shit!'"

Goebel started off as just another faceless freshmen before gradually working his way to the point that his teammates considered him enough of a leader to vote him captain. With those captains, Meyer felt he had a core of leaders who would help navigate through what might be a trying season. Meyer had coached long enough to have a feel for a team entering the season. He still wasn't sure what he had. He knew the nonconference part of the schedule wasn't particularly taxing. But as he looked at the schedule, he knew road games at Michigan State, Penn State, and Wisconsin would be tough. He knew Nebraska would be a major challenge. And of course, there was resurgent Michigan under Brady Hoke at the end. The Buckeyes were ranked 18th in the preseason Associated Press media poll. (Because of their postseason ineligibility, they were excluded from the coaches poll and were ineligible for the Bowl Championship Series standings.)

Meyer scoffed at the notion that the Buckeyes deserved to be ranked. He had coached long enough to know what he had and what he didn't. He didn't voice this publicly, but he had an expectation for how many wins his first Buckeyes team would likely achieve. Eight or nine, he thought.

· 11 ·

MIAMI: THE MEYER ERA BEGINS

EVERYONE HAD JITTERS on the morning of September 1, 2012, but nobody's could have been worse than Nathan Williams'. For the previous 13 months, he'd battled his right knee and his own demons. Football had sustained and inspired him during a difficult childhood. His parents divorced when he was young, and he bounced around in a seemingly endless quest for stability. He and his two brothers and sister lived in Ohio; then Sacramento, California; then Bakersfield.

"I went to a new school pretty much every year, sometimes three schools a year just because of how much we would move around," Williams said.

He leaned on his siblings, and he leaned on football. When he was in kindergarten, his teacher asked her students what they wanted to do when they grew up. Williams said he wanted to play in the NFL. In the sixth grade, he wrote a plan, detailing step-by-step how he would fulfill that dream. He returned to Ohio before his sophomore year to live with his dad and attend Miami Trace High School, which produced the wondrously talented but ill-fated quarterback Art Schlichter a generation earlier. Before Williams even went home after arriving at Port Columbus airport, he went to Ohio State. Former Miami Trace coach Sonny Walters, a mentor to Williams and fixture in Ohio high school football circles, picked him up and drove him to meet Buckeyes coaches.

"Just to give him some hope because [Walters] knew football was a big part of helping him grow," Luke Fickell said.

Williams became a star at Miami Trace and was a contributor as a freshman for the Buckeyes. But Williams was an enigma. A hard worker who was considered a good teammate, Williams was nonetheless a bit of a loner. Early in his career, he was arrested on misdemeanor theft charges at a Dayton-area mall, though he pleaded guilty to a lesser charge.

"It was a total misunderstanding," Williams said. "I made sure nothing like that would ever happen to me, and it never has and it never will."

Williams and the Buckeyes expected to have a big year in 2011. He would play the pass-rushing end, called the "Leo" in Ohio State's scheme. Defensive coordinator Jim Heacock said at the end of the season that the Buckeyes had designed their strategy for 2011 in large part on Williams' versatility. He had the speed to beat tackles off the edge. He had the football instincts to be moved around and cause offenses headaches.

But one afternoon in the middle of two-a-days in training camp, Williams awoke from his nap at the team hotel and fell as he got out of bed. His right knee had given out. Williams tried to tough it out at practice that afternoon but couldn't. He suited up for the season opener against Akron and played in the first half. The pain was unbearable. Williams suspected that his coaches didn't believe the injury was as serious as he felt it was. Williams had arthroscopic surgery. It didn't help. A coin-size lesion was spotted on his MRI. He was told he'd need microfracture surgery. Microfracture procedures involve drilling small holes in a knee in hopes of regenerating cartilage. Most players don't make a full recovery from the surgery. Even those lucky ones who come back successfully—about a third—face a grueling rehabilitation. The first phase lasts two to three months. Patients are not permitted to put any weight on their affected leg. For eight hours a day, Williams lay in bed while a Continuous Passive Motion machine gently exercised his knee. Meanwhile, his teammates' 2011 season was imploding. Williams felt isolated from his team, and there were some hard questions directed his way, as well.

"He didn't have a great attitude," Fickell said. "He struggled with, 'I'm not playing. How can I help?' He was in such a bad mood that it was hard on him. I was probably a little hard on him. I wanted him to realize he needed to help the team in a different way."

Fickell worried that playing football was so paramount in Williams' life that he couldn't envision a life without it. Football ends for every player at some point, usually sooner than he expects. Fickell knew that from his own experience, when an injury ended his chances for a pro career before it could start.

"I kept telling him," Fickell said, "'You need these guys on the team. They need you. You can't base your whole emotional being on, 'Well, if I'm not on the field, I'm not happy.'"

The relationship between Williams and Buckeyes coaches deteriorated.

"We kind of butted heads and stopped communicating," Williams said.

But his resolve to return never wavered. Ohio State had hired a new physical therapist, Kristin Holbrook, and she was assigned to work with Williams daily. Slowly—very slowly—Williams began to recover.

"She's a very demanding person who wants the best out of every person she works with," Williams said. "It was hours upon hours that I worked with her."

As training camp approached, Williams was hopeful he'd be able to play. But he was discouraged by his progress. In practice, he was limited to individual drills. As late as mid-August, he suspected that he wouldn't return until midseason. Then the week before the opener, he had progressed enough to think that maybe, just maybe, he might be able to play in the season opener against Miami University.

"We'd gone through the game plan, and they weren't sure if I'd be part of it," Williams said. "As the week went on, I finally got to participate in a little bit of [full-team] practice—not very much and not nearly enough to be fully ready and prepared."

But he'd take his chances. A couple hours before the game, Mike Vrabel put Williams through drills to test his agility and strength. He passed. Three hundred and sixty-four days after his last action, Williams would be released from his own personal purgatory.

*   *   *   *

URBAN MEYER had been inside Ohio Stadium—The Horseshoe, as it's commonly known—once since his graduate assistant days in the 1980s. But broadcasting a game, as he did Ohio State's opener against Akron in 2011, was a bit different than being in charge of the program.

"Every head coach feels an overwhelming obligation and responsibility, and I even had more of it because this is my home state," Meyer said. "I felt it to the former players, to the fans, to my great state where I grew up."

The stadium, which opened in 1922 with a capacity of 66,000, looked considerably different than it did when Meyer would attend the occasional game as a kid, soak in the band performing "Script Ohio" and watch his heroes like Archie Griffin. Back then, the stadium really was the shape of a horseshoe, with a track on the outside of the field and small bleachers in the south end of the stadium. The track was now long gone and the south stands had been expanded to reach the top of the stadium. A new video board had been installed above the south stands as part of a $7 million audio-visual upgrade completed in the summer. As he strolled on the field before the game, he gazed around the stadium.

"I just loved the way they had the retired numbers up there now," Meyer said. "It wasn't like that before. I just thought the stadium was as beautiful as it's ever been."

He wasn't as sure about the product he would be unveiling. The same went for the crowd of 105,039 that filed in for Meyer's debut. They'd heard about this new Meyer offense. But except for those who'd attended the spring game—and that's hardly a definitive gauge—no one had seen it in action. The 18th-ranked Buckeyes were a 26-point favorite against the RedHawks, who were 4–8 in 2011. No in-state team had beaten Ohio State since 1921.

Meyer was familiar with Miami's program from his two years in the Mid-American Conference at Bowling Green. He had considerable respect for RedHawks quarterback Zac Dysert and wide receiver Nick Harwell, who he believed were future NFL players. Miami also ran the spread, though with a completely different aim. The RedHawks were a finesse team. Miami made little attempt to try to show that it could run against Ohio State's rugged defensive line. The RedHawks knew that to have any chance, they'd have to ride Dysert's arm with quick-release passes that would neutralize the Buckeyes' pass rush. That's exactly what they did, at least early in the game. Dysert threw for 165 yards in the first quarter. It should have been more. The RedHawks dropped several passes, including two that almost certainly would have gone for touchdowns. They also missed a 24-yard field goal. The Buckeyes' offense, meanwhile, did nothing early. It looked like a repeat of 2011's feeble offense. Ohio State managed only two first downs on its first four possessions. Braxton Miller threw incompletions on six of his first seven throws. The Buckeyes were quite fortunate to trail only 3–0.

The poor start defensively didn't faze Luke Fickell.

"That's what we wanted to see, how they'd handle it," he said. "They were so hyped and energized to take the field with all the new stuff we're doing in the program. Then all of a sudden you get kicked in the mouth, and you see how you respond. That's what I said to Coach Vrabel before the game: 'I want to see how our guys respond when the first adversity hits.'"

That was kind of the same thing the Buckeyes' offensive linemen wondered about their coach. But as they came to the sideline after each failed drive, they were struck by something. They had worried about how Ed Warinner would react to problems in a game. To their surprise, he wasn't a screaming maniac.

"On game day, he was the most cool, calm, relaxed guy," center Corey Linsley said. "He had his shit down and knew what he was going to do. He had this level of confidence that just relaxed us. This guy is a total 180 [degrees from what we expected]. Obviously, his level of intensity was there. But he wasn't screaming or shouting at us at all. His level of confidence from coaching us up to that point, he just kind of let us take the reins and go after it."

But just as the Buckeyes' early struggles caused the crowd to start to murmur, one drive—and in particular, one play—changed the game's momentum for good. Ohio State took possession at its 17 early in the second quarter. Carlos Hyde ran for 16 yards on the first play. Braxton Miller then connected with Philly Brown for a 38-yarder to the Miami 23. On the next play, Miller took the snap, saw Devin Smith in man-to-man coverage with Dayonne Nunley, and let it fly toward the deep right corner of the end zone. Nunley was behind Smith, and the pass seemed too high. Miller certainly thought so. In his mind, he thought, *Damn*. But twisting his body, Smith leaped and snared the ball one-handed behind his head, retaining possession in his right hand as he fell.

"When he initially threw it, as I was looking for the ball, I was thinking in my head, *This ball's about to go out of bounds*," Smith said. "It started to fall and I was like, just let me jump for it. I jumped for it and it fell in perfect. It's one of those catches you always dream of. Since I was growing up and watching football and seeing guys make top 10 on *SportsCenter*, I've always wanted that to happen. Like every kid, you dream about that moment and practice."

For the Buckeyes, it was a needed sign that the receivers could make big plays under pressure.

"I don't know if Devin has been saving that, but I've not seen him do that," Meyer said after the game. "That was a wild moment. And that was a moment that ignited the stadium."

Once the fuse was lit, the offense took off. They drove 57 yards for a touchdown on their next possession, and 73 for another score on the one after that. The defense, after missing tackles and blowing coverages early, settled down. When Evan Spencer caught a 44-yard pass at the Miami 1-yard line with three seconds left before halftime, Meyer didn't hesitate to go for the touchdown and apply the knockout punch.

"Coach Meyer brought us together and said, 'If you guys can't convert this, you're worthless,'" left tackle Jack Mewhort said.

Mewhort lined up next to Fragel to provide extra beef on the right side, but it didn't matter. Miami stuffed Hyde at the goal line. "We were blocking down and someone just didn't block down," Mewhort said. "They blocked out, and it ruined the play."

It also ruined the day for Mewhort.

"That's probably the only thing I'll ever remember about that game," he said. "That play was on my mind the rest of the game. As an offensive line, we were really disappointed we didn't convert that."

So was Meyer.

"Really pissed," he said. "To the point I can't get it out of my mind. I let the offensive coaches and players know my displeasure."

The Buckeyes had to settle for a 21–3 halftime lead. Ohio State did blow the game open in the second half. On the Buckeyes' first play, Miller ran an option left, found a seam, and got to the sideline, then left the final Miami tackler flat-footed with a nifty stutter-step move on a 65-yard touchdown.

The Buckeyes extended the lead to 35–3 when Bradley Roby emerged with the ball in the end zone following a botched Miami punt. The score was 35–10 at the end of the third quarter. Then Meyer the coach became Meyer the childhood fan and alum. As is tradition, the band played "Hang On Sloopy" before the start of the fourth quarter.

"I stared at that for a while," he said. "I told a couple people that had never seen it to check it out."

The Buckeyes added three more touchdowns in the final quarter for a 56–10 victory. There were plenty of reasons for excitement. Miller ran for 161 yards—a record for an OSU quarterback—and threw for 207 despite the shaky start, though he left the game early with leg cramps. Hyde scored two touchdowns. Travis Howard intercepted two passes. Fullback Zach Boren, who somehow managed to go the entire 2011 season without getting a single carry, scored his first rushing touchdown of his OSU career. (He'd caught an eight-yard TD pass as a freshman.)

Happiest of all was Nathan Williams. He entered the game in Miami's second possession.

"I remember running on the field and being more nervous than I've ever been, just because of all the hours of rehab I had to do," Williams said. "It was definitely a rush."

His teammates, who knew how long he'd struggled, greeted him enthusiastically in the huddle. "They were all pumped up," Williams said. "They knew how bad I wanted it. They were saying, 'Nate's back! Nate's ready to go!'"

Williams played far more than expected. He took about 30 snaps and had two unassisted tackles, including one on third down to end a Miami possession. Yes, he was rusty. He allowed Dysert to slip from his grasp when he had a chance for a sack. But he was out there, contributing, feeling whole once again.

Early in the game, Williams had been hit on the knee by a helmet and would miss the next game as a result. At first, he thought he had reinjured the knee. But as painful as it was, he kept playing. The adrenaline made the pain tolerable. Williams would have to be treated gingerly the rest of the year. His practice time would be limited. That would have its effects on him and the entire defense. But those would be issues for later. Now he just wanted to soak it in.

"It was unbelievable," Williams said. "I can't really put into words how excited I was being able to play after all that rehab."

Meyer's emotions about his team's overall performance were less than unbridled joy. Yes, he was thrilled to have coached his first game for the school he'd grown up loving. His team had won by 46 points.

But coaches know that scores can be misleading. Miami did not have the physical talent to go toe-to-toe with Ohio State in the trenches. It was almost inevitable that the Buckeyes would wear the RedHawks down. Ohio State had been sloppy, and that gnawed at him. In his postgame news conference, he was gracious toward Miami and generally put on a happy face. It was a façade.

"I didn't let on with the team," Meyer said. "But I was kind of crushed with how we played. All the way through, we just didn't play very well. At the end of the game, we kind of blew them out. They didn't match up with us. But we played poorly. That was not a good game."

· 12 ·

CENTRAL FLORIDA: RIDING BRAXTON

THE PLAN WASN'T for Braxton Miller to run 27 times against Central Florida.

Then again, few things went according to plan for the Buckeyes in 2012. When improvisation was needed, it usually would fall on the sophomore quarterback to provide it. Miller would prove to be far better equipped to handle it than he had been as a freshman when he was thrust into an impossible situation after Terrelle Pryor abruptly left and Joe Bauserman faltered.

"Coming in as a freshman from high school, with Terrelle here, I thought I was going to sit back and take notes from him," Miller said. "In the back of your mind, you have that question: I don't know if I'm ready for this big stage of football yet."

He wasn't intimidated by playing in front of huge crowds. He could block that out. But trying to lead players who were several years older was a definite challenge.

"All the guys were 22 or 23 years old," Miller said. "An 18-year-old coming in trying to run the show, it's different."

His teammates noticed the difference with a year of experience.

"He grew a lot, being a leader and speaking his mind and putting guys in their place and keeping everybody where they need to be," left tackle Jack Mewhort said. "He's really maturing into a student of the game, and he really cares about his guys and wants to be better."

Though it took some time for coaches to adjust to the reality that Miller wasn't a fiery leader, his teammates appreciated his level-headedness.

"He's the smoothest operator you'll ever meet," Mewhort said. "You'll never see the stress get to him. In the heat of battle, he's always so calm. He could have the world on his shoulders, and he'd never flinch. He always has a smile on his face. If he is ever nervous, nobody will ever know that."

As impressed as they were by his demeanor, they were awed by his talent, particularly his innate ability to elude tacklers.

"It's amazing to watch," Mewhort said. "It's like watching a video game."

Miller first became aware that he was a gifted athlete when he was seven years old. He was playing football in his Springfield back-yard with his brother, Breyon, who's five years older, and Breyon's friends. It's not unusual for a big brother to let a little brother score a couple of touchdowns. Give the kid a thrill. But it soon became apparent that Braxton didn't need their charity. He could score even when they were trying their hardest.

"That's when I knew, dang, I had something special," Miller said.

He and his slightly older cousin would go to different neighbor-hoods seeking games. They'd always dominate.

"People would be like, 'I don't want y'all playing with us no more,'" Miller said with a chuckle.

It wasn't just in football. As a Little League pitcher, Miller threw so hard and with such natural movement that opponents accused him of throwing a curveball. He was so dominant that he was forced to move up to an older age group.

As his athletic ability became apparent, his father, Kevin, wanted to make sure that Braxton's head didn't swell. He drilled into Braxton that athletic prowess can be fleeting, that he should always carry himself with modesty. That was never a problem for Miller.

"When I score a touchdown , I just toss the ball to the ref and trot back to the sideline," he said. "People would say, 'You've got no commotion, no celebration.' I'm used to scoring so much, and it comes natural, so there's no need to celebrate."

The Millers moved to Huber Heights before Miller started high school. Wayne coach Jay Minton said that Kevin Miller told him he didn't care if Braxton played quarterback as a ninth-grader. He said he'd be satisfied if his son got his feet wet playing wide receiver or defensive back. But it didn't take long for Minton to see how talented Miller was. In the season opener against perennial power Colerain—cornerbacks coach Kerry Coombs' old school—Wayne fell behind. Minton put Miller in at quarterback after halftime. Miller rallied Wayne, and though the comeback fell short, there was little doubt that the future had become the present.

"I remember [Colerain coach] Tom Bolden came over to me after the game," Minton recalled, "and said, 'That kid is a freshman? Are you kidding me?' From that point on, there was no going back."

Despite battling several injuries, including a broken leg as a sophomore, Miller established himself as an elite prospect. He would have numerous close calls with injuries throughout 2012, but he managed to answer the bell to start all 12 games. That might have been impossible if he'd been used the way he was against Central Florida.

*　　*　　*　　*

THE AVERAGE Ohio State fan might have had trouble distinguishing Central Florida from some of the generic opponents the Buckeyes face in their nonconference schedule. But Ohio State coaches were worried about UCF. The Golden Knights would be hungry and unafraid. With George O'Leary, they had an accomplished coach who probably didn't figure to be in charge of Central Florida at age 66. He'd been hired by Notre Dame in 2001 after a successful stint at Georgia Tech. But his days at Notre Dame proved to be just that—days. Shortly after he arrived in South Bend, it was discovered that he had lied on his résumé about his academic and football achievements. Notre Dame fired O'Leary after only five days on the job. After two years as the defensive coordinator of the Minnesota Vikings, Central Florida hired O'Leary in 2004 to rebuild its program. In his first year, the Knights went 0–11. But they quickly improved and became a power in Conference USA. Their 2011 season and aftermath would be similar to the Buckeyes'. They finished with a losing record and ended up on NCAA probation. UCF was banned from a 2012 bowl game (though the school would successfully appeal and win the Beef 'O' Brady's Bowl against Ball State to cap a 10–4 season).

In its opener, Central Florida routed Akron and was confident of success in Columbus. Certainly, O'Leary didn't fear heading into the Horseshoe. The week of the game, he compared Ohio State fans to the staid ones at Michigan.

"It's not a loud stadium," O'Leary said. "They sit on their hands in that stadium. I've been there before, and you take Wisconsin, you take Iowa, you take UCF. It's much louder than that stadium. It really is, as far as noise is concerned, because it is so far away from the field. But a lot of stadiums are louder than that place. I didn't even [pipe] in music this week or any type of noise, because I think we should be able to execute without it."

That was Meyer's fear, as well. He considered the Golden Knights to be on a par with a middle-of-the-pack Big Ten team or slightly below. At that point, that's about where he thought of the Buckeyes.

"The talent differential wasn't that much," he said. "They were a good team. I knew that going into it. I know this team coming in here has got players. If we don't play well, we've got real problems."

Meyer knew it might be a hard sell for his players. To his players, UCF was just another unfamiliar school from a non-BCS conference.

In most ways, Central Florida would match up well against Ohio State. But the Golden Knights did not have Braxton Miller.

*   *   *   *

MILLER OPENED the scoring with a 37-yard run that gave a glimpse of how the spread can work with a quarterback like him. Ohio State opened the field by lining up with five receivers. Center Corey Linsley and right guard Marcus Hall opened a running lane at the line of scrimmage. Jake Stoneburner made a nice block downfield to seal off a linebacker. With Miller's speed and shiftiness, that was all he needed to race untouched to the end zone.

The Buckeyes drove inside the UCF 10 two possessions later. On third-and-five, Miller threw an incomplete pass to Carlos Hyde, and the Buckeyes had to settle for a field goal for a 10–3 lead. The failure to convert the touchdown was hardly the worst thing that happened on the incompletion. Hyde sprained a medial collateral ligament in his right knee and was done for the day. That left the Buckeyes without a proven running back. With Jordan Hall still recovering from his foot injury, redshirt sophomore Rod Smith and true freshman Bri'onte Dunn were the only available scholarship tailbacks. Smith was still working his way into good graces after missing a flight to the Gator Bowl and failing to arrange his own way to Jacksonville. Dunn's start at Ohio State was marred by a summer incident in which he was arrested and charged with traffic violations after a small amount of marijuana was found in the car that he was driving. The car was his mother's, and Dunn was later acquitted. But neither Smith nor Dunn had earned the trust of OSU coaches. Smith would fumble late in the game, continuing an issue he'd had in 2011.

"I'd be lying to you if I told you we did [trust them], simply because of the newness of us and amount of reps they'd had," offensive coordinator Tom Herman said.

Had the defense shut down Central Florida, the Buckeyes wouldn't have needed to rely so heavily on Miller. But the same issues that had plagued Ohio State against Miami cropped up again. Without Nathan Williams and sophomore Michael Bennett, who was out with a groin injury that would linger, the defensive line lacked depth. Like Miami, UCF designed its passing game on having its quarterback, Blake Bortles, get rid of the ball quickly. So Ohio State's pass rush was again mostly a non-factor. Missed tackles and assignments again were a problem. The Knights tied the score at 10 on a drive aided by the Buckeyes. Cornerback Bradley Roby whiffed on a screen pass to Storm Johnson at the line of scrimmage on a play that went for 20 yards. Safety Christian Bryant took a poor angle on a 48-yard run by Johnson. Linebacker Ryan Shazier then bit on a play-action fake, allowing tight end Justin Tukes to sneak behind him for an easy one-yard touchdown catch from Blake Bortles.

The teams traded turnovers—a fumble by fullback Zach Boren followed by a Travis Howard interception after Bortles' pass was tipped by Orhian Johnson—before Miller again took over. He completed passes of 14 yards to Philly Brown and 10 to Devin Smith. On third-and-16, Miller than ran 24 yards on a quarterback draw and then went the remaining six yards for a touchdown on the next play to give Ohio State a 17–10 halftime lead. On the Buckeyes' first drive of the second half, the virtual one-man show continued. With his arm or legs, Miller accounted for 64 of the 76 yards on a touchdown drive that extended the lead to 14 points. When Etienne Sabino intercepted a Bortles pass and Miller capped a 32-yard drive with an eight-yard touchdown run for a 31–10 lead, the Buckeyes seemed in control. But Central Florida answered with an 84-yard touchdown drive. Adolphus Washington blocked the extra-point kick to keep it a 15-point margin.

After Miller was intercepted at the Ohio State 36, the Knights drove to the Buckeyes' 9 when safety Orhian Johnson made the game's key defensive play.

"We were in a red-zone Cover 2," Johnson said. "I was trying to read the quarterback's eyes and play my zone and broke on the ball."

Bortles threw a dart, but Johnson snagged it for an interception.

"I had missed a pick that Travis had picked off, so I knew I had to make the most of the next one that came to me," he said.

The Buckeyes would struggle all year with blown interceptions, but Johnson was the exception to the hands-of-stone problem. That wasn't by accident. When he was a kid, his father, Oscar Johnson III, would throw footballs at his son in the front yard of their St. Petersburg, Florida, home.

"He'd put me on the wall so I couldn't back up or run nowhere, and he'd throw the football as hard as he could," Johnson said. "I either caught it or I tore my chest up. After a couple times of getting hit in the chest, you realize that you've got to stick your hands up there."

Orhian had to catch 10 in a row, or at least have five catches twice before his dad would end the drill. His hands may have grown reliable, but the rest of him wasn't. Johnson was always viewed as a guy with unfulfilled potential at Ohio State. Before his junior year, Fickell named him one of three Buckeyes to represent the team at the Big Ten media days in Chicago. It's a big honor, especially for a non-senior. But Johnson had a disappointing junior season and was a backup by year's end. He blew his chance for a clean slate by being late to Meyer's first meeting and compounded that by being late for another meeting soon afterward. Knowing he'd put himself in the crosshairs, Johnson flirted with the idea of transferring.

"I think it was mainly me talking because I was frustrated," he said. "I just threw names [of schools] out there just to say them, but I was so close to these guys, I couldn't leave."

He came to realize and accept that even if his career wouldn't play out exactly as he dreamed, he could still be an integral contributor. Johnson had shown enough that Meyer gave him an expanded role as the nickel cornerback, which is called the "star" in Ohio State's scheme.

"Everybody, when they come to college, wants to be an All-American, wants to be a starter, that guy their team depends on," Johnson said. "Coming in as an 18-year-old, you start thinking, *I'm not playing. I'm not good.* It can mess with you. But you get around this kind of program and you learn that everybody's valuable.

"This thing can't run without every piece. You start to buy into it and you start see your role increase so it makes you feel comfortable in your role. Like coach says, it's a meritocracy in everything we do. If you do your job well, to the best of your ability, you're going to get praised for it. I enjoyed the group of guys I played with. I didn't mind swallowing my pride to go out and play certain roles for those guys. I feel the position I was put in was important, even though I wasn't a starter. Whether it was on special teams or nickel back or safety, I wanted to be someone the team could depend on and someone the younger guys could look at and say, 'Okay, that's how you're supposed to handle it.'"

That he had done. Christian Bryant, who beat out Johnson for the starting safety spot as 2011 wore on, said Johnson helped him even at the expense of his own playing time. "When we were fighting for playing time, he never gave me the cold shoulder," Bryant said. "He got me to understand the defense and schemes. I have a lot of respect for Orhian. Orhian is always a positive guy. He always tries to bring the best out of somebody."

The Buckeyes' defense thwarted Central Florida the rest of the game. Cornerback Doran Grant, in because Howard had suffered a shoulder stinger, broke up a fourth-and-four pass from the Ohio State 47. The next Knights drive ended with four straight incompletions. The 31–16 Ohio State victory ended on an incompletion under heavy pressure from the Buckeyes' 9.

Miller finished with 141 yards and three touchdowns in his 27 carries. He completed 18 of 24 passes for 155 yards. Of Ohio State's 69 snaps, Miller ran or threw on 51 of them. No other Buckeye had more than seven carries.

"I was running some of the running back plays, Carlos' plays," he said.

"*Carlos, hurry up and get healthy and come back*," Miller remembers thinking, "*because I don't want to carry that rock 27 times again*. But it's a role you have to take on sometimes when things go bad."

That was Tom Herman's feeling. He knew it wasn't ideal to have Miller run 27 times. But what was the alternative?

"Braxton's always going to be the best player on the field, so you're tempted every game to put the ball in his hands every snap," Herman said. "But you know that's not in the long-term interest of the team or the offense. But in that instance, if the ball was not in his hands in that game after Carlos got hurt, then we would have been doing the team an injustice because the two kids in the backfield with him were so inexperienced. You call plays and you adjust, according to injuries or circumstances. You do whatever you have to do to win a football game."

So Miller had little choice but to suck it up.

"Everything," Miller said when asked what hurt afterward. "You get hurt carrying the ball 27 times. I took a couple of hits. You get sore. That's the name of the game. You get tackled, you get hurt. I was like, I can't do this anymore. I can't do 27 carries every game."

Hyde would miss the next two games with the MCL sprain. Miller would get some help, though. Jordan Hall would return the next week. But it was another player who gutted through an injury who'd make the biggest mark in the season's third game—or more accurately, after it.

· 13 ·

CALIFORNIA: BAD GAME, BIG SPEECHES

DURING TRAINING CAMP, John Simon sprained his ankle. Then he suffered a groin injury. That was followed by a rib dislocation injury.

"Some ribs kept popping out of place," he explained. "They'd snap out of place and the cartilage would pull them right back in. It was pretty painful. It was hard to breathe at times, but it never got to the point where I thought I would miss anything."

This lasted, he said, for the first four or five games of the season. If Simon admits that an injury is "pretty painful," that translates to "excruciating" in a Simon-to-normal-human dictionary. But against Central Florida, Simon suffered a shoulder injury that he realized might be beyond a matter of his Herculean pain threshold.

"I couldn't really move it at all besides more than an inch or two left or right," he said.

Simon being Simon, he kept it to himself.

"I didn't really tell anybody because I figured it'd get better," he said.

But as Ohio State's game against California approached, the shoulder wasn't improving much. On game day, he wasn't sure he could go. But he did play, even if he was essentially doing so one-handed.

*   *   *   *

OHIO STATE'S nonconference scheduling philosophy has been based on having one marquee opponent, with whom they play a home-and-home series. The other games essentially serve two purposes. They are tune-ups for the Big Ten season, and they generate sufficient revenue to keep the Buckeyes' 36-sport program—the largest in the country—in the black. The marquee games are added years in advance. Ohio State already has a series against the Texas Longhorns scheduled for 2022–2023. Such a long lag time means that a "marquee" opponent might be B-movie material by the time the game is played. Certainly, the California Golden Bears from the Pac-12 were not now the elite program envisioned when the schools agreed in 2002 to play. Jeff Tedford developed a reputation for developing quarterbacks as Cal's coach, most notably Green Bay Packers star Aaron Rodgers. But 5–7 and 7–6 records the previous two years made Tedford's job security tenuous. A loss to Nevada in the 2012 opener followed by an unimpressive win over Southern Utah only increased the heat. (In fact, Tedford would be fired by season's end.)

While the outside world saw an underachieving football team, Meyer saw a team that was at least as talented as his. Former Ohio State coach John Cooper serves as a scouting consultant for the Cincinnati Bengals. Every week, Meyer asks Cooper for an assessment of the Buckeyes' opponent. Cooper told Meyer that the Bears had several players likely to be taken in the NFL Draft. Keenan Allen, the half-brother of Cal quarterback Zach Maynard, was considered a likely first-round pick. (But he would slip to the third largely due to injury concerns.) To Meyer, the Buckeyes had so many question marks that any team with a modicum of talent would be a challenge.

His suspicions would be confirmed, though for the first 30 minutes the Buckeyes seemed to be on their way to a comfortable victory. Ohio State's offense got a boost by the return of running back Jordan Hall from his foot injury. With Carlos Hyde out with his sprained MCL and only green Rod Smith and freshman Bri'onte Dunn left, Hall was desperately needed.

"I was just happy to be back out there with my boys," Hall said. "I knew I wasn't really full speed, but just to be out there…"

Even showing plenty of signs of rust, Hall ran 17 times for 87 yards to provide some support for Braxton Miller. But it was still Miller who was front and center. He opened the scoring by adding yet another dazzling touchdown run to his highlight reel. On a third-and-four play, Miller started up the middle. He got a block from Zach Boren pushing the defender outside. Still, Miller looked to be hemmed in when safety Alex Logan came up in run support and had the angle on the quarterback. But Miller practically gave Logan a hip dislocation with a quick fake and raced down the left sideline untouched for the 55-yard touchdown. Drew Basil missed the extra point, keeping it 6–0.

Cal took a brief lead thanks to some shoddy tackling. The Buckeyes had Isi Sofele surrounded on the first play of the Bears' drive, but he escaped from middle linebacker Curtis Grant for a 26-yard gain. Grant would soon be replaced by Storm Klein, whose suspension had ended. Grant would not start the rest of the season for the Buckeyes.

"Curtis just would never take the spot," Meyer said. "To say why, I can't give you one reason. It's a multitude of things. He just didn't earn the playing time. It was very devastating because I knew we were struggling. When you have a very highly recruited player that's not taking a spot, it's very frustrating. And he's a good kid."

Grant blamed himself for failing to seize the job.

"I got too complacent," he said during spring practice in 2013. "I couldn't handle the glory, I guess, of being a starter. I should have kept working harder."

Five plays later, after Grant's missed tackle, Chris Harper scored on a 19-yard screen play and took the lead with the extra point.

Ohio State scored the next two touchdowns to take a 20–7 lead. First, Miller threw a perfect 25-yard back-shoulder throw to Devin Smith, who made a nice catch in tight man-to-man coverage for the second touchdown.

"During the week, he talked to the receivers and said, 'If they use this coverage, I'll throw it like this,' and he made a perfect pass," Smith said.

Miller and Smith connected again on a 35-yard completion that set up a one-yard touchdown catch by Jake Stoneburner. But the Buckeyes' offense then went silent. Ohio State had seven straight fruitless possessions, which each lasted fewer than six plays. Led by a little-used sophomore running back, Cal began its come-back. Sophomore Brendan Bigelow had just one carry in each of the Bears' first two games. He'd had only six as a freshman. But he came close to becoming infamous in Ohio State lore this day. Early in the third quarter, Bigelow took a handoff on a sweep left from the Cal 19. He slipped a tackle by Nathan Williams in the backfield. Orhian Johnson had Bigelow wrapped up at the 23, but Bigelow spun free toward the sideline, where several Buckeyes had a chance to make the stop. Ryan Shazier threw himself at Bigelow but missed. The running back turned upfield and raced untouched the rest of the way for an 81-yard touchdown run to cut Ohio State's lead to 20–14. It was the longest run ever by an OSU opponent in Ohio Stadium and swung momentum Cal's way.

Cal bounced back from kicker Vincenzo D'Amato's second field goal miss of the day late in the third quarter to take the lead early in the fourth quarter on a one-yard keeper by Maynard.

Ohio State's offense awoke to go on a 75-yard touchdown drive, sparked by a 15-yard run by Hall and 21-yard pass to Philly Brown. After Miller threw to Jake Stoneburner on a fake-run play that Meyer used to run at Florida with Tim Tebow, Miller dived into the end zone for a two-point conversion to put Ohio State ahead 28–21.

But then Bigelow struck again, once more aided by bad tackling from the Buckeyes. Shazier overpursued and missed Bigelow at the start of the run. Safety Christian Bryant had a chance to make the tackle, but he went for the big hit and fanned. Bigelow went untouched for a 59-yard touchdown. For the day, he would gain 160 yards on only four carries.

Cal had a chance to take the lead when it got the ball back at the Ohio State 44 after an ill-advised pass by Miller into double-coverage with just over seven minutes left. The Bears drove to the Buckeyes' 25. Facing third-and-one, Maynard handed to fullback Eric Stevens. But with Johnathan Hankins providing penetration, the Buckeyes swarmed Stevens and stopped him short of the first down.

Tedford then made a fateful decision. Despite D'Amato's earlier misses from 40 and 42 yards, Tedford elected to give him another chance. His kick, like his previous two, went wide left. With 4:20 left, the Buckeyes got the ball back at their 25. Ohio State faced third-and-seven when offensive coordinator Tom Herman called a play designed to hit Philly Brown on a short pass to move the chains. Miller was flushed from the pocket and scrambled right. What he saw next, he couldn't quite believe.

"I don't know what happened, but the corner, the linebacker, and the safety went straight to Philly like a little suction," Miller said.

The safety, Alex Logan, was the key. Was he thinking about being juked on Miller's early touchdown run and determined not to let Miller beat him with his legs again? Whatever, he abandoned his coverage responsibilities on Devin Smith, who did what he'd been coached to do in these situations. Wide open along the right sideline, Smith waved his arm to get Miller's attention. Miller saw him. He made sure to put plenty of air under the ball and keep it in bounds. Smith caught the ball at the Cal 35 and easily scored for the go-ahead touchdown.

Cal had one more chance. Two players who'd had their shaky moments earlier in the game combined to make the clinching play. Shazier would be credited with 13 tackles on the day, but he'd also had some critical missed plays. The sophomore's explosive hitting ability, especially for a guy still growing into his body, was obvious. But occasionally, his strategy seemed to be, "Ready, fire, aim." Christian Bryant, who'd missed the tackle on Bigelow's second long touchdown run, also had a tendency to go for the knockout blow when it wasn't wise.

Like Shazier, his talent was clear. But Bryant's transition with the new regime hadn't gone smoothly at first. "I actually got into a fight with him in the first workout," Mickey Marotti said. "He said something to one of my [assistants] or talked back. 'C'mon, brother.' I went off on him. 'He's not your brother! Who do you think you are?!'"

Marotti said Bryant reacted as if nobody had ever challenged him like that before.

"I thought he had a little bit of phoniness at first," he said. "He didn't work hard."

Bryant agreed that he and Marotti butted heads at first.

"When you have someone new coming in, you've always got to feel them out because you don't exactly know what the message might be or where they're coming from," Bryant said. "I was just trying to feel those guys out."

But their relationship warmed quickly, and Marotti said that Bryant became one of his favorite players. Now he would get his only interception of the season.

Cal had first down at its own 42 with 1:22 left. Maynard looked to throw a seam pass to Allen. But Shazier did a superb job forcing Allen off his route. Maynard didn't adjust, and his pass sailed over Allen to where Bryant was waiting. He caught the ball and returned it 38 yards to seal the 35–28 win.

"[Cornerback Bradley Roby and I] communicated before the snap that they were going to try to go to Keenan Allen," Bryant said. "They tried to bait Ryan into not carrying the second vertical [receiver], because there were two verticals coming up the field in the boundary. Ryan did an incredible job by holding off the second vertical for me to break on the first one. The quarterback made a mistake, and I read the play the whole time and broke to the No. 1 receiver and caught the ball."

The Buckeyes had survived, but nobody was thinking greatness as they headed off the field. Ohio State had spent much of the game self-destructing. The Buckeyes committed 11 penalties, including four personal fouls. Though their previously dormant pass rush came alive with six sacks, they still allowed 512 yards, the most by a Buckeyes defense since 2005.

"We got a little lazy in the second half because we thought we had a comfortable lead," Shazier admitted after the game. "We can't have that happen."

Clearly, something was missing from this team. In the postgame locker room, the void began to be filled with a speech by John Simon. He had managed to make it through the game, despite the pain.

"I could tell watching him that he was playing with one arm," Simon's father, John Jr., said. "But it would have hurt him more if he didn't play."

Simon had only one tackle—a sack to end a third-quarter drive. But he had played, been there for what the Buckeyes call their "sacred brotherhood." It is customary in a victorious Ohio State locker room for coordinators to single out deserving players and have them say a few words. Nobody was prepared for what Simon would say. He's more the strong, silent type, but he became emotional and teary-eyed, which made the words resonate even more.

"Everybody thinks it was a preplanned speech," Simon said. "I just spoke from the heart. I don't really remember what I said. I just told the truth and told them it meant the world to go out and play with them week in and week out."

His teammates, who already revered Simon for his relentless work, were blown away.

"He basically said that all week before game he wasn't sure he was going to play," senior linebacker Etienne Sabino said. "You could see in his eyes and his tone of voice how much it meant to him, how much the team meant to him, how much the game meant to him, how much the people around him meant to him. To see the love of one of our teammates has for each one of us and for the game of football itself, I think it brought us closer together. After that, our team really got closer overall."

Urban Meyer has heard his share of speeches. As he listened to Simon, he felt a pit in his stomach. As hard-driving as he was, it hit him that even he could give more. When he entered the postgame press conference, he was still soaking in Simon's passion.

"That's a grown-ass man," Meyer told the media.

He joked that if he had another son, he'd want to name him Urban John Simon Meyer.

"That's how much I love that guy," Meyer said. "I'm not ashamed to say I love him. Love that guy—man. [He] makes all of us look in the mirror and say, 'Are we doing enough for our team? As [a] coaching staff, are we doing enough? Are we doing as much as he's doing? No. We've gotta do more. Gotta do more."

Watching the Cal game was a former Buckeye with a particular interest in the game. Butler B'ynote'* was an OSU running back

---

*He went by the spelling By'not'e during his playing career. OSU misspelled it, and he never bothered to get it corrected. "I really didn't pay too much attention to it," he said. "It was really my dad who got on me about it. It just never crossed my mind to go to the equipment guy and ask him to change it. I probably had a million things on my mind."

in the early 1990s. After his brief NFL career ended, B'ynote' had a bumpy time until he found his calling as a minister. He was scheduled to speak to the team at the voluntary chapel service the next day. B'ynote' was disappointed by the Buckeyes' performance as he watched on TV. He was concerned that what he felt didn't seem to jibe with the message of his sermon. B'ynote' views himself not so much the writer of his sermons as a vessel for God's word.

"I just kind of meditate and pray about the situation and just let God, let the Holy Spirit really speak to me," B'ynote' said. "As strange as this may seem to some, I just hear it."

The message he heard that week was to deliver a speech about love. But that really wasn't what B'ynote' wanted to talk about, especially after watching the Buckeyes muddle through the game.

"Watching the game, I was like, if they don't get it together, they're going to lose some games," he said. "This is Cal, and they barely squeak by. And realistically, if certain things would have happened, they would have lost that game. They didn't lose on the scoreboard, but they lost on the field, as far as I was concerned."

To B'ynote'—and no doubt he was not alone—the 2012 Buckeyes resembled the underachieving 2011 team to that point, even with Meyer as coach. To give a message about love to the Buckeyes seemed poorly timed, he thought.

"I was like, the last thing these dudes needed to hear about is love," he said. "They needed to be hearing about toughness. Get them fired up. I remember saying to my wife, 'Man, I don't want to go in there and talk about love. These are football players.' Even when we got into the car before I walked into the facility, I was really apprehensive about it. This [speech] is so basic. I wanted to say something dynamic, come up with something really cool. But the Lord had already given me that."

But his sermon, titled "The Price Tag of Love," was the perfect complement to Simon's impassioned locker-room speech. B'ynote' told the Buckeyes that love wasn't a choice, but a command from God.

"Love is tough," B'ynote' said. "Love means suffering. Love means being challenged and sacrificing yourself."

As he delivered the sermon, B'ynote' wasn't sure whether it was resonating. He even felt the need to apologize for going slightly over his allotted 15 minutes. His concern was erased when Meyer gave him a high-five and a big hug.

"He said, 'Man, that was a home run. We needed that. You were right on point because that's exactly where we are as a team,'" B'ynote' said. "It was amazing."

Months later, Meyer views the Simon and B'ynote' speeches as the first turning point of the season.

"It was a really incredible speech," Meyer said. "It was almost like—I don't want to get overdramatic here—God put us through this, because I know our guys are better people for having gone through that three- or four-week period, and that was a big part of it."

· 14 ·

UAB: WARNING SIGNS

IF URBAN MEYER was hoping that the John Simon and Butler B'ynote' speeches would ignite his team right away, he was in for a major disappointment. The next week's game against Alabama-Birmingham might have been the low point of the season. A struggle against California might have been baffling, but it was understandable. The Golden Bears have a strong tradition and play in a major conference. They certainly had enough athletes to give themselves a puncher's chance against Ohio State. The same could not be said for UAB. The Blazers get leftovers from their state and region, if they're lucky. Alabama's best players head to Nick Saban's Crimson Tide program or to Auburn, which won the 2010 national title. UAB didn't start its football program until 1991 when it began as a Division III school. UAB lost 42 of 60 games from 2007 to 2011, prompting the firing of Neil Callaway. The Blazers hired Arkansas offensive coordinator Garrick McGee as their new coach a week after Ohio State hired Urban Meyer. Let's just say that McGee's hiring didn't generate quite the same buzz in Alabama that Meyer's did in Ohio. Like Central Florida, UAB plays in Conference USA. But while UCF wouldn't be overmatched against an average Big Ten team, Alabama-Birmingham would be. The Blazers, in sum, figured to be the worst team Ohio State would play in 2012.

So what happened on September 22 would provide little optimism for the Buckeyes as they headed into Big Ten play. Except for the last 10 minutes of the second quarter and a long touchdown drive in the fourth quarter, UAB outplayed Ohio State, a 37-point favorite. Worried about the pounding Braxton Miller had taken, the Buckeyes lessened the load on him as much as possible. Jordan Hall did much of the heavy lifting, running 17 times for 105 yards. Miller's first carry didn't come until midway through the second quarter. Just as their previous opponents had, Alabama-Birmingham threw a curveball at the Buckeyes. Ohio State had expected the Blazers to feature a deep passing game with quarterback Jonathan Perry. But after three possessions, McGee replaced Perry with Austin Brown, and UAB went with more of a short passing game.

"They're a fast, upfield-rushing defensive line," McGee said after the game. "We felt like we had to use quick screens to move the ball."

The strategy worked in some ways. Despite not scoring an offensive touchdown, the Blazers gained 403 yards to only 347 for the Buckeyes, who were without injured cornerback Bradley Roby and safety C.J. Barnett. Doran Grant played well filling in for Roby, but the injuries had their greatest effect on special teams.

Ben Buchanan's right foot paid the biggest price. Six minutes into the game, Buchanan stood at the Buckeyes' 25-yard line ready to punt. What happened next was simple math. Ohio State had only two blockers to the left of long-snapper Bryce Haynes. UAB lined up three to that side. The Buckeye closest to Haynes was freshman Joshua Perry, who was in because of the injuries. When the ball was snapped, Perry moved to his right without blocking anyone. That left three rushers against one on that side. Buchanan had no chance. UAB's Calvin Jones came untouched and actually swatted the ball *before* Buchanan could kick it. Nick Adams picked up the ball and ran in for the touchdown for a 6–0 lead. (Orhian Johnson blocked the extra point.)

It would have been better for Buchanan had the punt been blocked the traditional way. Because he didn't get a chance to kick the ball, his foot felt the full force of Jones. Buchanan hobbled to the sideline and consulted with trainer Doug Calland.

"I told him I didn't think it was broken, but that I definitely tore some ligaments and blood vessels and I know it's going to puff up if I take my shoe off," Buchanan said.

He kicked the rest of the game. Sure enough, when he took his cleats off after the game, his right foot did balloon. He joked that his foot looked like the Michelin Man's.

"I came in the training room the next day, and I think the guys were very surprised at the way it looked," Buchanan said.

But he was so concerned that he might lose his starting spot that he dared not miss a single practice, even though pain would shoot up from his foot with every kick.

"If something is tender, you want to keep off of it," Buchanan said. "With kicking, you're literally smacking a ball over and over on a bruise."

It was part of what could be termed a character-building year for Buchanan, though character has never been an issue with him. A devout Christian, Buchanan was a semifinalist for the prestigious Wuerffel Trophy, which is based on athletic performance, academics, and community service. He and his family undertook several aid missions, including one to provide medical supplies to Honduras after his freshman season.

Such trips gave Buchanan a sense of perspective that most college athletes don't have, and he needed it. He was frustrated that as much as Meyer cares about special teams, the kickers were left pretty much on their own in practice, with no one to give them individualized coaching. The graduate assistant, Wes Satterfield, who'd worked with kickers the previous two years had gotten his master's and moved on.

Even the ball itself became a source of frustration. College teams can choose the model of ball they want to use. Miller didn't like the Wilson 1001 model the Buckeyes used when Terrelle Pryor was the quarterback. So the Buckeyes switched to the Wilson GST, which was the one Miller used in high school.

"The other ball they had was slippery," Miller explained. "It had no tack to it. I'm like, 'I've got to change that ball. I've got to have a different type of leather.'" Miller said the 1001 ball contributed to his difficulty throwing spirals as a freshman.

"[The GSTs] are a very easy ball to throw," Buchanan said. "It's just not a real supple ball for place-kicking and punting. We [he and kicker Drew Basil] hated them. It's like hitting a wooden golf ball. It takes forever to break them in."

Buchanan said that a kicker using the GST ball loses at least five yards of distance. Studies have backed this up. "But I guess we know our place," Buchanan said. "If Braxton likes them, then that's the way it is."

Yes, it is. When told that the kickers hated the GST ball, Miller replied with a laugh, "I don't care what they hate. I'm throwing the ball."

Buchanan said the kickers and snappers would joke about how little pull they had to get to use a different ball. "We said that if John Simon liked *lining up* against the GST ball as opposed to us *kicking* the GST ball, he would win the battle," Buchanan said with a laugh.

Of course, it doesn't matter what ball is used if it gets blocked, which would happen twice more in 2012. Blocked punts happen, even by teams much inferior to their opponents. Surely, this would be a slap across the face that would awaken Ohio State, who would then dispose of the Blazers like the fodder they were paid $850,000 to be, right? Not exactly. UAB extended its lead to 9–0 on a 47-yard field goal by Ty Long. The Buckeyes' offense finally came to life after having to punt on its first three possessions. The Buckeyes drove 75 yards for a touchdown, with Rod Smith scoring from one yard out.

After a 54-yard field goal by Long, the Buckeyes needed only four plays to take the lead for good. Miller completed 20- and

25-yard passes to Philly Brown and then scored on a 12-yard run featuring one of his trademark spin moves. Ohio State made it 21–12 at the half after cashing in on a turnover caused by a jarring hit from Christian Bryant.

A week earlier, UAB had played South Carolina close in the first half before wilting in the second half to lose 49–6. If Ohio State figured the Blazers would collapse again, the Buckeyes would find otherwise. The Buckeyes were caught napping on the second-half kickoff when the Blazers recovered a pooched onside kick. UAB would cut Ohio State's lead to 21–15 on a 34-yard field goal. That came at the end of an 80-yard drive kept alive when the Buckeyes allowed a screen pass to gain 32 yards on third-and-16.

UAB had a chance to take the lead on its next drive, which was kept alive by a taunting penalty on Bryant on a third-down incompletion. But the drive ended when Long missed a 46-yard field goal. Ohio State would finally take control with a methodical, 71-yard touchdown drive to take a 29–15 lead with five minutes left. A Doran Grant interception extinguished the last flickers of UAB's upset hopes.

But a 14-point victory against a team that would finish with a 3–9 record was hardly a momentum boost. Meyer was dismayed at the lack of progress. Asked to narrow down the team's deficiencies afterward, Meyer replied, "Defense, offense, and kicking game."

After the season, Meyer expounded on his state of mind after the nonconference part of the schedule was over. "I didn't think we coaches did a good job," he said. "Fundamentally, I didn't think we were a great team. We were not good tacklers on defense. We struggled defending the pass, and getting pressure on the quarterback was not good."

Through the first four games, Ohio State ranked 104th out of 120 Football Bowl Subdivision teams in pass defense, yielding 277.2 yards per game. They ranked 112th in tackles for loss. They ranked 71st in total defense. For a unit that prided itself on its

"Silver Bullets" nickname, it was almost too easy to say that the Buckeyes were shooting blanks.

The offense, other than big plays resulting from Miller's stunning elusiveness, was mostly plodding. Ohio State had passed for 197.7 yards per game, 96th nationally. Even the punt-return game, Meyer's pride and joy in many ways, was dismal. The Buckeyes ranked 105th in that category. Only in turnover margin did Ohio State rank in the top 20 statistically.

* * * *

IN HIS FINAL YEARS at Florida, the prospect of such an undistinguished season might have driven Meyer to the brink. But all indications were that he was coping well with such an imperfect team. He was still abiding with the requirements of his daughter Nicki's Pink Contract, which was posted prominently in his office. A large picture of Shelley was another reminder.

"He said it's watching him every minute," she said.

Meyer's kids called him frequently, particularly Nicki. If he didn't respond, Nicki would immediately call Shelley, who'd call him. But Nicki said that her father almost always answered her calls and texts. Urban left the office at noon on Sundays to make sure he could watch Nate's football games. That would have never happened earlier in his career, he said.

"In the beginning of season, when we weren't doing so well and barely beat UAB, things just weren't clicking right," Shelley said. "That last year at Florida, he would have just been in the office almost all night long trying to draw up plays, trying to fix what's going on, not getting sleep, just worry, worry, worry that we're not scoring enough points and struggling with these teams we should be beating [handily]."

But that didn't happen last year. Part of it, she said, was that Meyer knew how flawed his team was. He knew that so much transition—a new coaching staff, scheme, and philosophy—would inevitably result in bumps.

Shelley was continually watching for danger signs. Running backs coach Stan Drayton said he also kept an eye out for trouble on the horizon. Drayton tried to be subtle, asking Meyer if he'd worked out, eaten lunch, or done his Bible study, often using humor to make his point.

"He asked me to do it the very moment he took this job," Drayton said.

"I can make him laugh, and he knew he was going to need some [help] in that [life balance] respect. I'm proud of the way he's embraced at least the attempt."

With players to coach, Drayton could only do so much. It was Hiram de Fries' primary job to make sure Meyer stayed on track. One of Meyer's first calls after deciding to accept the Ohio State job was to de Fries for just this purpose.

"Hiram watches that for me, because I don't want to go over the top," Meyer said.

De Fries is not listed in the Buckeyes' media guide. That's fine with him. He'd rather be in the background. "It allows me to observe," de Fries said. "You learn more by watching than talking, and I have a relationship with Urban where I can tell him exactly what I think. Because of that, I can be truthful."

As a businessman and attorney, de Fries understands that the best-laid plans often change and should change. What matters most are execution and the continual push for excellence in the face of adversity. De Fries also recognizes that a leader has to understand limits, including his own. De Fries served, in certain ways, as Meyer's coach. The Buckeyes were clearly a flawed team during the non-conference part of the schedule. De Fries wanted to make sure that Meyer kept his equilibrium as he figured out which buttons to push.

"I list things in this order: Urban, the team, the staff, the players, the program, and then Ohio State," he said. "I'd rather your health be really, really good than have an undefeated season. If you can have both, why not?"

De Fries said there were times when he sensed that Meyer might be in danger of veering off course. He never did. "I did not see anything get to that point," de Fries said. "If there had, I would have thrown myself in front of the train."

But a different sort of train awaited the Buckeyes if they didn't improve. The Big Ten season had arrived. The conference's reputation has taken a hit in recent years, justifiably. And 2012 was not shaping to be a banner year. Northwestern and Minnesota, two teams that Ohio State would not play, were the only other conference teams to go undefeated in non-league play. The only team to beat a ranked opponent was Michigan State, which edged Boise State in East Lansing. That's where the Buckeyes were headed next. Meyer knew that if his team didn't make a significant leap, the season would go south quickly. Michigan State and the next opponent, Nebraska, had beaten Ohio State in 2011. Meyer could see the potential losses piling up.

After the season ended, he gave his frank assessment of his team after UAB: "Awful. Fundamentally flawed and effort-flawed. I thought we were very poor tacklers. I was very concerned about the throwing game—receivers and quarterback play. [We were] very flawed. I'm thinking it's two or three years until we get good. I thought we'd be a 7–5 or 8–4 team. We were 4–0, but we were a really bad team."

· 15 ·

MICHIGAN STATE:
RIP YOUR CHEST OPEN

URBAN MEYER CALLS it his "Bob Newhart couch." Every day, he sits in Mickey Marotti's office and chats with his friend and strength coach to get the pulse of his team. After the UAB game, both knew what was urgently needed.

"I'm almost glad that happened," Meyer said of the lackluster performance against UAB, "because we hit the panic button. Coach Mick and I, that whole week, we grinded our players really hard. You go beat the hell out of UAB, and you're not in a panic. On Sunday, I hit the panic button. I said, 'We're about to lose the next two games.'"

In Meyer's mind, more than the 2012 season was in jeopardy. If the Buckeyes were to lose to Michigan State and Nebraska, everything could implode. The momentum that had been built toward the next recruiting class might be lost. The pessimism that pervaded the program in 2011 might return. With no bowl game, motivation for the rest of the season would wane.

"If we lose those two games, the season's over," Meyer said. "With all the negativity around this place, you just go like this [snapping his finger]. I could see it. The schedule is right in front of me, and I saw what was coming. I was worried about recruiting, and I was worried about our team. Then I'd have to make a decision: would I keep playing the seniors or start playing the young players?"

Meyer could tell from talking to Marotti that the coaching staff hadn't yet fully won over the players. They weren't disrespectful, and they weren't defiant. But they just as obviously weren't ready to embrace everything the new regime was preaching.

"It wasn't a team that was letting us coach them," Meyer said. "I call it 'evaluation.' They're evaluating us. When a player is evaluating a coach, that's a really bad situation. That means there's a lack of trust."

Meyer understood the reasons. The Buckeyes had enormous success under Jim Tressel. The 2012 seniors had arrived after Ohio State had gone to consecutive BCS title games. They expected to enjoy similar success. For a while, they'd been on track to do that. They were freshmen on a winning Rose Bowl team and sophomores that won the Sugar Bowl, though that victory was vacated as part of the NCAA sanctions, as was a Big Ten title. The contrast between the old and new coaching staffs was just as much a dividing line. Tressel was professorial and calm. He'd put his arm around players while making a point. Meyer made it clear he wasn't interested in being the players' buddy—at least not yet. Performance is what mattered. Practices even during the season were tough. He called the first full-scale practice of the week "Bloody Tuesday."

"There were times during the season and during camp when it was miserable," Boren said. "I was like, 'Oh my God, I have no idea how we're keeping up with this level of practices, with this grind.' There were some times you'd go into the facility and you'd be dragging. You'd be like, 'There's no way practice is going to be hard today. He's gotta know.'"

Finally, Boren and Sabino felt that they, as captains, needed to approach Meyer.

"Guys were coming up to me saying, 'Man, I'm not going to make it. I'm not going to make it,'" Sabino said. "We had been doing so much, and guys were just blown out. And it was still fairly early in the season. A lot of us were exhausted physically. I would say that more than 10 guys came up to me and said, 'You've got to talk to him.'"

When Boren and Sabino went to Meyer's office to plead their case, Meyer was empathetic. But he didn't change much. Sabino said a few reps might have been shaved off of practice. On the whole, though, Meyer believed he couldn't deviate from the plan. He believed he knew what was necessary. The harder it was, the more committed his players would become. It was like climbing a rope. The higher they'd climb, the harder it would be to let go.

"Knowing the type of kids we had here, quality kids, I thought they would come together," Meyer said. "It took longer than I thought. I thought it would come together during training camp, and it didn't, because the system was so good that was here before.

"It's human nature. 'Why are we doing this? We won the Rose Bowl two years ago and we didn't do this. We beat the Team Up North nine times or something. We've won the Big Ten. We've got rings. What's this guy doing?' It sounds good in January until you have to live it."

In hindsight, Meyer believes he may have been too negative early in the season, that the players didn't buy in during the nonconference part of the schedule because he was so hard on them. The Buckeyes could get away with mediocre play the first four weeks because the competition had been inferior. But entering the Big Ten season, even a weak Big Ten, Meyer knew his team had to come together.

"We couldn't just let it go," he said. "A lot of people said we're fine. It was not fine. It was bad."

Easing off the throttle now was not an option, he believed, not with the Buckeyes playing their toughest opponent so far and going on the road for the first time. He met individually with numerous players that week, beseeching them to raise their games. He challenged his coaches to ratchet up the intensity in practice and in meeting rooms. Michigan State had beaten Ohio State 10–7 in Ohio Stadium in 2011, and the score belied how outclassed the Buckeyes had been. Ohio State scored with 10 seconds left to avert a shutout.

The 2012 Spartans were considered among the Big Ten favorites. Michigan State had a stingy defense and a run game powered by 244-pound Le'Veon Bell from the Columbus suburb of Reynoldsburg. Bell had run for 253 yards the week before against Eastern Michigan and 210 in the season opener against Boise State. Given how shoddy the Buckeyes' tackling had been, Meyer had reason to be alarmed.

"Le'Veon Bell was on SportsCenter every single day, jumping over people and running over people, doing what he did the first half of the season," defensive end Nathan Williams said. "I think a lot of the coaches were iffy about how we'd do against that team. They had a lot of promise. I really felt like he thought Michigan State was a better team, and he had to do something to get us going."

The Buckeyes hadn't forgotten the sting of the previous year's loss to Michigan State. The Spartans, long considered underachievers, had seemingly turned the corner under former Buckeyes assistant coach Mark Dantonio. They had beaten in-state rival Michigan four straight times, shedding their "little brother" status.

"They said they were new kings of the Big Ten," safety Orhian Johnson said. "We knew we were the ones who let it go. We were real hungry."

*   *   *   *

THE MEETING ROOM at the Brighton, Michigan, Marriott seems an unlikely location for a turning point in a football season. But that is where the Buckeyes believe that the transformation sparked by John Simon's and Butler B'ynote's speeches crystallized into something real and lasting. Meyer could even pinpoint the time:

11:22 AM on September 29 during the team's pregame meal before driving to East Lansing.

Meyer stood up in front of his team and told them the moment of truth had arrived. The second-guessing had to stop, he said. He told them that the task that day and for the rest of the season was too difficult to accomplish if they weren't fully committed to the coaches and each other.

"Give us your heart," he told his players. "Let us coach you. Don't be so evaluative. You won't improve. We'll still be this lousy football team, and in our Big Ten season you're going to embarrass yourselves. Rip your chest open. Let us coach you. Take your heart out of your chest and hand it to your coach. Let them coach you as hard as they can and just do what they ask you to do."

At the end of the 15-minute speech, Meyer raised his glass of water—championship water as Marotti called it—and asked his players to join him in a toast.

"The whole purpose was, 'If you're all in, you're all in,'" Meyer said. "'Don't put your glass up, don't toast, if you're not all in.' The whole mantra was, 'We're one.'"

Something had clicked. They could all feel it. It was palpable—magical, to use Meyer's word.

"I'm not bullshitting," Williams said, "it was kind of like we were actually going into war. I know people say football is a war sometimes. But that's really how it felt. It was like we were about to give our lives up for a greater cause than ourselves."

By the time the Buckeyes drove to East Lansing and got to their locker room, they were practically frothing. Zach Boren gave a speech that built on what Meyer had said.

"I remember saying that it's time to put everything together and be one and become a family and have each other's back," he said. "It's not about yourself. It's not about just the offense or just the defense or just special teams. It's about all of us being one and all of us being one family.

"It was really the first time we told each other that we loved each other and had each other's backs. I kind of came across like that because I told the whole team that I loved them and that we were one family and we were going to get through the season together."

John Simon looked into his teammates' eyes and could sense something special was about to happen. "Guys were all fired up," he said. "That locker room got pretty rowdy before that game. I think that's when it really hit me that we're together, and we're going to take it as far as we can go."

Williams said that teammates were actually crying.

"Not crying out of sadness or happiness, but crying because there was a greater energy, a greater feeling that everyone felt that day," he said. "I remember people throwing chairs and breaking chairs in half, holding each other's arms and praying. It was truly amazing to see that."

The momentum carried into the game. On the game's first snap, Braxton Miller ran for 20 yards, starting a 75-yard touchdown drive. Miller wasn't around for the end of it. On a 13-yard run, Miller was tackled out of bounds by Isaiah Lewis, and the quarterback's helmet hit an equipment case on the Ohio State sideline. The personal-foul penalty on Lewis moved the ball to the Spartans 14. Kenny Guiton replaced Miller for the rest of the drive and handed off to Jordan Hall on three straight plays to get into the end zone.

Michigan State countered with a 50-yard drive that ended with a field goal to make it 7–3. The game then turned into a slugfest. The Buckeyes mostly stuffed Bell, holding him to a season-low 45 yards on 17 carries.

"They made sure they eliminated me from the game," Bell said. "They did a great job."

The game continued to be chippy. Late in the first quarter, Ohio State defensive tackle Johnathan Hankins got tangled with Spartans offensive lineman Jack Allen on a Bell carry. As both players lay on the field, Allen stuck his hand through Hankins' face mask and appeared to try to gouge his eyes.

"I was pushing him, and the whistle blew, and he pushed me over the pile," Hankins said. "I grabbed him. I guess he was mad. That's how it is in the trenches. I didn't even think about it or tell anybody. He was talking smack the whole game and trying to get into my head."

For Hankins, the Michigan State game was a special one. A Dearborn Heights, Michigan, native, Hankins wanted to become a Spartan along with high school teammate William Gholston. But wary of his weight, Michigan State did not offer a scholarship. Ohio State did, and he became a star and the first Buckeye taken in the 2013 NFL Draft (selected in the second round by the New York Giants, the 49th overall pick).

"Recruiting is an educated guess," defensive coordinator Luke Fickell said. "There's a lot of people who might have said about Johnathan Hankins, 'A 350-pound lineman, I don't know if he's good enough. I don't know if he can move.' But I remember Jim Heacock being adamant about, 'I love this kid. I love his personality, his desire, and his love for football.'"

Heacock said that the high school tape he saw of Hankins was of low quality, so it was difficult to analyze that much from it. But he was watching with a couple other coaches when they saw a play in which Hankins hustled to the sideline to make a tackle. That elicited a "Whoa!" among the coaches.

Hankins made an even deeper impression on his official visit to Ohio State. Heacock was impressed with Hankins' knowledge of the game as they studied tape. Heacock was getting ready to take Hankins back to the hotel to relax before dinner when Hankins asked if they could watch more tape instead.

"All weekend long, he couldn't get enough," Heacock recalled. "You could see he was very passionate about learning to be a good defensive lineman."

Heacock grew fond of Hankins' family. He was reassured when Hankins' teachers also spoke highly about him. "There were so many positives, even though you didn't see a whole lot on tape," Heacock said. "He was something special, I thought."

As a freshman, Hankins' girth limited him to about 15 plays a game. But he gradually lost weight and got in better condition, most dramatically with Sarah Wick's nutrition program. In 2012, he became an every-down player. "We used to rave how [ex-Buckeye] Cameron Heyward would go 70 plays," Fickell said. "But he was a 285- or 290-pound guy. Johnathan Hankins has that same kind of motor for a 325-pound guy."

Hankins took some criticism in 2012 for not piling up big stats. He had only one sack and four tackles for loss. But that, Fickell said, was largely a function of Hankins' role in the defense. He was asked mainly to control the line of scrimmage, to hold his gap and be disruptive so that others could swarm to the ball.

"If you let him line up as a nose guard across from the center, he probably could have been a bigger wrecking ball, a more dominating force," Fickell said. "But for us to get our best 11, we played him most of the time in three-technique." (A three-technique lineman lines up on the outside shoulder of the offensive guard.)

As valuable as Hankins was on the field, "Big Hank" was at least as liked for his upbeat personality. "Everybody does something wrong, but he just never does anything wrong," Meyer said. "He's just a wonderful kid. He brightens your day. I say that there are energy givers and energy takers. He's an energy giver. He walks into a room and he brightens that room."

Meyer and Hankins made it a point to stand together during the national anthem.

"Those were two of my favorite minutes of the game," Meyer said.

Hankins was not injured by the attempted eye-gouge, but the Buckeyes did lose a key player midway through the second quarter.

"It was a little option play," Jordan Hall said. "I got the pitch, and I remember I broke through and got tackled on the sideline, and he landed right on me."

Hall tried to keep playing. He lined up as a wide receiver on the next play, but he knew something was wrong. He tried to push off his leg and could do nothing more than hop and then hobble. He had partially torn a posterior cruciate ligament. PCL tears typically aren't as serious as ACL tears, but Hall would not return the rest of the season. It was a particularly cruel injury because he had returned just two games earlier from the torn tendon suffered when he stepped on glass in the summer. Hall believed the two injuries were related. Because he couldn't work out as hard after the tendon injury, Hall thinks his leg was vulnerable to another injury. Fortunately for the Buckeyes, Carlos Hyde was back from his knee sprain.

Ohio State maintained a slim lead until the middle of the third quarter when the Buckeyes' tackling woes resurfaced on one horrible play. On first-and-10 from the Ohio State 29, quarterback Andrew Maxwell threw a screen pass to Keith Mumphery. Orhian Johnson missed a tackle at the 20. Then Christian Bryant bumped Mumphery at the 10 but neglected to wrap him up, allowing him to stay on his feet. As several Buckeyes closed in on Mumphery, Sabino unsuccessfully tried to strip the ball free instead of tackling him. Mumphery then carried the remaining Buckeyes pursuers into the end zone to give Michigan State its first lead, 13–10.

Ohio State's offense had done little since its opening drive. The Spartans had two talented cornerbacks in Johnny Adams and Darqueze Dennard, and they trusted them enough to move their safeties up into the box to help stop the run game, something the Buckeyes saw plenty of all season. Against that defense, Philly Brown caught 12 passes—the most by a Buckeye in 15 years—but those receptions totaled only 84 yards. It would be the other wide receiver, Devin Smith, who would make the game-breaking play. With less than two minutes left in the third quarter, the Buckeyes had the ball at their own 37 after Miller got two yards on third-and-one. Herman decided that was the right moment to take a shot deep.

"It was a little against our MO at the time, throwing a dropback pass on first down," Herman said, "but it was the right thing to do at the time because it was so packed in at the line."

Devin Smith got a step on Adams, and Miller's pass couldn't have been placed any better. Smith caught the ball in stride at the 32 as Adams dived while trying to deflect the pass. Smith easily shook off Adams' desperate swipe of a tackle and cruised into the end zone.

"I have all the faith in Devin to get on top of the corner," Miller said. "I waited and waited until he slapped his hands down and then I threw it. It felt perfect. I knew from the release. It came out perfect."

The Buckeyes had a chance to extend the lead on their next possession but ended up lucky not to lose their quarterback to a serious injury. With the ball at midfield, Miller got free on a scramble. But he lurched to a halt when his left leg locked. By reflex, Miller dropped the ball, and Michigan State's Kurtis Drummond recovered.

"I planted wrong," Miller said. "It would have been a long run, maybe a touchdown if that hadn't happened. Everything went numb."

Miller grabbed his knee in agony. In the stands, his father, Kevin, feared that Braxton had blown out his knee. Once again, though, Miller had escaped serious injury. He'd merely hyperextended the knee and was able to return. The Buckeyes' defense, meanwhile, was up to the task. Etienne Sabino had ended the previous Michigan State drive with a sack, and Nathan Williams ended this one the same way. His sack of Maxwell forced the Spartans to settle for a 48-yard field goal after the Miller fumble recovery to make it 17–16. After a three-and-out by the Buckeyes, Michigan State got one first down before it gained only one yard in its next three plays.

In the press box, Ohio State's coaches openly dared Michigan State to punt.

"Pardon my French, but they were fucking jacked up like, 'We're going to go win the game. Give us the damn ball back,'" Herman said.

The Spartans did punt, a good one by Mike Sadler for 50 yards, fair caught by Devin Smith at the Ohio State 18. Four minutes and 10 seconds remained. The Buckeyes on the field were brimming with confidence. Offensive line coach Ed Warinner gathered his players together and told them it was on them to seal the victory.

"It was point of pride," left tackle Jack Mewhort said. "I remember standing out there, looking at the clock before the first play and looking at the dude against me and thinking, *Okay, let's party.*"

"We were so pumped," center Corey Linsley added. "The level of intensity was unbelievable. We all kind of locked arms and said we've been waiting for this for a long time."

What happened next would have brought a tear to Woody Hayes' eyes. Hyde banged ahead for seven yards and then six for a first down. On the next play, Miller found a crease created when Mewhort blocked his man to Grand Rapids and ran for 14 yards.

One more first down would clinch it. The Buckeyes faced third-and-four at the Spartans 49 when Herman called for a Hyde carry behind the right side of the line. Meyer, still not completely sold on right tackle Reid Fragel, questioned whether Herman was sure.

"I said, 'Is that the way you want to run it?' because Reid had to make the block," Meyer said.

Herman confirmed it. The play worked to perfection. Fragel extended both hands on the Michigan State defensive end, shoved him back inside and pancaked him. Zach Boren drilled Marcus Rush to open the hole for Hyde, who plowed ahead for five yards. First down. Game clinched.

"It was very rewarding because we weren't trying to trick anybody," Warinner said. "We knew exactly what we were going to do, and they knew exactly what we were going to do. They were coming at us with everything they had. They were blitzing and packing the box. So it was good we could still pound it out."

It was especially gratifying to Warinner. He'd coached for two years at Michigan State under George Perles early in his career. His wife and her family were all Michigan State alums. To see his unit perform at its best with the stakes highest allowed him to walk off the field beaming.

"He was just so proud of us," Linsley said. "He didn't have much to say, just a smile on his face, and he shook our hands."

The importance of the victory couldn't be overstated.

"If we win this," Linsley said after the game, "it starts to snowball in the right direction. If we don't win, it starts to snowball in the wrong direction."

After the game, the team gathered to celebrate with the Buckeyes' marching band and danced along with a song, "Buckeye Swag," that was a recent addition to the canon.

"We did 'Buckeye Swag' last year, I think," safety C.J. Barnett said. "But I don't think we ever celebrated that as much until Michigan State."

There hadn't been reason to. Now there was. The Buckeyes remained a flawed team. That would not change the rest of the season. But they'd finally come together, cast aside whatever lingering reservations they had about the new coaching staff, and survived a crucible of a game.

Suddenly, everything seemed possible.

· 16 ·

NEBRASKA: PRIME-TIME FIREWORKS

IN HIS POSTGAME news conference in East Lansing, Urban Meyer was asked about the increasing number of high-scoring games in college football. That day, West Virginia beat Baylor 70–63. Having just finished what he described as a sledgehammer of a game against Michigan State, Meyer said, "I'd like a 70 every once in a while."

Who could have guessed the Buckeyes would flirt with that total the next week, especially against a program like Nebraska?

The Cornhuskers joined the Big Ten the previous year. Their coach was Bo Pelini, a Youngstown native who played safety for Ohio State from 1987 to 1990. His freshman year was Meyer's last one as a graduate assistant. Pelini coached in the NFL until returning to the college game in 2003 as an assistant at Nebraska. He was LSU's defensive coordinator when the Tigers beat Ohio State for the 2007 BCS championship. Afterward, Nebraska hired him to revitalize a program that had fallen into mediocrity under Bill Callahan. For two generations, the Huskers had been one of the country's dominant programs, led by a potent running game behind a powerful offensive line and a stout defense nicknamed the Blackshirts.

But Nebraska's defense had been merely decent in 2011 and was looking vulnerable again in 2012. UCLA had gouged the Huskers for 653 yards in a 36–30 victory in the second game of the season. As had been the case against Michigan State, Ohio State had a score to settle with the Huskers. The previous season, the underdog Buckeyes dominated Nebraska in Lincoln for the first two and a half quarters. Carlos Hyde ran wild, and the offense showed rare creativity in building a 27–6 lead. But then Braxton Miller left the game with a sprained ankle, and the Buckeyes collapsed. Nebraska scored the final 28 points for a 34–27 victory. It was the biggest comeback in Cornhuskers history.

The Buckeyes hadn't forgotten. Now, just like in Lincoln, Ohio State and Nebraska would meet again in a nationally televised, prime-time game. Meyer loves such atmospheres and, after the season, would lobby the Big Ten to schedule more night games. The Buckeyes were ranked 12th, Nebraska 21st. Until the Michigan game, this would be the signature game on the home schedule.

Early in the game, there was little indication that Ohio State's offense would have its best game of the season. Its first two possessions were three-and-outs. But then cornerback Bradley Roby made the first of several huge plays for the Buckeyes. The redshirt sophomore from Georgia has always thought of himself as a receiver in disguise and longs to be used on offense. He might have been the best athlete on the team. He ran a laser-timed 4.31 in the 40-yard dash in the spring and said he's been hand-timed as fast as 4.2.

"That guy's a freak," fellow cornerback Travis Howard said.

Roby originally committed to play for Vanderbilt. But he had a Buckeyes connection. Roby went to the same high school, Peachtree Ridge, as former OSU star Cameron Heyward. Heyward's mom, Charlotte, clued Ohio State coaches in on Roby's potential. Roby took his official visit to Ohio State for the game in which the Buckeyes beat Iowa in overtime to clinch a Rose Bowl berth in 2009.

"It was crazy," Roby said of the Horseshoe that day. "I was like, 'This is kind of cool.' I thought Coach Tressel was a good dude. So I was like, 'Why not?'"

What may have clinched it was Ohio State's history of sending defensive backs to the NFL. "Why not come to the DBU if you want to be a DB?" he said. "Everything just lined up right."

Roby flashed his considerable ability as a redshirt freshman, but he believed that was only a prelude. Roby wore No. 25 as a freshman and asked to wear No. 1 in 2012. "That was a big deal to me," Roby said. "It signified the change I underwent, coming from a freshman to being up there with everyone else. If you wear No. 1, you've got to be good. I had to prove to everybody that I was No. 1."

Cornerbacks coach Kerry Coombs said that Roby backed up his ambition with a work ethic. "He is in the office every day watching film," Coombs said. "He is committed to absolutely being the best player in the country."

But cornerbacks who don't intercept passes don't get that kind of recognition, and Roby hadn't picked off a pass yet in 2012. "It was frustrating," Roby said. "Everybody was clowning me. 'Oh, you're supposed to be all this and all that, and you don't have a pick.' You know how people joke."

Against Michigan State, he blocked a punt, but that was quickly negated because Braxton Miller fumbled the ball back on the ensuing possession. Now, that film study was about to pay off. Nebraska faced third-and-10 from its 31. From the way the Huskers lined up, he sensed that an out route was coming. Quarterback Taylor Martinez's pass to Quincy Enunwa wasn't quite as close to the sideline as he wanted. Roby stepped in front of Enunwa, made the interception, and headed toward the end zone. With his speed, no one was going to catch him. In an instant, it was 7–0, Buckeyes.

"It was something we really needed at that point," Roby said. "To spark that first big play was a huge deal."

Roby's touchdown capped early defensive dominance by both teams. The first 13 snaps of the game gained a total of 17 yards. Neither team had a first down for the first seven and a half minutes. The offensive futility ended quickly and permanently.

After Roby's touchdown, Nebraska scored the next 17 points. Rex Burkhead, who'd pounded the Buckeyes in their 2011 game, ran 73 yards to set up a tying touchdown. The Huskers capitalized on a 43-yard punt return by Ameer Abdullah to go ahead 14–7. Facing fourth-and-seven at the OSU 25 on their ensuing possession, the Buckeyes took a chance on a fake punt. It looked as if Ben Buchanan had a seam, but Steven Osborne shed the block of Storm Klein and tackled Buchanan just short of the first down. On the sideline, Meyer slammed his play sheet to the ground in anger. Nebraska then drove 27 yards to the Ohio State 4. But the Buckeyes' defense stiffened. On third-and-goal, John Simon flushed Martinez from the pocket. Roby correctly read that that the tight end was running a crossing route toward him and picked him up. As Martinez, a gifted runner, tried to scramble for a touchdown, Ryan Shazier came up to tackle him. Nebraska had to settle for a field goal.

Still, down by 10, the Buckeyes faced the possibility of having the game slip away just as it had in Lincoln a year earlier. Then the Buckeyes' offense caught fire in a way it hadn't—and wouldn't again—all season. Ohio State scored touchdowns on its next five possessions. It began, not surprisingly, with the legs of Miller. Ohio State took possession at its 25. On a designed run, Miller got a block from right guard Marcus Hall, went upfield, and cut sharply to his right. As he raced down the sideline, Miller got a beautiful block from Philly Brown, who took out two potential tacklers. Miller was finally chased down at the Nebraska 3 after going 72 yards. Carlos Hyde ran in from the 1 to make it 17–14.

Roby then got his second interception of the game when he stepped in front of Kenny Bell in zone coverage to pick off a Martinez pass. "For whatever reason, somebody convinced that quarterback that it was okay to throw against Bradley," Ohio State cornerbacks coach Kerry Coombs said. "A lot of guys didn't do that. He challenged him three times. He had two picks and a drop.

Chris Fields said his days as a center fielder taught him how to make diving catches like the clutch one he made against Purdue.

Braxton Miller juked several Penn State defenders before diving in for a one-yard touchdown, adding to his highlight reel of stunning runs.

Jake Stoneburner had an up-and-down year, but his long touchdown catch broke the game open against Penn State.

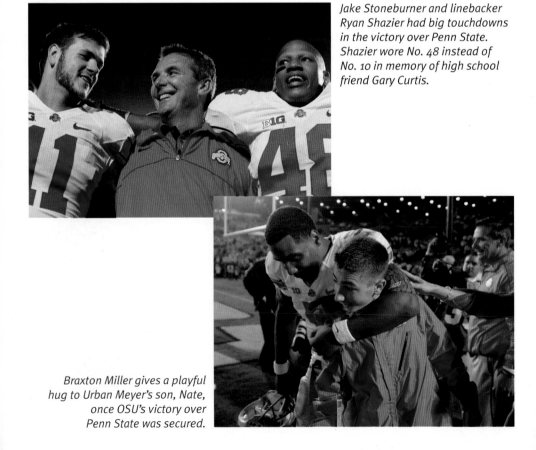

Jake Stoneburner and linebacker Ryan Shazier had big touchdowns in the victory over Penn State. Shazier wore No. 48 instead of No. 10 in memory of high school friend Gary Curtis.

Braxton Miller gives a playful hug to Urban Meyer's son, Nate, once OSU's victory over Penn State was secured.

Carlos Hyde's emergence as a workhorse runner relieved the load on Braxton Miller.

The midseason switch of Zach Boren, here against Illinois, from fullback to linebacker solidified a shaky defense.

Buckeyes left tackle Jack Mewhort holds the Illibuck Trophy given to the winner of the OSU-Illinois game. Mewhort was one of the leaders of an offensive line that made the most improvement of any unit on the team.

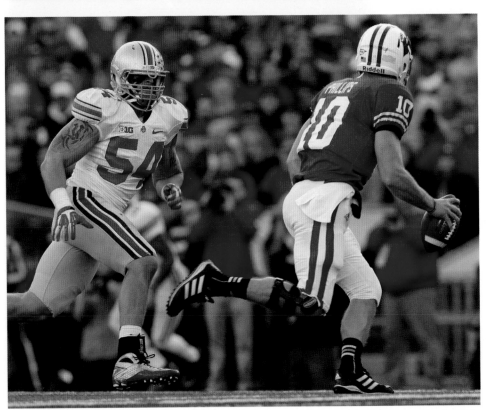

John Simon, chasing Wisconsin quarterback Curt Phillips, had four sacks against the Badgers in the last game of his college career.

Etienne Sabino jars the ball free from Montee Ball on a late goal-line stand against Wisconsin.

Nathan Williams, here congratulating C.J. Barnett, beat the odds by returning from microfracture knee surgery.

Unable to play against Michigan because of a badly swollen knee, John Simon is saluted by Urban Meyer as the defensive end is introduced on Senior Day.

C.J. Barnett, like most of the rest of the Buckeyes, struggled with dropped interceptions in 2012, but the junior safety held on to this one on Michigan's final possession in the Buckeyes' victory.

Zach Boren briefly stands over Michigan quarterback Devin Gardner after sacking him in the second quarter.

Left guard Andrew Norwell (helmet aloft) celebrates with the crowd after Ohio State's victory over Michigan.

Their perfect season realized, defensive coordinator Luke Fickell and Zach Boren savor the moment amid the swelling crowd on the field.

The structure of the defense is set up for Bradley to be challenged. It's just that a lot of guys aren't going to do it."

Two plays later, Miller threw to tight end Jeff Heuerman for an 18-yard touchdown to put Ohio State ahead. The Buckeyes and Huskers then traded touchdown drives.

Ohio State got the ball back at its 43 with 1:27 left before half-time. The Buckeyes moved to the Nebraska 31. Facing fourth-and-one with the clock ticking past 35 seconds, Meyer windmilled his arms on the sideline to signal that he wanted to go for it—quickly. But just as Hyde bulled ahead for a couple yards, whistles blew. Pelini had called for a timeout just before the snap.

He'd have been better off doing nothing. The Buckeyes called for a quarterback counter, and it couldn't have been executed any better. Left guard Andrew Norwell pulled to his right to seal one defender. Reid Fragel exploded off the line to head off a linebacker. Hyde, a willing and able blocker, plowed through safety P.J. Smith to make sure Miller was untouched as he ran for the touchdown to make it 35–24. For the first time all year, the Buckeyes were showing the full dynamism of the spread offense. With Herman's no-huddle tempo, the Huskers became physically spent.

The dominance started with the offensive line. The unit that had put itself in the doghouse in January had become a force by October. "The offensive line is one of the most unique groups in all of sport," Meyer said. "They're unheralded. They do a job most people would consider illegal. Just think what they do all game. They play the game of football and never see the ball."

Without all five players working in unison, the result can be "comical," Meyer said. But when everything is in sync, it's poetry. That's what he saw against Nebraska. "The Nebraska game this year, it was magical what that group did," Meyer said. "The foot-work—they all looked alike. They were well-coached. They were disciplined. They were all going hard. I'm convinced that the atmo-sphere that Coach Warinner created in his meeting room, about reliance on one another, is why they played so well. That pulled a guy in who didn't care before, Reid Fragel. I'll argue this as long as I live—and he'll admit to it—he didn't care. He cared this year."

It was clear that whatever reservations the offensive line had about Warinner, about how unrelenting he was with them, dissolved as they saw the progress they made. The linemen came to marvel at how Warinner could analyze the big picture and connect the dots for them.

"We'll be sitting there sometimes," center Corey Linsley said, "and I'll be like, 'Why in the hell is he talking about this?' And then two weeks down the road, it'll end up winning the game for us. He just comes into the meeting room on Sundays and kind of smiles. 'Didn't I tell you that?' It's like, 'Wow, all right. This guy's got the right idea.'"

The Buckeyes' 28-point scoring flurry in the second quarter ignited the crowd. Sometimes, the halftime intermission can halt such momentum. Not on this night. The Best Damn Band In The Land, as Ohio State's marching band is known, performed a tribute to classic video games that had the crowd roaring. The highlight came when the band formed a horse, complete with a gallop. The performance has been viewed more than 15 million times on You-Tube and was even honored in resolutions by both the Ohio Senate and House of Representatives.

* * * *

NEBRASKA got the ball to open the second half and drove 77 yards for a touchdown to cut Ohio State's lead to 35–31. But that would be as close as the Huskers would get. The Buckeyes went 75 yards to push the lead back to 11. Hyde's third touchdown, a one-yarder, was set up by Miller's 35-yard pass to Heuerman. Fellow tight end Nick Vannett had an earlier 32-yard catch, giving Ohio State big-play production from a position traditionally neglected in the Buckeyes passing game.

Klein sacked Martinez for a 12-yard loss on Nebraska's next possession, and the Huskers were forced to punt. What followed essentially put the game away. Philly Brown fielded Brett Maher's low 50-yard punt at the Ohio State 24. He headed upfield and found a crease. The only player with a chance for the tackle was Maher, and Brown blew past him at the Nebraska 40.

The reason Brown had a crease was because of an almost imperceptible block by a player who went mostly unnoticed—except by his teammates and coaches. Walk-on senior Taylor Rice, from nearby Dublin, had overcome family tragedy to remain part of the Ohio State team. On November 28, 2009, a month before the freshman left for the Buckeyes' Rose Bowl game against Oregon, Rice's 15-year-old sister, Lyndsey, was killed in a car accident. Support from his teammates helped Rice cope with her death, and her memory inspired him.

"It just makes you appreciate things more," he said. "If possible, it makes you love the people around you that much more. You see these people you saw prior to it, and it just hits you—like one day they might not be here, so you've got to make the most of every second you get to spend with them. More than anything, I'm grateful for having her for 15 years."

Rice had hoped to earn a football scholarship. The NCAA sanctions that reduced Ohio State's maximum to 82 probably prevented any chance of that. He had come to accept that and his role on the team. He was listed as a wide receiver, but he was strictly a special-teamer. Listed at 5′10″ and 185 pounds, he was hardly imposing physically. That didn't matter.

"Taylor was a real honest person," Brown said. "We had a team meeting, and they asked everybody what they would do rest of the year. Taylor Rice wrote on his paper that his man would never make the tackle. And I couldn't tell you one time when his man did make the tackle."

He certainly didn't on Brown's return for a touchdown. As Brown caught the punt and began his return, a Nebraska player had the angle on him. But Rice alertly darted alongside the would-be tackler to shield him away from Brown, who sped by him.

"If you don't have Taylor holding the guy up at the line and then hustling 45 yards down the field and laying that block, it doesn't go for a touchdown," Buckeyes punter Ben Buchanan said. "That's something you don't see pointed out on the front page of the [Columbus] Dispatch or ESPN, but it doesn't happen without that. I think Taylor took pride in that role, that he was kind of the unsung hero."

Brown went untouched into the end zone for a 76-yard score to give Ohio State a 49–31 lead. In film review, Kerry Coombs, who oversees the punt-return unit, showed that play repeatedly, according to Buchanan. "He said, 'This is what we're looking for. This is the kind of effort we're looking for.'"

The punt-return unit wasn't the only one that shined against the Huskers. The kickoff coverage unit had a banner night, as well. A new rule was instituted in 2012 that gave teams the ball at the 25 instead of the 20 on a touchback. Many teams decided to kick deep and get the touchback. Not Ohio State. Drew Basil was usually instructed to kick the ball high just inside the end zone, giving tacklers a chance to pin opponents deep. It was a risk/reward game that the Buckeyes were happy to play. Those on the coverage unit took to their responsibility with such fervor that they called themselves "the Piranhas." Coombs explained that they would have been called "the Sharks," if not for the fact that so many of the players were among the smallest on the roster. Freshmen such as Devan Bogard, Najee Murray, and Armani Reeves began to make names for themselves with their play on kickoff coverage. The leader of the Piranhas was Zach Domicone, a fifth-year senior who had overcome numerous severe injuries. As a redshirt freshman, he suffered an avulsion fracture in his groin, in which a piece of his pelvic bone was chipped. He battled recurring hamstring injuries. During practice for the Gator Bowl in 2011, he tore his ACL. Domicone said that Luke Fickell and athletics director Gene Smith approached him about taking a medical hardship, which would end his career but allow him to remain on scholarship.

Domicone was still on the fence after having surgery in January. He was sitting on a stationary bike with his leg immobilized in a brace when he first met Urban Meyer. "I was talking to trainers and teammates, trying to figure out what was best for me to do," he said. "Coach Meyer came over and introduced himself and said he'd watched film and wanted me to stick around and be a leader to the team."

He pushed himself to return, probably too much. His leg was too sore to play in the opener against Miami, but he gradually worked his way back. Domicone being Domicone, he strained his calf against Nebraska, which would keep him out of a couple of later games. Many of his fellow Piranhas would also become injured. But against Nebraska, Domicone was able to play through the pain to have probably his best game of the season. He had two tackles on kickoff coverage, including one at the Nebraska 15. The Buckeyes held Abdullah to a 16-yard average on eight kickoff returns as they continually forced the Huskers to start deep in their own territory.

That coverage proved pivotal in preventing Nebraska from mounting a serious comeback. Burkhead had left the game with an injury, a huge loss for the Huskers. As dangerous as Martinez was as a runner, he was an erratic passer with an unorthodox delivery. Sure enough, after Nebraska reached the Buckeyes' 35 down 18 late in the third quarter, Martinez heaved a pass deep over the middle that Orhian Johnson easily intercepted. It was Johnson's second interception in as many years against Martinez.

"He likes me," Johnson said with a sly smile. "He's my homie. He gives me one every year. He always shows me love, so I'm cool with him. I'll never say nothing bad about Taylor."

The same apparently goes for Nebraska.

"I don't have anything against Nebraska," Johnson said. "I think they're the best team added to the Big Ten. I like them."

After Johnson's interception, Hyde was stripped of the ball at the end of a rugged 15-yard gain, but a three-and-out by the Buckeyes' defense got the ball back. Ohio State needed only three plays to make it 56–31. Hyde ran for six and 23 yards before leaving for a breather. Rod Smith, who'd gradually earned his way back into good graces, then ripped off a run that displayed his vast potential. He took a handoff up the middle and shed three tackles on his way to a 33-yard touchdown. The Buckeyes tacked on their final touchdown when Carlos Hyde scored his fourth touchdown of the night on a 16-yard run with 48 seconds left. After that score, Meyer went over to Warinner on the sideline and shook his hand on a job well done. Warinner acknowledged it with a wink.

Ohio State finished with 498 yards of offense, including 371 on the ground. The Buckeyes averaged 7.7 yards per carry. Miller finished with 186 yards on 16 carries. Hyde ran 28 times for 140 yards. The Buckeyes threw only 14 times, with Miller completing just seven, but the catches went for 127 yards.

The offensive performance was a huge confidence boost to a team that had been denigrated for the last year and a half.

"I think it showed the country that we're an elite football team," left tackle Jack Mewhort said. "We have it in us. Maybe we don't show it all the time, but when we get it going and figure stuff out, we're as good as any team in the country. Coach Meyer would cite the Nebraska game and say, 'Let's play like that.' That was a big springboard for us. We saw what we could do. A big-time atmosphere on prime-time TV under the lights against a great opponent. It showed us we're big time. We're what everybody should be talking about. We obviously didn't play like that the rest of the season. But it showed us that we have it in us."

But in the heady glow of the win was some unfortunate news. In the first quarter, linebacker Etienne Sabino left the game with a leg injury. "To this day, I honestly don't know exactly what play it was that I got hurt on," Sabino said. "I want to say I was leg-whipped. Maybe I got cut by one of the linemen on a run play, but I honestly couldn't tell. I know something started hurting in my leg and I kept playing through it. A couple series later, I tried to get back in the game, and I was unable to run."

Sabino had fractured his fibula. He had surgery the next morning to implant a plate and titanium screws in his leg. Sabino had emerged as a team leader and a solid player at a position where depth was nonexistent. Meyer would have to look far and wide for a solution. It turned out that the answer was standing right behind his quarterback.

· 17 ·

INDIANA: BOREN'S MOVE

URBAN MEYER didn't plan the move.

When Meyer walked out to practice on Tuesday, October 9, he didn't intend to make any dramatic changes, certainly not like the one he'd make. But as he perused his linebacker corps as preparations began for the Indiana game, the grim reality of the situation hit him. Etienne Sabino would be out for several weeks with his broken leg. Ryan Shazier had been playing through some nagging injuries and was unavailable to practice. Storm Klein had a bulging disk in his back and couldn't practice. Now even some of the backups were hurt. Freshmen Joshua Perry and Camren Williams couldn't go. Defensive end Nathan Williams had volunteered to play linebacker, but his inability to practice because of his precarious knee made that unfeasible. In fact, soreness would keep Williams out of the Indiana game. The few linebackers who were healthy had been slow to grasp the defense. The situation looked dire.

Then Meyer walked over to fullback Zach Boren. Meyer had originally pegged Boren as a good player and a hard worker but a negative guy. By now, Boren had become one of his best leaders. His locker room talk against Michigan State after Meyer's "Rip Your Chest Open" speech had, in the coach's eyes, completed the transformation. Boren was all in. Now he was going to find out just how much.

"I looked on the practice field and saw all these guys hurt," Meyer said. "Here's Zach Boren, who's now the ultimate team guy.

I just went right over to him and said, 'What the hell are we going to do?' Someone had just told me that Josh Perry couldn't practice. I said, 'Zach, I need you on defense.' He said, 'I'll do whatever I can to help this team.'"

In truth, it wasn't all that much of a stretch and had been a request he'd waited his entire Ohio State career to hear. Boren had been a linebacker since he'd started playing football at age five. He was an all-state player at Pickerington Central, though his senior season was cut short because of an ACL tear. Growing up in a Columbus suburb, Boren was that rarest of species, a central Ohioan who was a true Michigan fan. Heck, he was really a Michigan Man, or at least a Michigan Son and Brother. His father, Mike, played for Bo Schembechler at Michigan in the early 1980s. His mother, Hope, competed in track and field for the Wolverines. Zach's brother Justin, an offensive lineman, started his career at Michigan under Lloyd Carr, and Zach intended to follow him there as a Wolverine.

"I actually verbally committed to Coach Carr," he said. "Coach Carr was a great man. He reminded me a lot of Coach Tressel."

But Carr retired after the 2007 season, beating Meyer's Florida team in the Capital One Bowl in his final game, and Rich Rodriguez was hired as his successor. Justin Boren soon became disenchanted. Claiming that Michigan's "family values [had] eroded" under Rodriguez, he transferred to Ohio State. That was practically heresy given the intensity of the rivalry. Once Justin left, Zach changed his mind about going to Ann Arbor. He would also become a Buckeye.

"I was bleeding scarlet and gray at that point," he said. "Once you're on one side of the rivalry, you learn to hate the other side real quick."

And all that Michigan stuff the family had accumulated over the years? "I remember cleaning everything out and my mom taking it to Goodwill," Zach said.

He graduated early from Pickerington Central and enrolled at Ohio State in January to get a head start. He hoped he'd be a linebacker and sat in the linebackers' meeting room as he rehabbed from his knee injury. But in preseason camp his freshman year, Luke Fickell said they needed him at fullback. It gave him an opportunity to play right away, and he took advantage. In 2009, he won Ohio State's First-Year Offensive Player award. The itch to play linebacker never left, though, even as he dismissed it as unlikely the longer he played fullback.

Boren took Jim Tressel's forced resignation hard. When Meyer arrived, Boren found it was a lot harder to switch his loyalty from old coach to new coach than it had been from Michigan to Ohio State. "I wouldn't say I didn't buy in right away," Boren said. "But I had so much respect for the previous coaching staff."

When Boren declared, "You can't break us!" during that first week of 5:00 AM punishment workouts, it looked like he'd have a rocky relationship with the new regime. Boren said that his declaration was misinterpreted.

"I was saying it to be motivational to the guys," Boren said. "So many guys were hurting and wanting to stop because they didn't think they could go anymore. I was just saying it to be motivational, that you can go farther. A lot of times when you think you can't go anymore, you really can. You have to tell your body that you can do more and that you can't be broken as a person and that you have a lot more left."

Boren said that he and Meyer sat down after the season and laughed about the misunderstanding. At the time, there was nothing amusing about it. Meyer continually harped on Boren to be more positive, with his actions, words, and even his body language. He had responded, but now he would be asked to put that to the test. As much as he always wanted to play linebacker, a switch midway through his senior season was not how he envisioned it. It would have been understandable to ask if Meyer was serious. After all, Meyer said he consulted with Fickell about the change "for 10 seconds" before approaching Boren. He was stunned, but immediately agreed to switch to the other side of the ball.

"It totally came out of left field," Boren said. "I was just shocked. There was so much going through my mind. I was so nervous. I had no idea what even the calls were. But there was a sense of excitement. There was a sense of being a freshman again."

When Boren lined up as a linebacker, the doldrums of a Tuesday practice evaporated.

"People were hooting and hollering," Boren said. "It felt like some of the excitement had come back to the defense."

He remembers his first play of practice on defense. Boren said he read the play like he did in high school and made the tackle for a one-yard loss.

"I think it took the coaches and everyone by surprise," Boren said.

At least one teammate wasn't surprised that Boren could make the transition.

"I had all the confidence in the world," Sabino said. "Zach is a great football player. Honestly, I didn't doubt it at all. I knew he could do it. Knowing his background and his football IQ, you could put him anywhere on the football field."

Meyer didn't publicly announce the move of Boren during the week. Why give Indiana information that it could use against the Buckeyes? Since practices are closed to the media, it wasn't until close to the game that word began to leak out about the Boren switch.

*   *   *   *

INDIANA has long been the doormat of the Big Ten. The Hoosier State's passion is basketball. John Wooden was from there. OSU grad Bob Knight was Indiana's dominant personality the three decades he coached IU. Football is a secondary sport, and the other two major programs in the state—Notre Dame and Purdue—have richer gridiron traditions. Indiana has played in one Rose Bowl—in 1968. Ohio State hadn't lost to Indiana since 1988. But the Hoosiers made what looked like a wise move by hiring Kevin Wilson in 2011. Indiana went only 1–11 in Wilson's first year, though they threatened Ohio State at the Horseshoe until the Buckeyes pulled away late for a 34–20 victory. The 2012 Hoosiers, despite losing quarterback Tre Roberson to a season-ending injury in the second game, were a more competitive team. The previous week, Indiana had Michigan State on the ropes before the Spartans rallied with 14 unanswered fourth-quarter points to win 31–27.

Meyer knew Wilson well and admired him. Wilson was an assistant under spread guru Randy Walker at Miami University and in 2008 won the Broyles Award as the nation's top assistant coach while offensive coordinator at Oklahoma. As Meyer built his playbook over the years, he borrowed concepts from studying Wilson, and they became friends.

"He's an innovator," Meyer said before the game. "I have a lot of respect for him as a guy. Indiana's got the right coach now."

Meyer was worried that his team might be flat after two emotional wins. The Buckeyes would spend the night in Indianapolis and then take buses for the final hour of the trip on game day, which Meyer didn't like having to do. Also, Memorial Stadium is not known for its atmosphere. It's not unusual for traveling Ohio State fans to outnumber Hoosier fans when the game is in Bloomington, although, as both teams' colors are variations of red, it can be tough to tell. When the teams were introduced, the Buckeyes did get a louder ovation from their fans than the Hoosiers did from theirs. That reinforced the disparity between the programs. Ohio State was Ohio State and Indiana was Indiana. Whatever momentum Wilson was building in the program, there was little reason to think that the Hoosiers would seriously threaten the now eighth-ranked Buckeyes.

If Ohio State could score 63 points against Nebraska, it figured to be able to score against the Hoosiers.

But overlooked in the offensive explosion against Nebraska was the fact the Buckeyes surrendered 38 points to the Cornhuskers. With the linebacker situation in flux—who knew how well Boren would play in real competition?—the Buckeyes figured to be tested by Indiana's offense. But to surrender 49 points, the most ever against the Buckeyes by the Hoosiers, would have seemed incomprehensible.

There was little sign of trouble at first. The Buckeyes jumped to a 10–0 lead in the first quarter and forced three-and-outs on Indiana's first two possessions. Klein started despite his back injury. Boren entered on the second possession, playing weak-side linebacker. The middle linebacker calls the defensive signals, and Buckeyes coaches didn't believe Boren was ready for that responsibility just yet. Shazier played middle linebacker instead.

Then things went downhill quickly. After Indiana finally got a first down, quarterback Cameron Coffman handed off to Stephen Houston for a seemingly simple run up the middle. It turned into a disaster. Shazier blitzed and was swallowed up by the pulling right guard. Klein went to the outside instead of filling toward the middle. Right defensive end Noah Spence, in for Nathan Williams, was pushed out of the play. Defensive tackle Michael Bennett was blocked to the inside. Cornerback Bradley Roby, coming up in run support, took a step to the outside, taking himself out of the play. He dived but barely got a hand on Houston, who raced otherwise untouched for a 59-yard touchdown.

What made the play especially maddening was that it did not take the Buckeyes by surprise. "We spent Friday and Saturday morning talking about how we were going to defend that play and actually put in a wrinkle for that play, because other teams had used that against us," co–defensive coordinator Everett Withers said.

Indiana had put three wide receivers on the right side of the field. Ohio State's coaches knew that the Hoosiers would either throw in that direction or run to the left of their center. But none of it mattered because the Buckeyes took improper angles or were manhandled.

"We had schemed them and then didn't execute it," Withers said.

Another recurring problem cost Ohio State the lead. A blown blocking assignment allowed Indiana to block Ben Buchanan's punt after the Buckeyes' next possession. Injuries that began affecting the punt-block unit in the Alabama-Birmingham game continued to mount. Forced to mix and match, the Buckeyes had to scramble to find enough suitable bodies.

"We had a lot of guys on the punt team who were not prepared to be on the punt team," said Zach Smith, who was in charge of that unit. "It was a depth issue. We had guys out there who were not ready."

Houston capitalized on the block, scoring on a seven-yard run to give the Hoosiers a 14–10 lead. Drew Basil then missed a 35-yard field goal—his first unsuccessful kick of the year.

The Buckeyes needed a big play to reverse momentum, and they got one from a player who came perilously close back in the winter to being written off as a non-factor. But Travis Howard, out of anyone on the defense, might best have exemplified the turnaround from underachiever to conscientious standout.

"Travis is a remarkable story," cornerbacks coach Kerry Coombs said. "When I got to Ohio State, Travis was a mess. He was [academically] ineligible. He was a wonderful kid—friendly, smiling, and happy, and very happy to be mediocre. I think he thought there was a pot at the end of the rainbow that really wasn't there. His footwork was bad. His attention to detail was bad. His effort in pretty much all areas of his life was poor."

On Coombs' first week on the job, he and Howard had what he called "a good, hard" conversation. Coombs had watched tape.

He'd seen Howard's academic record. "I told him, 'I can't under-stand why you're like this. My job is to help you become an NFL player, help us win a lot of football games, and [make sure] you're going to graduate. And if you don't do X, Y, and Z over the next short period of time, I'm going to find someone else [who can].' I said that we can clearly be 6–7 with you, so we can probably be at least that without you."

Painful as it was, Howard knew that the criticism was justified.

"I felt like I didn't put my all into it," he said of his junior sea-son. "I took the year for granted. I knew there were plays out there that I could have made to help us win certain games if only I was focused and took it more seriously. [This year] I wanted to be all the way in and see what I could get out of it."

Coombs said that, even when he went on vacation, he and Howard talked every day on the phone. Howard became a sponge, Coombs said, devouring all of his coaching. Howard regained his academic eligibility during training camp. From the start of the season, he was a much-improved player, but the stinger issue in his neck threatened his progress. On the first play against Indiana, the stinger flared up again when he made a tackle.

"I was coming in and out of the game because there were certain times when I would make a tackle, if I'd turn my head the wrong way, my whole left side would go numb," Howard said. "It got so bad that at times they told me not to play on defense, to just play special teams."

Desperate to make an impact, he got his chance with the blocked punt.

"I remember being off on defense for a couple series, and Coach Mickey [Marotti] said, 'Are you in on punts?' Something told me to just go. I just remember lining up, and I had my head more to the right side because I couldn't put any pressure on the left side since it was numb. I remember saying, 'I'm going to take off and try to block it.' When he snapped the ball, the guy who was supposed to block me didn't see me, so I knew for a fact it was going to be a blocked punt. All I had to do was get my hand on the ball."

He did, and Roby recovered for a touchdown to put Ohio State back ahead 17–14. The Buckeyes' offense then got revved up. First, Braxton Miller and Devin Smith connected for a 60-yard touchdown using the same play that beat Michigan State. On Ohio State's next possession, Miller then took it himself up the middle for a 67-yard touchdown. Tight end Jeff Heuerman and pulling guard Andrew Norwell had key blocks, but the biggest might have been an inadvertent one. Linebacker Jacarri Alexander was closing in on Miller a few yards past the line of scrimmage when he ran into umpire Steven Woods.

Leading 31–17, the Buckeyes had a chance to extend the lead when they had first and goal at the Indiana 3. But on second down, Miller unwisely forced a pass into the end zone, and Indiana cornerback Greg Heban made a diving interception. What could have been a 21-point lead quickly became only a seven-point advantage soon afterward. Coffman threw to Shane Wynn on a short crossing pattern. But another Indiana receiver sprung Wynn free from Klein and Christian Bryant. Wynn raced up the left sideline for a 76-yard touchdown.

Once again, the Buckeyes' offense gave Ohio State some breathing room. With Miller briefly shaken up, Kenny Guiton came in for another one of his brief relief spots and executed a beautiful shovel pass to Carlos Hyde for a 14-yard touchdown. Hyde, who ran like a freight train all game, scored on a one-yard run after rumbling for 21 on the previous play to make it 45–27 early in the fourth quarter. He would finish with 156 yards in 22 carries.

After the season, running backs coach Stan Drayton described the 21-yard run as the perfect encapsulation of Hyde's growth as a runner.

"It was an inside zone play," Drayton said. "We ask these guys to press the line of scrimmage, run off a hill, make a jump cut, and burst through a seam. He did those things, and it was just like practice. Then he burst in the open field and got one-on-one with a safety, and there was a linebacker who had a pursuit angle on him. Probably about 10 yards downfield he met this linebacker and safety at the same time, and there was this demeanor that changed where he dropped and exploded and ran through them.

"There was an unbelievable sound from these three bodies hitting each other. And all of a sudden, you saw Carlos torque his body. You saw the knee lift and the drive, and you saw the safety's head hit the ground and the linebacker bounce off him.

"That type of skill set is everything we talk about—ball security and competing at an excellent level by anticipating where the hole and the safety are going to be. And all that happened with a torn MCL. That's when I knew Carlos had the ability to be as good as any back I've ever coached."

The Buckeyes' final score showcased another tantalizing talent. Devin Smith had caught the 60-yard touchdown pass but had also dropped two other passes that likely would have gone for touchdowns.

"I tell him all the time that he's the typical ridiculously fast guy who doesn't win at the line of scrimmage with the defensive back because [he knows] he's faster than the defensive back," wide receivers coach Zach Smith said. "He's trying to turn his eyes away and look upfield and see what he's going to do."

But Smith described the sophomore as "the most talented wide receiver I've been around other than Percy Harvin," and his second touchdown against Indiana showed it. He caught what looked to be a harmless pass on a crossing route. Three Indiana defenders looked to have him boxed in, but Smith planted, reversed field, and shed three tackles on his way to a 46-yard touchdown for a 52–34 lead.

That score should have put the Buckeyes in command of the game for good. But again, the Hoosiers wouldn't fold, aided by the injury-depleted Buckeyes defense. Howard was in and out of the lineup. Bryant also got hurt. Fellow safety C.J. Barnett was back after missing three games with a sprained ankle, but he was not 100 percent.

But it was the lack of effort that rankled Buckeyes coaches. Ohio State led 52–34 with less than four minutes left, when Indiana, using backup quarterback Nate Sudfeld in what was considered mop-up duty, drove 76 yards for a touchdown in less than two minutes. Indiana's ensuing onside kick looked to be headed out of bounds. Roby could have fielded the ball, but he assumed it would go out of play and stopped. Indiana's Nick Stoner didn't give up on the play, leaping as he reached the sideline to tap the ball back to a teammate. Five plays later, Sudfeld threw a short pass to Houston, who broke a tackle by Boren and went for a 25-yard touchdown.

Suddenly, with 1:05 left, it was a three-point game. Indiana tried another onside kick, this time a pooch. Philly Brown had to go back to retrieve it. Fortunately, he was able to cradle the ball in before Indiana could get there, clinching a Buckeyes victory that didn't feel like one.

"Winning games in college football is hard," Coombs said. "You shouldn't be miserable when you're winning. But, man, we couldn't have been more miserable."

Other than the last play, Boren had a credible performance. He had eight tackles, including five solo. "I was the leading tackler, but I blew a lot of assignments, as you would imagine," he said. "I was out there kind of like a chicken with its head cut off. It got to the point where I was just trying to go with my instincts, just play football."

Boren had a reason for a spotty performance. Most of the others on defense didn't. Indiana gained 481 yards, which told only part of the story.

"I knew they would gain some yards," Withers said. "What was frustrating more than anything else was the missed opportunities. I think we missed six or seven interceptions."

Safety Orhian Johnson said after the season that the Buckeyes had grown complacent because of being undefeated. The Indiana game revealed their weaknesses.

"I hate that game," he said. "At no point did we feel we were going to lose. But the whole time it was like, 'What is going on? Why is this happening right now?' It was unreal. You can't even put into words what happened. It was one of those games you just want to survive it. You just want to get out of it."

Meyer was distressed by what he'd seen. "I was very surprised and disappointed," he said, "because I saw us not go hard. Even early in the year when we were awful on defense, we went hard. That's the first time I saw us not play hard."

The bus ride home was a somber one. A reckoning of sorts was due. It came the next day. Meyer had what he described as a "hard meeting" with his defensive coaches. He also had one with defensive players. Feelings weren't spared.

C.J. Barnett said he was one of the targets.

"He wasn't happy with how I was doing," Barnett said, "and I guess since I was a starter and looked to as a leader, he kind of let me have it in front of the team. He said straight up, 'You need to play better.'"

Barnett could handle the criticism. His teammates regarded him as one of the smartest guys on the team.

"He's always in the film room and always seems to be a step ahead," backup safety Zach Domicone said. "I've been on sideline with him and seen him make offensive calls, and then it happens. In spring ball, he'd say, 'It's going to be a post route,' and he'd be right."

But not everybody was as able to avoid being stung by Meyer's bluntness.

"He'll go off sometimes," Orhian Johnson said. "I've done heard some stuff that would make people quit football and stuff that'll make them cry to their mama. But it's all honest. You may not like, but you've got to respect it."

Meyer reserved some criticism for himself. After the season, he blamed himself for some of the defensive problems that peaked with the Indiana game. He said he'd been so consumed with his responsibilities on offense and special teams that he didn't devote the attention to the defense that he should have.

"That was my fault," Meyer said. "I should have been over there, but on offense we were bad [earlier]."

But it was also true that the defensive coaches needed time to get into sync. Fickell had been on the staff for a decade, but this was his first year as the sole defensive coordinator. He and Mike Vrabel had switched position group responsibilities from the year before, with Vrabel handling the linemen and Fickell the linebackers. Withers and Coombs were new.

The process of having a coaching staff in alignment that Meyer had come to value as essential hadn't been completed. It wasn't that the coaches didn't get along personally. They said they did. But they came from different backgrounds and had different philosophies. Withers, for example, had served under coaches like Carl Reese at the University of Texas and Jeff Fisher with the Tennessee Titans. Their philosophies included highly aggressive defenses with an emphasis on blitzes. Ohio State traditionally had not been a team that blitzed extensively, believing—usually correctly—that its superior athletes would win enough battles that blitzing would be an unnecessary risk.

"I don't think it's a coincidence we didn't play well early," Coombs said. "I think we had to come to grips with each other as far as the mechanics of the game plan and who's calling what and who's responsible for what—how to impose our individual wills on practice and game plays. I definitely think there was a feeling-out process taking place, not one of conflict but everyone trying to find that alignment, that role for the good of the collective group."

Withers and Coombs needed time to get to know their players, and the installation of the spread on offense slowed the defense's growth. The Buckeyes worked against nothing but the spread in the spring and summer. It left them largely unprepared for some of the offenses they'd face, which was compounded by the fact that many of their early opponents surprised Ohio State with changes in their scheme and personnel. The inability of certain players like Nathan Williams (knee), Roby (shoulder), and Howard (neck) to practice much also hurt attempts to develop cohesion. Everything came to a head in the Indiana game.

"That was the big eye-opener to us," Fickell said.

Meyer decided to become more involved in the defensive game-planning.

"He was more visible during practice periods," Coombs said. "He's obviously an intense motivator. The kids and coaches want to perform better when he's watching. He started coming for specific periods of practice, running the scout team against the defense. That helped make some changes."

The coaches came to a consensus that they'd have to become more aggressive with their scheming. Roby and Howard had proven they could cover. The pass rush hadn't been consistent, so coaches decided to trust their cornerbacks in man coverage more often, which would free linebackers to blitz. In other words, the Buckeyes intended to dictate to offenses rather than react to what offenses did to them.

It was more than scheme that needed to change. Coaches can diagram schemes all day, but sometimes it takes a player to say what needs to be said. Withers said that happened after the Indiana game.

"I could feel that the players started to take a little more ownership," he said. "Guys like Christian Bryant stood up and called out some guys, to be honest. It was good for us to see that. Christian Bryant is a pretty passionate guy about playing the game.

"He didn't have a great game. I think he was a little hurt that game. But he'd seen enough, and he's a pretty vocal guy. At that time, I'm not sure if we really had any vocal leaders in the defense. John [Simon]'s not a talker. He's not a vocal guy. Zach would have been perfect, but he just got there. You think about that defensive football team and who are the guys who stood up and said, 'Hey, we've got to stop it. We've got to get this done.' We didn't have that guy. We had guys who did it by example, but we didn't have that true bell cow."

So Bryant, the guy who drew Mickey Marotti's ire early in January with his "C'mon, brother" comment, would emerge. His message, he said was that his teammates needed to correct their mistakes from the Indiana game but also keep their heads up.

"I wanted everybody to get on the same page," Bryant said.

The next week's game against Purdue figured to be a perfect opportunity to right the ship. The Boilermakers had been beaten by a combined 55 points in their first two Big Ten games against Michigan and Wisconsin. Purdue figured to provide a breather, a chance to get some playing time. Heck, maybe even Kenny Guiton would get in at the end for more than just a couple plays.

· 18 ·

PURDUE: GUITON'S MOMENT

PRAIRIE VIEW A&M.

That was where Kenny Guiton was likely headed until that unexpected offer from Ohio State.

Guiton had been offered scholarships by such schools as Kansas, Iowa State, and his hometown University of Houston, but those vanished when other quarterbacks committed first. Guiton wasn't on Ohio State's radar until quite late in the recruiting process in 2009, either. The Buckeyes wanted Tajh Boyd or Austin Boucher to serve as an understudy to Terrelle Pryor and then possibly succeed him. But Boyd went to Clemson and became a star. Boucher turned down Jim Tressel's late offer and stuck with his original commitment to Miami University, where he spent his first three years as a backup. With Joe Bauserman the only other scholarship quarterback on the roster, Ohio State was desperate to sign someone else, even if all he contributed was another arm for practice reps.

With the other offers gone, Guiton had resigned himself to settling for Prairie View, a Football Championship Subdivision school northwest of Houston that plays in the historically black Southwestern Athletic Conference. Its stadium holds 6,000. When Ohio State offered, Guiton couldn't quite believe it.

Not much was expected of Guiton. He certainly wouldn't challenge Pryor for the starting job, and the Buckeyes figured to recruit Pryor's heir apparent later, which turned out to be Miller. Guiton did have a chance to win the starting job in 2011 after Pryor left and with Miller a raw freshman, but he didn't do much to distinguish himself. He appeared in one game all season—against Nebraska—and had no statistics. When Urban Meyer arrived, he knew little about him as a player but was thoroughly unimpressed by Guiton's reputation. It didn't help that Guiton was one of the players late for Meyer's first team meeting the morning after the Gator Bowl. That he was tardy only because he'd stopped to pick up Orhian Johnson after the safety's car wouldn't start wasn't much of a mitigating factor in coach's eyes.

"In January, I called him in and said we had some things happen here that a quarterback shouldn't do," Meyer said. "I said, 'I'm not coaching you. It's time for you to go.' It was a bad meeting. I found out some things he did in the past."

Guiton doesn't recall being told he was on the verge of being booted. But he knew he was in the doghouse. "I'm not really sure [why]," Guiton said. "I guess I had a history of partying. This is what I was told: I was known as the guy who got people together for parties." His parties weren't wild ones, Guiton said, but Meyer impressed upon him the need for a quarterback to set an example in all ways.

"At the time, I didn't get it and didn't know why I was being pointed out as that [negative] guy," Guiton said. "Now looking back on it, I see the effect I have on teammates and how much of a leader I can be. If my actions were that, I didn't mean for them to be that. That's what the coaches had heard, and that's the mentality they'd come in with, thinking that I was. I didn't think it was a fair characterization of me, but I like to have fun, just like anybody else."

With an easy-going personality and an ever-present smile, Guiton was always liked by his teammates. Now he had to earn the respect of his coaches.

"I definitely thought that they didn't want me around at the time," Guiton said.

The only way he could prove his value was to work hard in the off-season, and he did. Mickey Marotti quickly identified him as one of the team's leaders, despite his backup status. By the end of spring practice, Meyer's opinion of Guiton had changed 180 degrees.

"Kenny Guiton is a very powerful guy," he said. "Kids migrate to him. They listen to him. They like him. He's a unique kid, and a great kid. He was a critical guy to [buy in]."

Guiton had another incentive to get with the program. He learned in February that he would become a father. "I was a little scared but excited at the same time," he said.

He knew he wouldn't be playing just for himself anymore, and his dedication reflected it. When Meyer had his post–spring practice individual meetings—many of which were unpleasantly blunt—his review with Guiton was glowing.

"I don't know if he was expecting that," Meyer said. "Throughout spring practice, I saw the growth of a young person into a young man, which was really cool. He was a very unselfish player, a player who can lead this team. I don't know if he'd ever been told that. He had this look in his eye like, 'This is unbelievable.'"

Even with that ringing endorsement, he wasn't going to beat out Miller. But at least the Buckeyes entered the season knowing they had a viable alternative if anything happened to Miller.

Something would against Purdue.

* * * *

OTHER THAN PLAYING undefeated Notre Dame tough in a 20–17 defeat, Purdue gave little indication that it would be the team that would throw the biggest scare of the season into Ohio State.

The Buckeyes were 17-point favorites against the Boilermakers. Purdue usually gives Ohio State fits at Ross-Ade Stadium in West Lafayette. At Ohio Stadium, it's typically a different story. The

Boilermakers hadn't won in Columbus since 1988. The Boilermakers had rotated three quarterbacks, none of whom had been able to seize the job. Purdue had some talented players, most notably nose tackle Kawann Short, but its season was already in the midst of a slump that would cost coach Danny Hope his job.

For the first 59 minutes of the game, however, it was the Buckeyes who could do little right. On the game's very first snap, the Boilermakers called for a wheel route to fullback Akeem Shavers. Co–defensive coordinator Everett Withers said the Buckeyes had schemed for a version of that play, but to the boundary—short side—of the field. Purdue ran it to the far side, trying to exploit Orhian Johnson and Storm Klein, who was still starting instead of Zach Boren. Purdue sent a receiver in Johnson's direction hoping to isolate Klein in man-to-man coverage. Johnson did as Purdue hoped, going to that receiver. Klein, especially with his ailing back, couldn't keep pace with Shavers. He caught the pass from Caleb TerBush in stride. Klein made a futile dive at Shavers, who ran for the 83-yard touchdown for a 6–0 lead.

"They were really trying to take advantage of our Mike linebacker," Withers said. "It was a little bit of a thing throughout the year, because of that position. It was one of those plays that they really schemed us. They got us. It might have gotten a lot of teams not prepared for that play."

Garrett Goebel blocked Purdue's extra-point kick, and that would loom huge by game's end. It was the sort of overlooked-but-significant play the unassuming defensive tackle made all season.

"I just remember being really pissed off that they scored," Goebel said, "and I was trying to come off the ball hard. I got out on the guy across from me, and I ended up getting my hand up and blocking it."

If the Ohio State offense had played the way it had in Big Ten play so far, that quick touchdown might have become a mere blip. But a Purdue defense that had given up 771 yards rushing the previous two weeks suddenly became stout against the Buckeyes. Carlos Hyde ran for 91 yards in 19 carries, but Miller was held in check. Until his fateful final carry, Miller was limited to 11 carries for 10 yards.

"They made a decision to take away our quarterback, a little bit like Wisconsin did [later]," Meyer said. "Something we call zero hole. No safeties deep. We should have thrown it all over the place. [But] that's not who we were. They did a good job. Purdue had good players and they schemed us pretty good, and we weren't playing well."

Even when Ohio State's offense got on track, the Buckeyes couldn't enjoy it for long. Ohio State took a 7–6 lead later in the first quarter on a 67-yard touchdown drive capped by an eight-yard Miller touchdown run. But Akeem Hunt—the Buckeyes had a tough day stopping guys named Akeem—took the ensuing kickoff and ran it back 100 yards for a touchdown.

In the third quarter, Ohio State went 80 yards in eight plays. On third-and-10 from the Buckeyes' 44, Miller threw to Philly Brown for a 19-yard completion. But Brown sustained a concussion when tackled and left the game for good. Chris Fields replaced him. The junior started eight games in 2011 without distinction. This year, he'd been almost a forgotten player. He didn't even play the UCF, Cal, or Michigan State games as he battled shoulder and shin splint injuries. Fields hadn't caught a pass all season.

"It was very humbling to me," Fields said.

Braxton would give him a chance to make an impact on the very next play, and he did. Fields caught a pass along the left sideline for a 35-yard completion. That set up a two-yard touchdown run by Hyde.

Again Purdue countered. The Boilermakers drove from their 18 to the Ohio State 31. On first down, TerBush threw a quick wide screen to Gary Bush. Purdue blocked C.J. Barnett and Travis Howard, and Bush raced between them for the touchdown to make it 20–14.

Purdue had a chance to extend its lead when it forced a fumble by Miller at the Ohio State 37. But Johnathan Hankins blocked Paul Griggs' 34-yard field-goal attempt to keep it a one-possession game with 29 seconds left in the third quarter.

The next play, however, looked like it might doom Ohio State for the day—and the season. Miller finally broke free on a keeper. As he ran past the Ohio State sideline, Miller tried to stiff-arm Purdue cornerback Josh Johnson. Miller and Johnson battled for leverage until Johnson grabbed Miller's jersey and body-slammed him to the ground. Miller had dodged serious injury numerous times in 2012. Instantly, this looked different. Miller didn't move as the stadium hushed.

"My eyes were blurry," Miller said. "I couldn't really see. I looked up and tried to hear stuff and couldn't hear. I couldn't hear, I couldn't see. So I just closed my eyes and tried to blink. When [trainer] Doug [Calland] came out there, I actually opened my eyes. 'Okay, cool. I'm good.' But I couldn't walk because everything was shot down from my spine. When you get slammed down on your neck like that, it's really dangerous. I didn't know what was wrong because I couldn't walk by myself."

Miller has had his share of injuries, but this, he said, was the scariest he'd ever had. "On a scale of one to 10, it was a 10," he said.

Miller was helped to the sideline, though he was clearly in agony. His father, Kevin, came down from the stands to be with him before he was taken to the locker room and eventually by ambulance to the hospital.

*　　*　　*　　*

KENNY GUITON had watched the play unfold from the sideline. He stood behind the Purdue defense to get a better angle of the play.

"He made the long run, and it went right past me," Guiton said. "I'm thinking it's a touchdown. 'Touchdown, Braxton!' Then the dude got him. Once he hit the ground, I could tell he was hurting a little bit. But I didn't know what the extent of it was. I saw how long he was down, and that's when the nerves kind of took over, like, 'Oh, man, he might not be coming back in. We're down and I'm going to have to try to win this game for the team.'"

October had already been a whirlwind for Guiton. His son, Jordan Zyaire, was born on the first day of the month in Dayton.

"It was a great feeling," Guiton said. "Holding him in my arms, I realized I was a dad and all kinds of thoughts ran through my head, like how when I was a child my father was a great father to me. At that moment, I thought how good of a father I wanted to be."

Now he had a chance to provide a memory he could share with his son forever.

"I felt like that whole game was just for him," Guiton said. "I got in and wanted to do so good."

But first he had to conquer his nerves. Guiton may have looked calm on the outside, but the butterflies were buzzing inside of him. It took a while for Guiton to settle into the game. Guiton's first pass was an incompletion on third-and-four from the Purdue 33. Drew Basil's 50-yard field-goal attempt hit the left upright. Things would get even worse. Purdue's punt after its next possession was downed at the 1. On second-and-five, Guiton dropped back to pass in the Ohio State end zone. Tight end Jeff Heuerman pushed a Purdue rusher in the back to keep Guiton from being sacked, and Andrew Norwell did the same to another pass-rusher after Guiton stepped up in the pocket. The umpire threw his flag for holding. The referee announced that the penalty was on Heuerman, though the game log would say it was on Norwell. It didn't really matter. Holding in the end zone is a safety, and the Buckeyes now trailed 22–14 with 10 minutes left.

After a four-minute Purdue drive ended with a punt, the Buckeyes took over at their 20. On third-and-13, Guiton rolled out and saw Jake Stoneburner deep near the Purdue sideline. He heaved the ball, but it was underthrown. Stoneburner went up for the ball with the Boilermakers defender, and the ball deflected high in the air into the waiting arms of Purdue's Landon Feichter.

With 2:40 left, a difficult outlook now became dire. Buckeyes fans sensed that, too, and many of them left the stadium. The Buckeyes had only one timeout left. One of the two they'd used was called early in the fourth quarter because they lined up on defense with only 10 players.

Sometimes the biggest rallies begin almost imperceptibly. Ohio State's began with a flinch by a Purdue player. Fullback Brandon Cottom moved just before the Boilermakers' first play after the interception. The false-start penalty made it first-and-15 and changed the entire dynamic of the series.

"It was huge," Meyer said. "When I saw that, I knew it was a big play."

Running for a first down now would be difficult, and Ohio State knew the Boilermakers were unlikely to throw a risky pass that could be intercepted. Purdue's next play was a short pass. Bradley Roby made the tackle for a gain of only one yard. The Boilermakers ran twice more and didn't come close to a first down. Cody Webster's low punt bounced a couple of times and then rolled before Fields, also Brown's backup as a punt returner, wisely picked it up. He raced to the right sideline and gained nine important yards.

Still, the Buckeyes faced steep odds. They had the ball at their own 39 with 47 seconds left and no timeouts. The Buckeyes' offense gathered.

"It was just sort of like, 'We've got to do this,'" center Corey Linsley said. "Everyone was screaming and yelling, but you could just see the look on Kenny's face. He was cool, calm, and collected. He was pumped up for the opportunity he had. It kind of calmed us down. We were like, 'We're about to win this.' We had a level of confidence about ourselves that we hadn't had to that point."

Guiton took command in the huddle. He told his teammates they needed a big play and reminded them that it was essential to get out of bounds. The first-down call was called "Cross Country," Guiton said. Devin Smith would run a deep crossing pattern behind the linebackers.

They were confident it would work if he could get protection, because the play required time. Meyer sensed that Purdue wouldn't blitz.

"We practice that every week," Meyer said. "That's what we call one of our chunk plays. It takes forever to open up. You just hold it for so long that a lot of times you get sacked. If you can hold on to it long enough, it's usually open."

Guiton did look to be threatened for an instant when Purdue defensive end Ryan Russell got around left tackle Jack Mewhort and got an arm on Guiton. But Mewhort pushed Reynolds before he could really grasp Guiton, who stepped up in the pocket and floated a pass in stride to Smith. The receiver caught the ball at the 38, saw he had room to run, and went upfield instead of stepping out of bounds. He was finally tackled at the 22 with 37 seconds left. The Buckeyes hurried to the line, and Guiton completed an eight-yard sideline pass to Evan Spencer, who got out of bounds. After Guiton threw the ball out of the end zone with no open receiver on second down, the Buckeyes faced third-and-two with 23 seconds left. They handed the ball to Hyde, who bulled ahead for the first down, barely. If he hadn't, the Buckeyes would have had to scramble just to get off a fourth-down play.

Guiton spiked the ball on the next snap. The Buckeyes averted disaster on the next play when Guiton threw a slant-in to Spencer at the Purdue 2. Had Spencer made the diving catch, he would have been a yard short of the first down, and time would have expired. The 2012 SEC Championship Game ended on a similar play when time ran out on Georgia against Alabama after a Bulldogs' completion.

"I had pressure in my face, and I made a bad decision to throw that one," Guiton said. "So I was happy that went into the dirt."

Guiton went back to Spencer on the next play. This time, Josh Johnson was called for an obvious pass-interference penalty, giving the Buckeyes the ball at the 2 with eight seconds left. Ohio State then called the same play that Spencer caught for an eight-yard gain on the second play of the drive. This time, though, Guiton looked in the other direction. Fields lined up inside on the left side. Guiton rolled out to his left. Hyde blocked a Purdue pass-rusher to give his quarterback more time. Fields was open, but Guiton's pass was low. Fully extended, Fields dived and cradled the ball in for the touchdown.

"I used to play baseball," Fields said. "I played center field for 13 years. I always taught myself to get that glove under [the ball]—scoop and score."

Guiton felt as though Fields bailed him out.

"That was a little powder-puff pass," he said. "I should have put more on it. I wish I didn't make it so hard on him. He was wide open."

The play was reviewed to make sure the ball didn't touch the ground, which it clearly didn't. That gave the Buckeyes extra time to debate the two-point conversion needed to tie the game. A year earlier, their season-ending losing streak began when a blocked extra-point kick against the Boilermakers kept Ohio State from winning in regulation. Now the Buckeyes needed to execute a more difficult conversion. On the sideline, their offensive linemen lobbied Meyer to run the ball.

"Our offensive line, which was our bread and butter, and Carlos had that look in their face," Meyer said. "They were saying, 'Run the ball, run the ball.' So I told Tom, 'I'm thinking about running the ball here.'"

But in the press box, Tom Herman was adamant. The Buckeyes had practiced for this situation with a delayed-action pass to the tight end. Ed Warinner, who'd normally be predisposed to side with his linemen, agreed that the pass was the right call. As co-coordinator, Warinner had been involved in making sure that was part of the game plan. Warinner said he'd used that play while coaching at Army, at Kansas, and at Notre Dame.

"That play has never failed me," he said. "I consider it to be undefeated."

The key to the play is to make the defense think that the tight end is a blocker. That means that the tight end, Heuerman in this case, does have to block at the beginning of the play. Then he sneaks to the opposite side and catches the pass once those in pass coverage follow other receivers. Meyer weighed all the vehement voices and decided to go with the coaches and stick to the pass.

"Tom said, 'We've practiced the wide play. It'll be there,'" Meyer recalled. "My concern was if we ran the ball, they'd put too many in there to block. Tom said that we've practiced that play for three weeks now. I said, "Okay, let's go with it.'"

The play may have worked in practice, but that was with Miller at the helm. Guiton had never run the play. But his diligence in taking mental reps in practice and studying in the meeting room gave him confidence.

"I knew how to execute it, so I just tried my best to go out and do it," he said.

The play, like most, did not go exactly according to plan. According to the play design, Heuerman was supposed to block defensive end Ryan Russell, and then go toward the goal line before crossing to his left. That's not what happened, and Heuerman jokingly blamed right tackle Reid Fragel, his roommate.

"We were supposed to double-team the guy for a minute, and then I was supposed to go over top," Heuerman said with a laugh. "But Reid's big ass came through and just annihilated the dude and threw him in front of me. So I got a little stuck behind him for a second and had to find a way out, one way or another. There's no second option. I had to find a way out."

So Heuerman decided to cut under Russell and Fragel and run his route that way.

"When you watch it on tape, it was the smart thing to do," tight ends coach Tim Hinton said.

But because he had to fight through the muck of linemen, Heuerman was a split-second later than expected running his route.

"While I was at the top of my drop, I was wondering, 'Where is he? Where is he?'" Guiton said. "I couldn't find him. Then I saw him coming out and I was like, 'Oh, yeah, this is it.'"

Hinton had momentary panic in the press box while waiting for Heuerman to break open.

"I'm screaming my lungs out, 'Get out! Get out! Get out!'" he said. "You can see the defense starting to collapse on Kenny, and you're like, 'Oh my gosh, this could go bad.' Then the ball comes out and Jeff is wide open."

Guiton lofted the ball over defensive tackle Bruce Gaston into the waiting hands of Heuerman.

"I better catch it, or I'm not making it out of the stadium," Heuerman told himself.

He did. Tie game. Basil squibbed the ensuing kickoff to Akeem Hunt, and he was quickly tackled to send the game to overtime. Purdue won the toss and deferred. On the first play from the 25, the Buckeyes almost got into trouble when Guiton bobbled Linsley's high snap. But he secured it and dived back to the line of scrimmage. Guiton then zipped a pass to Stoneburner for a 17-yard gain. Three plays later, Hyde dived in for a two-yard touchdown.

Now it was Purdue's turn. TerBush threw to Gabe Holmes at the Buckeyes 10, but C.J. Barnett drilled Holmes, jarring the ball free. On second down, Ryan Shazier's blitz up the middle forced TerBush to throw earlier than he wanted, and his short throw to Dolapo Macarthy sailed high. Purdue tried a wide-receiver screen to Holmes on third down, but Johnathan Hankins alertly sniffed out the play and tackled Holmes to keep the gain to only five yards.

It was the kind of play that endeared Hankins to his coaches, even if it looked like just another tackle in the play-by-play log.

"You watch him and say, 'Wow, a 325-pound guy on play No. 65 of the game just chased down a screen from behind,'" defensive coordinator Luke Fickell said. "You're not going to find a whole lot of those. It goes down as a tackle for a four- or five-yard gain. But when you really watch the game of football, you say, 'Holy shit.'"

Hankins was shaken up on the play. That gave both teams a chance to contemplate the fourth-down play, and Purdue took a timeout after seeing how Ohio State lined up. It didn't help. Freshman defensive end Noah Spence, whose mom's dream about "Urban Meyers" caused them to believe that divine intervention had sent him to Ohio State, beat his man off the edge. That forced TerBush to step up in the pocket and then roll right as John Simon pursued. TerBush barely got the pass off before Simon decked him. Safety Christian Bryant stayed right with tight end Crosby Wright, but it didn't matter. The hurried pass carried over the end zone, clinching the 29–22 victory.

The victory was a backup quarterback's dream.

"I can't even explain it," Guiton said. "It was so fulfilling. You want to come out and win the game as a quarterback. You want to take control of a game and try to win it. As a backup, you're not given that chance many times. So when you are given that chance, you have to have taken advantage. Just to see all the faith my coaches and teammates had in me—they all rallied behind me and believed in me—it's an experience I'll never forget."

While Guiton was leading the comeback, Braxton Miller was at the hospital, still shaken but, amazingly, not seriously hurt. He was given a sedative after taking an MRI and awoke to see Meyer and Mickey Marotti there to check on him.

"After my MRI, they gave me the medicine to make me drowsy. I fell asleep and woke up and felt better," he said. "Okay, I'm able to talk and see."

The game's outcome was never far from his mind.

"He kept asking, 'What was the score?'" Kevin Miller said. "He was trying to keep up with what was going on. He wanted to get back out there."

Guiton, whose supposed partying ways got him on the verge of being booted in the early days of the Meyer regime, had a low-key evening. "I didn't do much at all," he said. "I hung out with a few friends and went out to get something to eat."

He and Miller also exchanged texts.

"I tried to call him," Guiton said. "I don't think many people got to talk to him on the phone that night. I texted him to make sure he was okay. He texted me back and said he was okay and congratulated me on the win."

Guiton spent the next day with his three-week-old son.

"We had a great time just relaxing," he said. "We took a good long nap together."

Guiton would throw only two more passes in 2012. No matter. With one remarkable comeback, his legacy at Ohio State was secured.

Prairie View, by the way, defeated Alcorn State 52–37 that day to improve its record to 2–5.

· 19 ·

PENN STATE: FOR GARY

WHEN GARY CURTIS died on April 24, 2012, Ryan Shazier knew he wanted to do something big to honor his friend's memory. Curtis never played a game or took a practice rep for the Plantation (Florida) High School football team, but he was as instrumental to the Colonels as anybody in the program. Nobody loved football more than Curtis. Technically, he was a team manager. Really, he was the team inspiration. Despite the Duchenne's muscular dystrophy that confined him to a wheelchair, Curtis was revered as a full-fledged member of the team, complete with uniform No. 48. When Shazier transferred from Pompano Beach to Plantation as a sophomore, he didn't understand who Curtis was or why he was always at practice. The scorching south Florida heat didn't faze Curtis, nor did the torrential rainstorms that are a regular part of life there.

"He was in a wheelchair, and I always wondered who he was," Shazier said.

Shazier is an outgoing guy. Meyer said he's the kind of guy his wife always wants to give a hug. Curtis also had an upbeat personality as well. They struck up a friendship.

"I'd always talk to him," Shazier said. "He'd always play video games with us."

Gary was six when was diagnosed. He could still walk at that age, but as the disease progressed, he had to rely on a wheelchair. That wasn't all Curtis had to overcome.

"His mother was a drug addict and the courts took Gary away from his mom and gave him to me," said Pat Curtis, Gary's grandmother.

Pat wanted Gary to experience life fully, and she never treated his disease as a disability. Gary knew his life would be short. People afflicted with Duchenne's typically die by age 25. When Gary was 11, he came home from school and said to his grandma, "Do you know my disease is fatal? It means I'm going to die."

Pat told Gary that everybody dies eventually, that it was more important to live each day to its fullest. Gary replied, "Oh, okay," and that was that.

"As he got older and realized he was going to be in a wheelchair, he would be like, 'Why me?'" Pat said. "But we got through that and we never looked back. It probably took a couple years. He couldn't run. He couldn't play football. He couldn't do the things other kids could do. He would get disappointed, and we would talk it through.

"I said, 'God didn't give you anything you can't handle, Gary. God put you on this earth for a purpose. Maybe you're going to help someone and don't realize how much you're helping them.' Maybe that stuck with him, that he was put on this earth to help people."

Pat recalled how excited Gary was when a football player invited him to his birthday party. When Pat later saw the player at the grocery, she thanked him.

"Mrs. Curtis," the boy said, "if it wasn't for Gary, I wouldn't be where I am today. I was ready to quit, and Gary said, 'Absolutely not. Do you know how lucky you are, the way you can throw the football?'"

Shazier never needed to be encouraged to play football. He always loved it. But Curtis provided extra motivation.

"We used to always play for him in high school because he wanted it so bad but he could never get to play," Shazier said. "He was always there for us in football, so I was always there for him outside of football."

Shazier may have been especially empathetic to Curtis because he knows what it's like to be different. When he was five, Shazier was diagnosed with Alopecia, a condition that causes loss of hair.

"I was the only bald kid in kindergarten," Shazier said.

Shazier is now completely comfortable with having Alopecia—he even cracks jokes about it—but it him took several years to accept it fully. "Early in my football career, it helped me release my anger by playing instead of doing something stupid," he said.

Shazier comes from an accomplished family. His father, Vernon, is a pastor and motivational speaker who serves as team chaplain for the Miami Dolphins.

"Ryan has always been a kid who, whatever he gets involved in, gives 110 percent," Vernon said. "I've kind of raised him that way. Know what you're committing to, because when you do, you have a responsibility to give it your all."

If Ryan had a weakness as a kid, Vernon said, it was that he was too generous. He remembers having to replace his son's cleats in middle school because he'd given his to a needy teammate. In that sense, he was a bit of a kindred spirit with Gary Curtis. But as Shazier blossomed as a player, Curtis' health declined. In the spring of 2012, while Ryan was a freshman at Ohio State, Gary was put into hospice. He was 20 when he died.

"We had his memorial at the football field," Pat Curtis said. "We waited until June when all the guys came back from college. We set off balloons. It wasn't a morbid event. It was beautiful."

Shazier couldn't make it back for the memorial because of his OSU commitments. He vowed to do something to honor his friend and settled on wearing Curtis' No. 48 for a big game. He originally wanted to do it for the Nebraska game in prime time, but that didn't work out for reasons Shazier wasn't sure about.

The Penn State game would suffice just fine.

*   *   *   *

AS DIFFICULT as it had been for Ohio State to endure the tattoo-and-memorabilia scandal that cost the Buckeyes their coach and brought stiff NCAA sanctions, it paled compared to the unprecedented situation that had unfolded in State College, Pennsylvania, over the previous year. The sexual-abuse scandal involving former defensive coordinator Jerry Sandusky was so horrific in scale that it ranks among the worst in college history. Iconic coach Joe Paterno was fired. So were the university president and athletics director. The NCAA imposed harsh sanctions that included a four-year bowl ban and allowed Penn State's players to transfer without having to sit out a year. Many players did leave, including star running back Silas Redd to Southern Cal. The most costly might have been the departure of kicker Anthony Fera to Texas because the Nittany Lions had no capable backup.

After several high-profile coaching candidates turned down Penn State—Meyer was rumored to be among them but would neither confirm nor deny it—the school hired longtime NFL assistant coach Bill O'Brien. Much like Meyer did when he took over in Columbus, O'Brien had no tolerance for excuses because of the NCAA sanctions.

The sense of doom surrounding the program seemed justified when Penn State lost its first two games. Ohio University defeated the Nittany Lions 24–14 in the opener, though that wasn't a major upset considering that the Bobcats were expected to have a strong team. But the next week's loss to Virginia, 17–16, was particularly disheartening because Fera's replacement, Sam Ficken, missed four field goals. The last one came on the game's final play from 42 yards out.

Penn State rebounded against weak competition by beating Navy, Temple, and Illinois. Its first significant win came against Northwestern. Trailing 28–17 entering the fourth quarter, Penn State scored 22 unanswered points for a 39–28 victory. A 38–14 victory at Iowa set up a showdown with the Buckeyes for first place in the Leaders Division. Though neither Ohio State nor Penn State could represent the division in the Big Ten Championship Game, the divisional winner would officially be recognized as such.

This would be Penn State's de facto bowl game. Appropriate for the circumstance, kickoff was at 5:30, more prominent than an afternoon start but not quite prime time, either. This would be the Nittany Lions' biggest home game of the season, and they treated it as such. Seemingly every Penn State fan wore white, and the pom-poms created a stunning whiteout effect.

"That was probably the best stadium I'd ever been in," Braxton Miller said.

"The atmosphere was awesome," Ohio State center Corey Linsley said. "That had been my dream forever—to play a night game at Penn State. Everybody was pumped up. We knew Penn State was probably the best team we'd play all year."

No one was more pumped up than Shazier. As he put on the No. 48 jersey instead of his customary No. 10, memories of his friend rushed back.

"I looked in the mirror and started shaking my head, like he's gone but he's with me now and I know he's going to take care of me through the game," Shazier said. "I used him and used the Lord to carry me through the game. I did everything I could for him. It was like I know I'm going to have a big game if I do it for Gary. I wanted to do it for him on that stage."

* * * *

NEITHER TEAM could muster much offense for most of the first half. Ohio State punted on its first six possessions. Miller was particularly ineffective passing. After escaping serious injury against Purdue, Miller practiced all week with only minimal limitations. But in his desire to show that he was fine, he was over-amped. He completed only three of his first 11 passes and some of them were serious misfires. Philly Brown got open deep on one play, but Miller didn't put enough air under the ball and it sailed over the receiver. Another pass should have been an interception for a touchdown. Fortunately for the Buckeyes, Penn State safety Stephen Obeng-Agyapong dropped it.

The Nittany Lions drove to the Ohio State 25, where they faced a fourth-and-12. Lacking confidence in Ficken, Penn State went for it. Zach Boren sniffed the play out and made the tackle after an eight-yard gain. The former fullback was settling in at his new position and providing needed stability for the defense overall.

"I would say the Penn State game was the first game I really understood the defense," Boren said.

Still, Ohio State was pinned deep inside its own territory, and its offense was still stuck in neutral. Then came the game's first big play, which resulted from an old bugaboo for Ohio State—a blocked punt. Two linemen blocked the same guy, allowing Mike Hull to race in untouched. Ben Buchanan appeared to take an extra little stutter-step, and Hull blocked the punt easily. Michael Yancich recovered the ball in the end zone to give Penn State a 7–0 lead, sending the Beaver Stadium crowd into a frenzy.

It would prove temporary. Just as it had against Purdue, the momentum turned on a penalty. Ohio State was forced to punt but retained possession when Penn State's Brad Bars was called for holding long-snapper Bryce Haynes. Such an infraction against a long-snapper is rare, but Haynes had hustled to make the tackle on the Buckeyes' first punt. Perhaps the Nittany Lions were determined to make sure that didn't happen again and were overzealous in hemming him in at the line of scrimmage. Given new life on the drive, the Buckeyes kicked into gear. Rod Smith ran for 12 yards. Carlos Hyde gained three on third-and-two. Miller then broke his first big run of the game, a 33-yarder to the Penn State 6. Three plays later, Hyde plowed in from the 1 to tie the score with 34 seconds left before halftime.

At a friend's house in Florida, Pat Curtis and her family were watching. Pat is from Akron. She and her relatives remained Buckeyes fans, and they cherished seeing Shazier wearing Gary's No. 48. What happened at the start of the third quarter would send them into a tizzy. Penn State got the kickoff. After a short gain on the first snap, Nittany Lions' quarterback Matt McGloin dropped back to pass on second down. As he scanned the field, Shazier blitzed up the middle. McGloin never had a chance. Shazier swallowed him up for a nine-yard loss to the Penn State 8.

"Coach had called an inside blitz," Shazier said. "The main reason it opened up was because Zach Boren had played with the blocker a little bit and then bailed out. I got skinny through the gap and shot the gap."

That was only the prelude. On third-and-13, McGloin scanned the field before throwing over the middle. Shazier was waiting.

"We were playing zone," he said. "I didn't have anybody in my area, and I read the quarterback's eyes. I looked around to see if anyone was there and checked back on the quarterback. He threw the ball and I jumped the route." Shazier caught the ball at the 17 and ran untouched into the end zone.

"We were at the friend's house, and everyone was screaming," Pat Curtis said. "I was like, 'Shut up! I can't hear!' They were so excited."

After he scored, Shazier's thoughts turned to his friend.

"I thought, *This is crazy, the way he's watching over me, carrying me through this game*," said Shazier, who would earn co–Big Ten Defensive Player of the Week honors. "Once I scored, I was, 'Gary, thank you,' and, 'Jesus, thank you.' I wouldn't have gotten any of this if it wasn't for them."

Shazier's touchdown continued a remarkable streak by the Buckeyes' defense against Penn State. His score was the ninth time since

2001 that Ohio State had returned an interception for a touchdown against the Nittany Lions.

Penn State had a chance to tie the game when McGloin threw to Brandon Moseby-Felder along the left sideline. Moseby-Felder zigged through the Ohio State secondary and appeared to have a path to the end zone. But Bradley Roby made a diving tackle at the 4 after a 42-yard reception. A holding call then pushed the Nittany Lions back, and they had to settle for a 27-yard field goal. Ohio State still led 14–10.

Penn State got back in business when Miller's deep pass on third-and-five was intercepted at the Ohio State 44. But a Nathan Williams sack forced Penn State into fourth-and-nine. The Buckeyes planned a punt-block when a player with one of the most famous surnames in Ohio State history made the biggest play of his career.

Adam Griffin, the son of two-time Heisman Trophy winner Archie Griffin, was a redshirt sophomore backup cornerback. Lightly recruited, Griffin was offered a surprise scholarship by Jim Tressel. Adam carried what could have been a tough legacy to uphold with grace. His teammates called him "Young Arch." He didn't mind. Even Urban Meyer would refer to him as "Archie" without realizing it. What did bother Griffin was his lack of playing time early in his career.

"It was extremely frustrating," he said. "I remember going home at night mad at the world almost every day after practice."

In 2012, he worked his way into being a regular on special teams. On this Penn State punt, his job was to prevent a Nittany Lions blocker from hitting Corey "Pittsburgh" Brown so that Brown could try to block the kick. But when the blocker, Derek Day, made no attempt to block Brown, Griffin's instincts took over.

"As soon as he free-released down the field, I thought, *Oh man, they're faking this*," Griffin said.

He turned and sprinted backward. Punter Alex Butterworth threw to Day—Mike Hull was more open a few yards farther downfield—and Griffin broke it up. Ohio State took over at its own 43. From that point, the Buckeyes' offense rolled. Miller had a pair of 13-yard completions to Evan Spencer. Carlos Hyde ran twice for eight yards to get the ball to the 1.

Miller then made as spectacular a one-yard touchdown run as could be imagined. He was supposed to hand the ball off to Hyde. But when defensive end Sean Stanley broke through the line and drilled Hyde in the backfield, Miller pulled the ball back from his running back. Miller was now forced to improvise. Somehow, he sensed outside linebacker Gerald Hodges coming from the opposite side, closing in for a blindside hit. But as Hodges dived at Miller, the quarterback did a most unnatural thing. He stepped *backward*. Hodges tackled air. Meanwhile, star linebacker Michael Mauti had a shot at Miller until Reid Fragel pushed him in the back and out of the play. Miller now had a path to the end zone, but it would close quickly. Safety Malcolm Willis dived at Miller, who contorted his body to miss him and hurtled into the end zone to put Ohio State ahead 21–10.

Miller is not often impressed by his own moves, but that would be one he would savor.

"That was crazy," he said. "It shocked me, just rewinding the play, like, 'That's pretty sweet.'"

The crowd fell silent, in disbelief at what it had just seen. The pom-poms could be put away for good. The Buckeyes' defense got a three-and-out, and the Buckeyes went 58 yards—28 on a Rod Smith run—to take a 28–10 lead.

Penn State scored with 10 minutes left on an 80-yard drive to make it 28–16. The Buckeyes then applied the kill shot when Miller connected with Jake Stoneburner on a perfectly thrown seam pass. Stoneburner did the rest, outrunning two Penn State pursuers for a 72-yard touchdown.

For Stoneburner, it was a just reward in a season that provided plenty of tests. He'd endured the embarrassment of the summer incident with Mewhort that temporarily cost him his scholarship. He figured to be a major factor in the revamped passing game but went three games—UAB through Nebraska—without catching a pass. Even his position was changed, technically, when he became designated a wide receiver rather than a tight end. At one point, Meyer felt compelled to have a heart-to-heart with Stoneburner to light a fire under him. Meyer liked Stoneburner and respected his intelligence, but also thought he'd underachieved.

"He's a guy that I don't know how many times he's been told the truth about football," Meyer said. "He's been one of those guys, 'Well, Braxton didn't get me the ball enough. They didn't use me enough.' Our answer was, 'No, you don't play hard enough.' We showed him video of it."

That meeting marked a turning point. After Zach Boren switched to defense, the Buckeyes needed someone to pick up some of the slack as a blocker. Though he'd always been more of a pass-catcher than a blocker, Stoneburner embraced the challenge and became effective in that role. Against Penn State, with that touchdown catch, he showed his receiving skills were still intact, as well.

Penn State would add a late touchdown to make the final score a respectable 35–23. No one was fooled. Ohio State had dominated. The Buckeyes had scored touchdowns on four of five possessions when the game was in doubt. Miller had run for 134 yards and two scores in 25 carries. Hyde had pedestrian stats—22 carries for 55 yards—but video review would reveal that 91 percent of his yards came after contact.

Penn State gained 163 of their 359 yards on their final two possessions after the outcome was secure. Ohio State did not allow a run longer than nine yards. The Buckeyes coaches' decision to employ a more aggressive approach paid off. Ohio State had four sacks, two by Shazier. Cornerback Bradley Roby had seven pass break-ups.

During the spring, Meyer explained his philosophy of the ingredients necessary for a special season. Superior talent alone could get a team seven or eight wins. To get nine required strong discipline. Extraordinary leadership was needed for 10 or more. A reporter reminded Meyer of his pronouncement the Monday after the Penn State game. With three games left, the Buckeyes already had nine wins. But Meyer didn't need to wait for any more games to declare that his Buckeyes had passed a threshold.

"This is a special team," he said. "They're fighting for each other. It's a refuse-to-lose type atmosphere. Some of us have seen teams that play really well, and they're blowing teams out all the time. We're not that type of team. I can give you 150 reasons why. However, we're a bunch of guys who work really hard, [have a] blue-collar approach, who show up every Tuesday and want to get better. You don't want anything else as a coach."

· 20 ·

ILLINOIS: MASTER PSYCHOLOGIST

URBAN MEYER never mentioned Illinois by name all week.

Unlike his refusal to utter the name of Ohio State's rival to the north, Meyer has no particular distaste for the Fighting Illini. Heck, Tim Beckman, Illinois' first-year coach, is one of Meyer's protégés. As Toledo coach in 2011, Beckman's Rockets came into Ohio Stadium and had a chance to win in the final minutes before Ohio State prevailed. His 2011 Toledo team was better than his 2012 Illinois one. The Illini entered the November 3 game with a 2–6 record. They were 0–4 in the Big Ten, and conference opponents had outscored them 142–38.

Some coaches—okay, most coaches—facing an overmatched team like Illinois would stand in front of the media and insist that such an opponent was far better than its record and that it posed a grave threat. Joe Paterno, for example, drew snickers for years when he sang the praises of Temple before the Nittany Lions' annual thrashing of the Owls, who haven't beaten Penn State since 1941. That's not Meyer's style. Yes, he said that Illinois had talented players and that he had immense respect for the Illini's program. He pointed out that Illinois had beaten Ohio State seven of the last 11 times the teams had played in Columbus. The most painful to Buckeyes fans came in 2007 when the Illini stunned top-ranked Ohio State 28–21 behind a career game by quarterback Juice Williams. That Illinois team went to the Rose Bowl, the high-water mark for coach Ron Zook before the program slid. Zook was fired after the 2011 season. He also happened to be the predecessor to Meyer at Florida. But while he left Meyer considerable talent with the Gators, that wasn't the case for Beckman in Champaign. The 2012 Illini were clearly in rebuilding mode, and Meyer did not try to prop them up as world-beaters. He understood that probably the only way Ohio State would lose to Illinois was if the Buckeyes beat themselves. So all week, his main foe was complacency.

"I know Illinois," Meyer said after the season. "I know they have good players. But they were struggling, had a losing streak. So I wanted it to be about us. I didn't care who we played."

Cornerbacks coach Kerry Coombs said that practice that week was particularly hard.

"I remember playing Illinois and the entire week being so stressed out about how we were playing and what we were doing and the conversation about our improvement and what we needed to do," he said. "It never came up that we were playing Illinois. Nobody ever mentioned Illinois. Then all of a sudden we showed up on Saturday and there was Illinois, and guess what? We were a better team than the week before. Because that's what we focused on."

Adding to Meyer's sense of urgency was that the Buckeyes had an off week after Illinois before closing with Wisconsin and Michigan. An underwhelming opponent and the prospect of a break before the two biggest games of the year made Illinois a prime candidate to be a trap game.

"Coach Meyer really did a fantastic job pumping us up for that game," center Corey Linsley said. "We always said we have one shot, and it's a one-game season. Somebody's coming down the hallway of your home, and you have to knock them out with one punch. You have to take that punch and hit him square in the jaw and leave no doubt that guy is not harming you and your family. That was sort of the motto we worked by all week and played by."

The psychological angles Meyer deploys are often overlooked compared to the attention devoted to his use of the spread offense.

But it is an essential part of his coaching. Co–defensive coordinator and safeties coach Everett Withers believes what sets Meyer apart from most coaches is the way he uses psychology—Meyer's college major—to prepare a team.

"I don't think it's the Xs and Os, and I think he'd tell you that also," Withers said. "I think it's the psyche of the team and how he works that psyche from the off-season program to spring practice to summer workouts to two-a-days to the start of the season. I think he has a great sense and pulse of which way he goes and the psyche of each team."

That's why Meyer consults every day with Mickey Marotti. It's not to get the latest results from that day's bench-press drill. "Mickey is a psychologist," Meyer said. "Mickey understands people and understands it's a people-driven sport. It's not a scheme sport. It's all about motivation and pushing the right buttons to motivate people.

"Earle [Bruce] is a psychologist. Lou Holtz was a psychologist. Sonny Lubick is one of the greatest psychologists. I've worked for psychologists. I didn't work for scheme doctors."

If you want to see Meyer's eyes roll, mention the concept of a coaching "guru."

"There are no gurus," he said. "I love coaching against 'gurus.'"

But pit Meyer against a coach who understands motivation, and he knows he'll be in for a tough day. "I don't like coaching against the guys who 'get it,' because you know you're in for a tough day."

Those who believe Meyer's success is based on the spread offense are mistaken, he believes. "Of course, they are," he said. "It's [showing that you] care. It's truth. Absolutely. It has nothing to do with the spread offense. It has to do with how you treat people and motivate people and push the right buttons. [Yes], toughness, but also let them know that you genuinely care about them."

He'd always believed that, but his experience visiting different successful coaches while working for ESPN early in 2011 reinforced it. He'd seen those colleagues at conventions, but never in their own element. He appreciated the uniqueness of each school, but also came to believe that the one common denominator all successful programs have is that their staffs are all in "alignment." That means that the head coach is the CEO, and everyone is rooted to his philosophy. Not that every school has—or should have—the same philosophy. But whatever it is, the system for accountability and responsibility must be understood and followed by everyone on the staff. So when he took over at Ohio State, he made sure that all the coaches, most of whom hadn't worked together, were in sync.

"That was probably the biggest thing I learned from my year off," Meyer said. "I wasn't going to let that happen here. From A to Z, we crossed every *t*, dotted every *i*. We had six- to seven-hour staff meetings, which I never used to do, and covered everything in detail not once or twice but three times until they could almost regurgitate it back to me."

Meyer inculcated his philosophical approach into all his coaches. He reviewed expectations for everything from recruiting and discipline to the players' academic management, weight-lifting, and off-season workouts. Position coaches would do much more than teach players proper blocking or tackling techniques. They would essentially become their life coaches. Coaches would be expected to know whom their players dated, know their families, know when they went to church, know about their academics to the point of knowing when the next major test was. Meyer knew these were major demands. He made no apologies.

"That's fine if they don't believe in that," Meyer said. "Just don't coach here. I remind them all the time [that] their greatest gift is free will. If they don't like the way we do things, don't complain, move on. Because we do it different, and you're going to be held accountable for everything your players do."

The level of monitoring depended on the player. Players were classified into three categories—blue, red, and gold. Players in the gold category—John Simon, Etienne Sabino, and C.J. Barnett were among the first—had earned enough trust that they did not require much hovering. Those in the blue category were constantly overseen.

"We know if he's two minutes late for class," Meyer said. "We know if he's sitting in the back of the room or the front of the room. We know if he's wearing a hat. We know if he's got his iPod. And the coach better know that."

Soon after assembling the coaching staff, Meyer took them to Longaberger's Golf Club east of Columbus for an intense two-day retreat. Each coach had to stand up and detail his coaching philosophy. What were the core values of his position? What would be the standard that his players, and by extension their coach, must uphold? How would he teach fundamentals and technique? Meyer wrote down their answers so that he'd always be able to hold coaches accountable.

Stan Drayton's core values as a running backs coach, for example, consist of three components: 100 percent protection of the football, 100 percent protection of the quarterback, and the demand that his players "perform at a competitive excellence."

So that would be the standard to which Meyer would hold Drayton's players. Meyer doesn't shy away from putting his coaches in uncomfortable situations. In fact, it's part of the plan.

"I call it direct teaching," Meyer said. "It's not one way. We're going to have dialogue. I don't want yes-men. I want creative thinking. I want a creative environment where everybody sits on the edge of their seat. That's in our staff room, and that's also in our position meeting rooms."

If things get pointed, well, that's just the way it is.

"He knows how to push your buttons," Fickell said. "I think that's what great leaders do. They're not degrading you as a person. They're just evaluating what they see."

Wide receivers coach Zach Smith, who, as Earle Bruce's grandson, has known Meyer since birth, said Meyer believes that reaching immediate consensus can be a problem.

"He knows that there's more accomplished through controversy and hard conversation than there is through agreement," Smith said. "If you feel a certain way about something, whether it's a recruit, a play, a player, a philosophy—whatever it is—if he challenges that and you fight back and stand up for it and have fire and conviction, he knows that deep down you really believe that. But if he challenges you and you back down, you don't feel that strong about it. So...if you stand up to it and stand up to him and show how you feel, there's deep conviction in that, and it's something he should consider."

Drayton said that when he's on the road, he'll often hear murmurings from coaches from other schools about Meyer's reputation for grinding his assistants.

"If I'm working for a guy whose sole purpose for me is to be the best at what I can do, then what's wrong with that?" Drayton said. "I think that's awesome. I think there's times when grown men need to be shaken up in their craft a little bit and challenged a little bit. If it's going to bring the best out of us, why not? He keeps us on edge. It's uncomfortable at times. But at the same time, how can you argue against it with the legacy of head coaches he's created in his years as head coach? It's all good, the way I look at it."

The expectation is that coaches know their position and know their players so well that they anticipate what Meyer needs before he requests it. Smith recalled his early days as an unpaid intern at Florida. He'd been doing such menial tasks as washing dishes and helping set up tents when Meyer brought him into his office. Smith was eager to start his coaching career, and Meyer offered him a graduate assistant job helping out with special teams, and along with it, some words of wisdom.

"He said, 'Here's the only advice I'll give you: if I ask you to do something, you should be offended that I had to ask. And you should do it and lay it on my desk as if you're saying, 'Here's your freaking report. It's better than you ever thought I could do, it's better than you wanted, and you'll never have to ask me for anything ever again because I'll have it done before you ask and I'll be offended if you have to ask, because that's my job.' That's when I was 22 years old. To this day, it's best advice that I've ever been given."

With expectations like that, no one should have been surprised that Ohio State was more than ready for Illinois. After a typically slow start—Illinois took a 3–0 lead midway through the first quarter—the Buckeyes finally did what they should do to an inferior team. They mauled the Illini.

After a three-and-out on its first possession, the Buckeyes rolled. The Buckeyes took a 7–3 lead on a 79-yard drive. Carlos Hyde and Rod Smith, running behind that potent offensive line, did most of the damage. Braxton Miller had a 24-yard completion to Jake Stoneburner just to add a dash of variety before Hyde bulled in from the 3. Whatever hope the Illini had of keeping Ohio State in check probably died when their star linebacker Jonathan Brown suffered a shoulder injury that knocked him out of the game.

The teams traded field goals on their next possessions before Ohio State left the Illini in the dust by scoring three touchdowns in seven minutes as the Buckeyes' offensive line dominated. The first came after Miller completed a 32-yard pass to Philly Brown. Hyde scored his second touchdown from five yards out as the right side of the offensive line pushed the Illini practically into the end zone before Hyde was touched.

On their next possession, the Buckeyes scored on a 51-yard wheel route from Miller to Smith out of the backfield, a play almost identical to the one Purdue used for its opening touchdown against Ohio State.

The Buckeyes made it 31–6 with 1:56 left in the half after taking over at midfield after Illinois shanked an 18-yard punt. Not that field position mattered a whole lot at that point. Ohio State's offense was humming. The Buckeyes gained 11 (Miller run), 11 (Hyde run), 14 (pass to increasingly productive tight end Nick Vannett), and 10 (Miller run) on their first four plays before Hyde scored again, this time from the 3.

Hyde would finish with 137 yards on 18 carries, running behind a line that hummed again. The game had particular significance to left guard Andrew Norwell. He had attended the 2007 Illinois game decked out in orange and blue because his brother Chris played defensive line for the Illini. He was one of the few in Ohio Stadium delighted by the Illinois upset.

"I was pretty fired up," he said. "I was sitting in the Illinois section with my parents."

Now he was one of the players on a line that was dismantling the Illini. Norwell was the only lineman playing the same position he played in 2011, and he did so at a high level. He would be a first-team All–Big Ten selection by the media. Even on Ohio State's line, Norwell stood out. He cultivated a warrior look by letting his long, curly hair flow out from his helmet. His somewhat offbeat personality also set him apart.

"He's a crazy dude," center Corey Linsley said. "He plays with the utmost intensity. You don't want to get in his way on game day."

Left tackle Jack Mewhort said, affectionately, that Norwell has "just a touch of insanity to him. He's just a different kind of guy. He always keeps mood light in the room."

Norwell invented an alter ego for himself—the Great White Buffalo.

"He'll make this buffalo call that's just out there," Mewhort said. "We'll be running, and he'll say stuff like, 'Oh, the Buffalo is thirsty. The Buffalo has to go to the watering hole.' Little quirky stuff like that."

Norwell got off on the wrong foot with the new regime when he was among the tardy ones at Meyer's first team meeting after the Gator Bowl, but that was uncharacteristic for him.

"He's really loyal," Mewhort said. "He loves football, and he really tries to get better every day. You may not know from the long hair and big beard, but he's a sophisticated dude when it comes to techniques and really studying the game and getting better. He's my favorite guy. I love playing next to him."

Norwell and company kept rolling in the third quarter to end any suspense. Miller's day ended early in the fourth quarter with a 37-yard touchdown pass to Philly Brown, who eluded several Illini tacklers with some nifty moves to push Ohio State's margin to 45–14. It was the kind of play Meyer had expected Brown to make all year. So, after the receiver came to the sideline, Meyer made a point to be matter-of-fact with him.

"Well, that's his job," Meyer explained. "I'm trying to develop that with everybody. I think it's a mindset we're trying to develop here, that it's not, 'Great!' [It's] nice job, Philly, move on to the next play, as opposed to 'Oh, my gosh, what a play!' It wasn't that good. It's just you're supposed to do it."

While the offense rolled, the defense stuffed the Illini. Illinois had only three plays all game that went for double-digit yards. The longest was a 12-yard pass from Nathan Scheelhaase to Dami Ayoola on the Illini's final drive. For the second straight week, the Buckeyes didn't allow a run of 10 yards.

"We felt the quarterback was a good threat as a runner, even though he hadn't run as much in the last couple weeks because of his ankle," co–defensive coordinator Everett Withers said. "We felt they had a good zone-read offense like ours. We wanted to make sure we stopped that, and then stop the play-action pass game, and we were able to do that."

Early in the fourth quarter, Kenny Guiton took over at quarterback for the rest of the game. He led the Buckeyes to the Illini

16 on his first drive before he botched an option pitch that was picked up by Illinois' Ashante Williams, who ran it all the way for a touchdown.

The Buckeyes added their final score when they handed to freshman Bri'onte Dunn for all seven plays of a 56-yard touchdown drive to make it 52–22. Dunn had 13 carries for 73 in his two possessions, which was good enough to earn him Big Ten Freshman of the Week honors.

He wasn't the only one to win conference honors. With Zach Boren comfortable at middle linebacker and stabilizing the defense, Ryan Shazier blossomed. Against Illinois, Shazier had 14 tackles, including 11 solo, to repeat as a Big Ten Defensive Player of the Week honoree.

A defense that in September caused cringes had become sound. That raw potential had finally been harnessed.

"Shazier was the poster child," Meyer said. "He went from a bad player to All–Big Ten."

The next week, the return of another linebacker would make the defense completely whole—and just in time.

· 21 ·

WISCONSIN: NARROW ESCAPE

THE FIRST 10 GAMES were really the prelims. Nobody on the team would say that, of course. But anyone looking at the 2012 Ohio State schedule would come to that conclusion. Sure, Michigan State figured to be tough, and was. Nebraska would be a challenge. Going on the road to Penn State is never easy. But the circle-the-calendar games were the last two—Wisconsin and Michigan. Ohio State's rivalry with the Badgers doesn't have the same passion as the Buckeyes' feud with the Wolverines—what could?—but it is quite intense. An Ohio State victory over Wisconsin would clinch the Leaders title for the Buckeyes.

"I hate Wisconsin just as much as Michigan," Philly Brown said before the game. "Ever since I've been here, they've been a nightmare. They've ruined our perfect season. [We had] a heckuva game last year. We're going to Wisconsin, and we don't want a repeat of what happened freshman year."

In 2010 Ohio State was the newly minted No. 1 team in the country entering its game in Madison. Wisconsin returned the opening kickoff for a touchdown, manhandled the Buckeyes at the line of scrimmage, withstood a Buckeyes rally, and pulled away for a 31–18 victory.

"It was just silence in the locker room," recalled safety Christian Bryant, a freshman on that team. "Everyone was so disappointed in their performance. I didn't want to feel that again."

In 2011 Wisconsin was considered the superior team. The Badgers had suffered a heartbreaking loss the week before on a Hail Mary at Michigan State. After stunning Ohio State with two quick touchdown drives late in the fourth quarter to take a 29–26 lead, Braxton Miller heaved a 40-yard touchdown pass to Devin Smith for the game-winning touchdown.

Wisconsin had been viewed as a darkhorse national championship contender in 2012, but the Badgers had a rocky start to the season. Heisman Trophy candidate Montee Ball was the victim of an assault on campus during the summer, and it took the running back time to get back into a groove. In 2011 the Badgers rode the play of Russell Wilson, who was able to transfer from North Carolina State and play right away because he had graduated. They hoped to have similar success with another rent-a-QB, Maryland's Danny O'Brien. But he proved to be a disappointment. Wisconsin barely beat Northern Iowa in its opener and lost to Oregon State 10–7. That prompted Bret Bielema to fire first-year offensive-line coach Mike Markuson, a move akin to Penn State firing its linebackers coach. Wisconsin steadfastly and successfully clings to the kind of old-style power football that Woody Hayes espoused. Its offensive line has been the foundation for the Badgers' success since Barry Alvarez revived Wisconsin's program in his 16-year tenure starting in 1990. To jettison Markuson and replace him with a quality-control assistant, Bart Miller, who'd never been a position coach, was stunning. The Badgers bumbled for a few more weeks. They blew a big lead in a loss to Nebraska and fell to Michigan State in overtime. Bielema benched O'Brien. Joel Stave failed at his chance to earn the job. So Bielema turned to Curt Phillips, a career backup who'd endured three torn ACLs in a little more than a year.

When the Badgers crushed Indiana 62–14 on November 10, they looked to be rejuvenated. Because of Ohio State's and Penn State's ineligibility for the Big Ten championship, Wisconsin was already assured being the Leaders Division representative in the title game. But the Badgers wanted legitimacy. They also wanted Ball to break the all-time NCAA career touchdown record for Football Bowl Subdivision teams. Ball had 77 touchdowns, one shy of the record set in 1999 by Miami University's Travis Prentice.

Adding to the storyline was the supposed dustup between Bielema and Meyer during recruiting. Offensive lineman Kyle Dodson of Cleveland originally committed to Wisconsin. Ohio State pursued him, and on signing day, Dodson became a Buckeye. Bielema was never specific about any transgressions he believed Ohio State had committed, and both he and Meyer downplayed any lingering issues in the week before the game. Ohio State fans would find it curious when Bielema suddenly bolted Wisconsin right after his team defeated Nebraska in the Big Ten Championship Game to take the job at Arkansas in the SEC, where recruiting is so gentlemanly.

Meyer did not feel compelled to deliver a "Rip Your Chest Open" speech for the Wisconsin game. Motivation was not going to be an issue. If Ohio State's players had any doubt how the Badgers fans felt about them, their arrival at Camp Randall Stadium answered it.

"I just remember pulling up and walking out of the tunnel and people were screaming at us and cursing us out," linebacker Etienne Sabino said.

Sabino had been in Madison in 2010 when Ohio State lost its top ranking there, but only as a spectator. He didn't play a snap that whole season. Sabino was a five-star linebacker coming out of Miami's Dr. Krop High School, where he was a teammate of Travis Howard. An assistant coach at Dr. Krop was Sonny Spielman, father of legendary Buckeyes linebacker Chris Spielman. Sabino's blue-chip status did not result in instant success. Intelligent and mature, Sabino nonetheless had a hard time translating his talent into production. In camp before his junior season, it became apparent he was going to lose a position battle with Andrew Sweat. So Sabino decided to redshirt to save a year of eligibility. Redshirting as a freshman is common. Volunteering to take a year off in the middle of a career is not. As much as he believed it was the right decision logically, going through a season knowing he wouldn't play gnawed at him. He likened it to "starving."

Being confined to the sideline at Camp Randall Stadium was particularly excruciating.

"Probably one of the hardest things I've had to do thus far in my career," he said. "Standing there and not being able to help out was tough."

Sabino became a starter in 2011, but it was a difficult season and not just because of the Buckeyes' struggles. Sabino broke his hand in the preseason scrimmage. He played through it, though it affected his play, which he described as mediocre. He had a strong Gator Bowl performance, though, and was off to a strong start in 2012. Against Michigan State, he was the Buckeyes' defensive player of the week, and Meyer had come to depend on him as a leader.

"He played very well, but as well as he played, his intangible value in practice and the locker room was awesome," he said. "He was not very 'evaluative' at the start. I didn't feel a pushback from him, and the players respected him because he worked so damn hard. He was not a great player. His career was very average. But he became a very good player."

Then came the fractured fibula against Nebraska.

"I felt my season was over, to be honest," Sabino said. "But doctors explained to me that it was a fairly common injury that people come back from in six to eight weeks," he said. "But if I had surgery, I could come back a little sooner, and that's what I did."

Sabino hoped he might be ready for the Illinois game, but that didn't happen. He finally got the green light for Wisconsin. "I can't even put that into words," he said of his excitement level.

The "warm" reception the Buckeyes received upon their arrival only added to it. "I remember having goosebumps from being so amped up for that game," Sabino said.

He estimated he was only 75–80 percent for the game. Sabino knew he didn't have that extra gear. But his presence gave a psychological boost to his teammates.

"That was a big deal," Christian Bryant said of Sabino's return. "We knew it was 'Bino's last season. Just having him back as a spiritual leader—he and Orhian always hold Bible study in their room—and him being a leader and a senior, it was big for us. We needed him. We needed that energy from him."

While Ohio State was getting Sabino back, the Badgers were hit by the news that their star linebacker, Chris Borland, would be unable to play because of a hamstring injury. Still, Wisconsin figured to be a formidable challenge, and the first play brought back painful memories. Kenzel Doe fielded Drew Basil's kickoff, broke through the first wave of tacklers on a 36-yard return to the Wisconsin 43. Then came a series of blown opportunities for both offenses. The Badgers went right at Howard on the first possession, and the Buckeyes barely dodged disaster on both. Howard fell while covering Chase Hammond on a deep route. Hammond caught the ball momentarily, but it came loose when he hit the ground as he got tangled up with the Buckeyes cornerback. Two plays later, Howard was beaten on a hitch route by Jared Abbrederis, but Phillips' pass was too long. On Ohio State's first possession, Braxton Miller threw to a wide-open Jake Stoneburner deep near the sideline, but the ball went through his hands, as Stoneburner evidently lost the ball in the brightness as it appeared from out of the stadium shadows.

Given the flow of the game, it wasn't surprising that the game's first score didn't come from either team's offense. Late in the first quarter, Ohio State forced Wisconsin to punt. Philly Brown fielded Drew Meyer's 43-yard punt, surveyed the field for an alley, and found one right up the middle. Blocks by Taylor Rice and Evan Spencer opened a wide gap up the middle, and Brown darted through it. He was never threatened as he went 68 yards for the score.

Early in the second quarter, the Buckeyes' offense finally got on track. Miller threw consecutive completions to Philly Brown for eight and 14 yards. Miller converted a third-and-two with a 10-yard pass to Devin Smith. A face-mask penalty by Wisconsin on Miller gave Ohio State the ball at the 15. The next play was an example of textbook blocking. Carlos Hyde took the handoff and ran through a gaping hole created by the line for an easy touchdown. It was 14–0, and the Buckeyes looked in control.

Typical for this Buckeyes team, however, looks were deceiving. Ball got in the groove on Wisconsin's ensuing possession. He gained 38 yards in the first four plays of the drive. After Phillips threw to tight end Jacob Pedersen for a 29-yard gain, Ball ran in from seven yards out for the touchdown, tying the NCAA record.

The game then settled into a defensive struggle. Wisconsin did a superb job containing Miller's runs. They brought safeties near the line of scrimmage and bracketed the quarterback. Ohio State could have tried to make the Badgers pay by taking shots down the field, but the Buckeyes' field position made that risky. On Ohio State's final 10 possessions of regulation, its average starting field position was its 19-yard line. The Buckeyes did little to improve it.

"No excuses whatsoever," center Corey Linsley said, "but they were running and executing an excellent defensive scheme to combat all of our biggest offensive attacks. They were playing some great defense. I wouldn't say they were taking it to us physically. But they were taking it to us fundamentally, and outexecuting us and outscheming us."

In hindsight, Meyer faulted himself for becoming too conservative. "I was really disappointed with [the strategy against] Wisconsin," he said. "I was so upset with the way I called it. The safeties were down, but we had such negative field position that I didn't want to lose the game."

That was an understandable strategy given the way Ohio State's defense responded after the Ball touchdown. John Simon played like a man possessed. He tied a Buckeyes record with four sacks, despite a knee that was becoming increasingly painful because of a swollen bursa sac.

"All the swelling hadn't coagulated yet," Simon said. "It was still fresh. I had full movement. It was just a pain issue, which usually isn't that big an issue for a football player."

Or at least a football player like him.

Ryan Shazier and Zach Boren each had 12 tackles. Safety C.J. Barnett had 11 tackles in what coaches said was his best game. With six minutes left, Bradley Roby broke up a touchdown pass when he alertly left his assigned man to break up a pass intended for Derek Watt in the end zone. It was one of 17 passes Roby broke up in 2012. According to the website cfbstats.com, Roby had more passes defended per game than any player in the country.

But the game's signature play would come later in the drive. Wisconsin drove to the Ohio State 2 with just under three minutes left and faced a fourth-and-one. It was no secret to whom Wisconsin was going to give the ball. Everyone knew Ball would get it. But Shazier did that one better. From film study, he had a sense of exactly what Ball would do. He figured Ball would try to dive into the end zone. Sure enough, that's what happened. The Buckeyes were ready. The defensive line got good penetration. As Ball leaped, so did Shazier to his left and Sabino to his right. The three collided and the ball popped free into the waiting hands of safety Christian Bryant coming on a blitz.

"From what we saw on film, it looked like it was my helmet," Sabino said. "Ryan hit him probably about a split second before I did, because I jumped over the top of him. It looks like it was my helmet, but it's hard to tell. It was one of those plays you think belong in a movie. It was a great feeling."

Alas, it would prove temporary. Ohio State couldn't muster the first down needed to run out the clock, and Wisconsin took over at the Ohio State 41 with 1:33 left and no timeouts. The Badgers faced only a slightly less dire situation than Ohio State had against Purdue. Like the Buckeyes against Purdue, they would come through. Wisconsin overcame a first-down sack by Simon to convert a fourth-and-three pass to Abbrederis in front of Roby for 14 yards. Another Abbrederis reception, this time for 11 yards, moved the ball to the 5. After an incompletion, Phillips threw a pass to Pedersen, who, despite being blanketed by Boren, sprawled out to make the catch in the end zone with eight seconds left.

The Buckeyes had to go to overtime if they were to keep their perfect season alive. Given the way Wisconsin moved the ball on its final two possessions and Ohio State's offensive problems—the Buckeyes didn't have a first down in the last 14 minutes of the fourth quarter—the momentum was clearly with the Badgers. But Ohio State's resolve was unshaken.

"I can't say I know [for sure], but in overtime everybody wearing scarlet and gray thought we would win the game," Meyer said. "That doesn't just happen. That's leadership of players. Behind me, I could hear them. They knew we were going to score and that we were going to stop them. That's the psychological warfare that goes on inside a team. That's Zach Boren, Sabino, John Simon, Goebel. That group of leaders had that team believing. There was no doubt who was going to win the game."

The "Jump Around" between the third and fourth quarters has become a venerable tradition at Camp Randall in the last two decades. The stadium does actually shake as fans do what the song says. In overtime, the Buckeyes did their own version of it.

"There are pictures of them on our sideline jumping around," Meyer said.

Then the Buckeyes did what they believed they would do. They needed only four plays to score. Hyde started with an 11-yard run on a sweep to the right. Miller ran for four yards and then scrambled for eight to the Wisconsin 2. Hyde then ran in easily for the touchdown to make it 21–14.

"It was crunch time," Miller said. "That's the kind of game I love."

Now it was the defense's turn to respond, and it did. On third-and-four, Sabino tackled Ball for a two-yard loss. Now the Badgers would probably have to pass. Bryant was ready, anticipating a pass to Pedersen.

"I knew their primary go-to receiver was the tight end, No. 48," he said. "They'd been trying to run the hitch to get the first down the entire game. They'd probably tried to run it four or five times. I just knew that was their go-to play at crunch time."

Sure enough, Phillips threw toward Pedersen. Bryant, who'd been guilty of going for the knockout blow at times instead of the fundamentally sound play, played it perfectly. He timed the throw perfectly and batted it down, making sure he didn't interfere with Pedersen.

"It felt like the ball was in the air forever," Sabino said. "I saw Christian's eyes, and when I saw him knock the ball out, it was just a great feeling. It was kind of a sigh of relief. "

The Buckeyes had survived—again. But there would be a cost. Sabino had played in serious pain, and he had company.

"Oh man," he said. "I remember waking up Sunday, and it felt like I had a peg leg. I remember talking to Johnny [Simon]. We were both like, 'Man, I'm sore.' But it would've felt a lot worse if we'd lost."

Only one of them would be able to play the next week for the biggest game of all. As big as Wisconsin was, as satisfying as it was, their thoughts—and those of their fans, had already turned to the season finale. After the Wisconsin game ended and reporters made their way through dejected Wisconsin fans, a throng of Buckeyes fans could be heard singing. They weren't basking in the glow of a hard-fought victory. They were already looking ahead.

"We don't give a damn for the whole state of Michigan," they sang, "the whole state of Michigan, the whole state of Michigan…"

As soon as the Wisconsin game was over, despite how dramatic it had been, Meyer's thoughts turned immediately to the same opponent as those Ohio State fans.

"Right to the rival," he said. "Absolutely."

· 22 ·

MICHIGAN: THE GOLDEN DOOR

"CLOSE YOUR EYES."

That's how Urban Meyer began the pregame speech he had begun preparing in earnest two days earlier. In truth, the idea for it began forming in his head as a boy in Ashtabula with Archie Griffin posters on his bedroom wall.

Bud Meyer loved Woody Hayes and raised his son in the way Hayes coached his players, with love encased in toughness. As a graduate assistant, Urban Meyer got a chance to meet Hayes before the coach's death in 1987.

"He was in failing health a little bit, but his mind was sharp," Meyer said. "He would speak at recruiting dinners. I would always walk up to him and say hello. He knew who I was. To me, it was reverence. It wasn't just a coach. I grew up in an era when that was an untouchable. I treated it as such. It took me a while to get over the untouchable. 'I'm actually shaking hands with Woody Hayes.' I was very childlike. It was the way I was raised and the respect I had for him."

When he became coach at Bowling Green, Meyer got a portrait of Hayes that still hangs in his office at home.

Meyer also had a deep admiration for Michigan coach Bo Schembechler, Hayes' protégé who revitalized Michigan's program and coached against Hayes in the Ten Year War from 1969 to 1978 during Meyer's formative years. Now Meyer would get to coach in his first Michigan game against Brady Hoke. Many were predicting that the 2012 Ohio State–Michigan game would be the start of another peak for the rivalry.

Like Schembechler, Hoke was a native Ohioan. He grew up in Kettering, a Dayton suburb. Unlike Schembechler, Hoke's allegiance has always been with the Wolverines.

"I don't understand being from Ohio and not following Ohio State [but] the rivals to the north of us," Meyer said. "I just don't understand that. It was so strong. Woody Hayes. Archie Griffin. The Ohio State Buckeyes. That's our home school. That's our home state. Let's cheer for the home team. That's all I knew growing up."

Not only did Hoke not like Ohio State, he wouldn't even refer to the school by its name, calling it "Ohio" instead. Well, Meyer wouldn't refer to Ohio State's archrival by name, either. Just as Hayes had done, Meyer would only call the Wolverines "That Team Up North." Players occasionally slipped and referred to Michigan by name, chastising themselves when they realized their sin and doing the 10 pushups required as penance.

While Meyer was getting plaudits for his turnaround of the Buckeyes from a 6–7 season, Hoke had received the same for resurrecting the Wolverines from the depths of the Rich Rodriguez disaster. Michigan had gone a surprising 11–2 in 2011. The Wolverines started 2012 ranked eighth in the Associated Press media poll, even getting one first-place vote by a Champaign, Illinois, writer. Any hope for a national title evaporated when Alabama routed Michigan 41–14 in the season opener. (That score had some resonance to OSU fans. It was the same score by which Meyer's Florida team beat Ohio State in the national title game in January 2007.)

Michigan later lost to Notre Dame and Nebraska. The Wolverines were eliminated from Big Ten championship contention when Nebraska beat Iowa the day before the Ohio State game. But league title hopes are always secondary for the Ohio State–Michigan game. The Game, as it's known, is all the motivation either team needs.

*   *   *   *

THE FINAL full-scale practice on Thursday, known as Senior Tackle, is one of Ohio State's cherished traditions. It's a time when seniors traditionally speak about what their years as a Buckeye have meant to them. Former coaches show up, as do parents. Meyer tweaked the traditional format. This year, he had each senior's position coach speak about the player, followed by an underclassman, and then the player himself.

Given the roller coaster these seniors had ridden during their careers, the stories were impassioned. Meyer said that safety Orhian Johnson's speech was among the high points.

"Orhian was real emotional," he said. "He kind of lost it a little bit. He came a long way. He talked about how appreciative he was. He said we saved his life because he was maybe headed in the wrong direction."

Mickey Marotti stood in the back amazed at the eloquence he was hearing from his seniors.

"Coaches were crying," he said. "Urban kept looking at me. I'm looking at him. He was maybe 20 yards away and he kept looking at me going, 'Wow!' meaning that these kids are great kids, man. They're talking about their experiences and what the young kids have to look forward to and how this was such a special year and talking about blind faith.

"It's not like we took over a program that was dogshit. There are a lot of banners hanging in this weight room. There are a lot of Big Ten championships and great success. For those older kids to have come back for their senior year—they could have left—to have blind faith in the new staff, in Coach Meyer, in all of us, it's pretty special. That's why he got choked up."

John Simon's father, John Jr., said Senior Tackle was the most touching thing he experienced all year as a parent. "That's when it really sunk in," he said. "You had something special here besides winning football games. I could really feel how close the coaches and boys were. It's corny to say this, but they all do love each other."

Which made Senior Tackle for his son all the more poignant. The bursa sac injury that flared up during his four-sack game against Wisconsin had gotten worse. Simon had played through injuries all year, but it was becoming increasingly obvious that this would be one that the team's heart and soul couldn't overcome.

Meyer had seen Simon on Sunday. The bursa sac had inflamed so much that it was larger than a grapefruit. Simon's skin was black and blue.

"It was as bad as I've ever seen," Meyer said.

Medical tests had shown the damage wasn't structural, and doctors were optimistic he'd be able to play. Meyer sensed otherwise, and his pessimism grew throughout the week despite almost round-the-clock rehab. Friday morning, he visited Simon.

"The kid's got tears in his eyes, and I know he's not going to play," Meyer said. "Tears are coming out of my eyes, too."

During his visit, Meyer had forgotten about an obligation to speak at Earle Bruce's Beat Michigan Tailgate luncheon. He was driven there with his mind in a fog.

"I'm just thinking about John Simon and those seniors," he said.

For seven minutes, he gave an emotional speech praising those seniors. He finished by saying, "Let's beat the shit out of Michigan." As soon as he said it, he thought, *Oh no.* He knew that social media would pounce, as it did. It wasn't clear whether he was more worried about the profanity or that he actually said the word "Michigan."

On game day, Simon went to the stadium early, hoping for a miracle.

"We tried everything," he said. "Saturday morning we did some drastic stuff, and nothing was working. Everything in the book, we tried."

The knee was so filled with fluid that Simon could barely move it. Remember the scene in *Rocky* when Rocky Balboa (Sylvester Stallone) begs his cornerman to cut his eye so that he can continue his fight with Apollo Creed? Meyer invoked another Stallone character for what happened next.

"It got so big that they couldn't drain it anymore," said Meyer, who was still at the team hotel at the time. "It was actually a mass in there, like putty. They performed a little surgery in the stadium. Unbelievable. Even he said it was like a Rambo thing."

It was two hours before kickoff, too late to get Simon to the hospital, so doctors applied a local anesthetic and went to work.

"They pulled this stuff out of his knee and sewed him up," Meyer said. "Here's the toughest guy I've ever met, and *he* said it was crazy. He said it was the most painful thing he's ever gone through in his life. But he asked for it. He said, 'Do it.'"

The procedure didn't provide a miracle. Fifteen minutes before kickoff, Simon finally accepted that he'd be on the sideline for the final, most important game of his career.

"I could barely walk, let alone get in a stance," he said.

In his heart, it was beyond painful. It took a brief talk with former Buckeyes linebacker Bobby Carpenter to convince Simon to accept being sidelined in the biggest game of his life. Carpenter could identify with Simon's emotions. Carpenter broke his leg early in the 2005 Michigan game, an injury that thrust then-unknown freshman James Laurinaitis into significant action for the first time.

Now Carpenter was telling Simon to let go.

"You could tell he was torn up and felt like he was letting his teammates down," Carpenter said. "I told him that you've got to put it behind you. You can't be out there today. Your teammates know you want to be out there and would try anything to get out there. All you can do at this point is to be their cheerleader."

Carpenter said Simon looked at him and nodded.

"John is a very emotional guy, but he keeps it inside," Carpenter said. "I could tell it was killing him. It was definitely tough and an emotional experience for me to see that. You never want to see a guy end his career that way."

Simon said that not attempting to play—no matter how futile—was one of the toughest decisions he's ever had to make. But the last thing he wanted to do was hurt his team's chance to win. So he accepted his fate.

"As soon as I made that decision," he said, "I dealt with some demons there pretty quick."

Meyer was emotional enough about coaching his first Michigan game. Knowing that the team's leader, the guy he likened to Tim Tebow, could not play added an emotional underpinning to his pregame speech.

Meyer began by asking his players to close their eyes. He told the story of a Green Beret, Colonel Wolf, whom he'd befriended in Florida. Colonel Wolf's actual beret has a prominent place in Meyer's office. Meyer described how Wolf explained the necessity of precise teamwork in special-forces operations, using the Seal Team Six killing of Osama bin Laden as an example. Meyer was careful not to trivialize the bin Laden raid to his players by comparing it to a football game. But he did cite it as a model of teamwork.

The Seals methodically went door to door in bin Laden's compound before killing him. Meyer said the Buckeyes had gone game by game to reach this point in their season. Now Ohio State's final "door" awaited them. The grand prize was behind it, and it had to be seized.

"He said, 'This is the one behind the big golden heavy door. Behind it is rare air,'" right tackle Reid Fragel said. "Obviously, he was referring to 12–0 being rare air that very few teams get to breathe."

Again, Meyer invoked Colonel Wolf.

"If your job is to protect your left flank and you feel a red dot on you from someone's gun, you can't turn, because you'd rather take it yourself and die as opposed to everyone going," Meyer told his team.

OSU strength coach Mickey Marotti has known Meyer for 25 years. He's heard most of his pregame speeches. This was, Marotti said, "the best I've ever heard in all our years together. You could hear a pin drop. No movement whatsoever. He was so animated and graphic. His arms [moving].... His voice.... It was awesome. The kids are still talking about it."

Meyer knew his speech was a bull's-eye.

"You don't know it's good until it starts flowing," he said. "And you watch your players. If they're into it, I'm into it."

In truth, Meyer probably didn't need to deliver a captivating speech. His players were plenty motivated anyway. The Buckeyes' domination under Jim Tressel over Michigan had ended in 2011 with a 40–34 loss in Ann Arbor. It was the Wolverines' first victory over Ohio State in eight years.

Seven victories out of eight against Michigan aren't sufficient in the Buckeyes' eyes. A losing streak to the Wolverines—even a two-game one—would be intolerable.

"I think everybody was pretty focused," linebacker Etienne Sabino said. "Everybody could visualize it. Everyone could see in their mind the golden door and what we had to do to knock it down, to be what we wanted to be."

They were also resolved to do it for Simon, to whom Meyer had promised the game ball.

"When the team came back after warmups, they picked me up fast," Simon said. "I appreciated that. They made sure they had my back. By the time I hit the field for the Senior Walk, I was pretty much over it and ready to do whatever I could to help."

Meanwhile, his parents stood with the other parents waiting for the seniors to be introduced, greeted by Meyer, and join them.

One by one, the 21 seniors, from walk-ons Kharim Stephens and Dalton Britt to starters, were announced and given hearty ovations. Meyer met all of them with handshakes and hugs. Simon, of course, was the last introduced. Wearing black sweatpants instead of his full uniform, Simon limped toward his coach. Meyer walked from midfield past the 20-yard line to embrace him as the crowd chanted Simon's name.

"We were on the field with the other parents and still didn't know whether John was going to be running out of the tunnel or not playing," his father said.

When Renee Simon saw that her son wasn't in uniform, she teared up.

"She would have been in tears, anyway, no matter what was going on," the younger John Simon said.

Senior days are tricky things. The culmination of a four-year career (or five-year, for redshirts) has arrived. After greeting Meyer, they exchange hugs and kisses with their parents, who've accompanied them throughout their football journeys. Emotions can get heavy. Then, in an instant, all that must be put aside for the game that will define their careers. The Buckeyes seemed to draw inspiration from the pregame festivities, not jitters.

Meyer wanted to strike immediately. Determined not to become conservative as he'd been against Wisconsin, he intended to put the Wolverines on their heels with a deep pass on the first snap. But when Ohio State started at the 25 after a touchback on the opening kick, Meyer had Tom Herman call run plays to start the drive. Three Carlos Hyde runs gained 15 yards, and then Meyer took his shot deep. The play worked perfectly. Michigan's safeties bit on Braxton Miller's play-action fake, giving Devin Smith single coverage on cornerback J.T. Floyd. Smith got past Floyd and made the catch for a 52-yard completion. Hyde then bulled in for the touchdown. Quickly, it was 7–0 Buckeyes. It couldn't be this easy, could it?

Of course not. All week, Meyer had fretted about the ways Michigan might use Denard Robinson. While at Florida, Meyer gained an oral commitment from Robinson to become a Gator. But the quarterback changed his mind and had a storied career in Ann Arbor. His senior year had not gone as envisioned. Robinson had suffered nerve damage in his throwing elbow against Nebraska. Robinson hadn't thrown a pass in a game since, but Meyer couldn't eliminate that as a possibility. Besides, Devin Gardner was dangerous as a quarterback himself. Who knew what gimmick plays Michigan might concoct?

Then again, Robinson showed on Michigan's first play that he didn't need any gadget plays to be a game-breaker. Robinson took the shotgun snap. Defensive lineman Michael Bennett, starting in place of Simon, beat his man and had a clear shot at Robinson. Bennett grabbed Robinson around the thighs, but the quarterback slipped away. He then faked safety C.J. Barnett, who appeared to have the angle on Robinson. Despite losing his left shoe— Robinson's nickname is "Shoelace" because he doesn't tie his cleats—he outraced the Buckeyes down the right sideline until pushed out of bounds after a 30-yard run. This would not be easy.

The Buckeyes foiled the drive when freshman defensive lineman Adolphus Washington beat All-America left tackle Taylor Lewan and stripped the ball from Gardner. Zach Boren recovered.

But the Buckeyes' problems with big plays would flare up again in the second quarter. On Michigan's next possession, Barnett bit on a shallower receiver and couldn't recover to make the tackle on Roy Roundtree, who caught a sideline pass from Gardner.

"It was bad communication," Barnett said. "I wasn't where I needed to be in my zone."

Escorted by Drew Dileo, who blocked Christian Bryant all the way down the field, Roundtree finished a 75-yard touchdown play.

Not all the drama occurred during play. Between the first and second quarter, Ohio State's 2002 national championship team, including Jim Tressel, was introduced in the north end zone. Tressel waved to the roaring crowd and then was carried off the field by his former players.

"Surreal," said Carpenter, a freshman on that '02 team. "When Kenny [Peterson] and Craig [Krenzel] lifted him up and the crowd began chanting his name, it brought a tear to my eye."

That 2002 team was famous for making things difficult for itself before finding ways to win, and the 2012 team seemed determined to follow the same path. Early in the second quarter, Philly Brown muffed a punt deep inside Ohio State territory. Michigan recovered and scored five plays later on a keeper by Gardner to give the Wolverines a 14–10 lead. After the Buckeyes were forced to punt, Michigan looked to build on its momentum. A face-mask penalty on Ryan Shazier moved the ball to the Wolverines' 38. On the next play, Gardner dropped back to pass. He couldn't find an open receiver, and Boren came on a delayed blitz. He sacked Gardner, momentarily standing over him à la Muhammad Ali in the famous photo of him after knocking out Sonny Liston.

"I remember getting yelled at by Coach Meyer after that play for standing over him," Boren said. "That play was such a blur. It was one of those plays where I was just reacting. I was expecting him to bootleg, but he pulled up in the pocket and I just took off. I don't think he even saw me. The cameraman got a good shot. I've got to thank him for that one. He got it perfectly."

That image is now displayed prominently in the Woody Hayes Center.

"That picture of him, it'll forever go down in history," Meyer said, clearly over his initial unhappiness at Boren's brief posing.

Another sack by Shazier forced Michigan to punt, and the Buckeyes rode the running of Hyde to the Michigan 14. Miller then threw to Philly Brown for a 14-yard touchdown with 1:30 left in the second quarter for a 17–14 Buckeyes lead. When Michigan ran on its first play after the kickoff, the Wolverines seemed content to run out the clock. But on the next play, Robinson took the snap and went around right tackle behind three blockers. When Travis Howard and Bryant converged on Robinson from opposite directions, the play looked harmless. Problem was, they hit Robinson at the same time, which had the effect of keeping Robinson upright. And off Robinson went for a 67-yard touchdown with 40 seconds left.

"That play was unreal," Howard said.

Howard said he assumed from the formation that Robinson would run the ball and knew his challenge would be to beat the block of the Michigan wide receiver, which he did. As he closed in on Robinson, he thought he could force a fumble with a jarring hit. Of course, he didn't see Bryant coming from the opposite direction with the same intent. The collision left Howard discombobulated.

"All I remember is getting off the ground, and I looked and heard everyone screaming, and my eyes went black. I couldn't even open my eyes. I was stumbling, and Orhian was telling me, 'Are you all right?! Are you all right?!' I'm like, 'Yeah, yeah, yeah. But I can't see.'"

Howard is on the kick-block unit, and Johnson helped him get lined up. Howard normally is the end on the play and the designated kick-blocker, but Johnson took his spot.

"So I'm lined up on the field-goal block, and I couldn't see anything. As I walked to the sideline, Christian was saying, 'Man, if only one of us had hit him low, we could have messed him up.' At the time I didn't know what he was talking about. I got to the bench, and my coach explained the play to me and said, 'You and Christian ran into each other.'"

Howard had been so disoriented that he thought he'd actually tackled Robinson. It wasn't until film review a couple days later that Howard saw the play.

"I was like, 'Oh, that's what happened,'" he said.

The Buckeyes got a semblance of momentum back when Drew Basil kicked a career-long 52-yard field goal to end the half. But the Buckeyes still trailed 21–20.

Robinson had run for 124 yards on six carries. Michigan had gained 219 yards. What had happened to the defensive progress Ohio State had shown late in the season? The defense had been dented, but their resolve hadn't been.

"They promised us when we went into halftime that they wouldn't give up a point, and they didn't," Brown said.

Meyer said that his pointer at halftime was the same one that the 105,899 fans at the Horseshoe would have given: tackle the quarterback. The Buckeyes would. The game turned on Michigan's first possession of the second half. The Wolverines faced a fourth-and-three at their own 48. At first, Hoke sent in the punt team. Michigan then called timeout, and Hoke changed his mind. But his play call was, to be kind, curious. Instead of having Robinson run to the edge to take advantage of his speed, he called for a run up the middle. The play had no chance. Ryan Shazier, with help from Sabino, drilled Robinson for a two-yard loss.

Meyer was surprised by the decision, especially the choice of plays.

"I thought they were going to try to draw us offside," he said. "Just running right at us, I didn't think they were going to get it. I was worried about an edge play, with Denard on the edge. We're not a great space team. We're pretty good against Wisconsin-type stuff."

Given excellent field position, the Buckeyes drove to the Michigan 11 before stalling. Basil kicked a 28-yard field goal to put Ohio State back ahead 23–21. This time the Buckeyes would not relinquish their lead. Michigan would gain only 39 yards the rest of the game, including only nine in the fourth quarter. Not that Ohio State's offense exactly supplied the hammer, either, blowing chances to take control. Ohio State had a first-and-goal at the Michigan 4 and somehow managed not to get any points when a blindside sack, botched snap, and missed field goal followed. Miller lost a fumble at the Michigan 36 at the start of the fourth quarter.

Six minutes later, another Buckeyes drive stalled at midfield. In came Ben Buchanan in hopes of pinning Michigan deep. It had been a difficult year for the senior from Westerville, but he wanted to finish on a high note.

"I was like, 'All right, Lord. Please just let me hit a great punt here,'" he told himself. He did. "I think I hit probably best tear-drop, perfect-spiral punt I've ever hit in my life."

The ball hit at the 1 and bounced back to the 8.

"I pointed upstairs as I ran off the field and hugged my team-mates, because a lot of them knew that was probably the last punt of my career," he said.

When Travis Howard recovered a Gardner fumble caused by a hit by Johnathan Hankins at the Michigan 10, the Buckeyes couldn't punch it in. Basil's fourth field goal made it 26–21, keeping it a one-possession game.

"Heck yeah, I was worried about that," Meyer said. "It's funny the sense of calm, though, when you're playing good defense."

The Buckeyes' defense made its final stop when Barnett inter-cepted a pass. It wasn't a particularly difficult interception, but Barnett had been among those in the secondary afflicted with stone hands. He estimated that he dropped six or seven potential inter-ceptions in 2012. He'd caught only one all year.

"The D-line got good pressure," Barnett said. "Orhian got a good reroute. The ball was up there, and I went up there and made a play. Thank God I caught it. I had trouble catching the ball all season. But I came up with it when I needed it."

The offense got the ball with 4:50 left. Just as it was against Michigan State at the start of the Big Ten season, the running game was up to the challenge. When Hyde ran for a first down with 1:57, the crowd began to erupt in a triumphant cheer. Meyer threw off his headset briefly to soak in the moment before putting it back on to make sure the Buckeyes could run out the clock. As the time ticked down to 54 seconds left, Meyer said, "It's over, Tom," on his headset to offensive coordinator Tom Herman in the press box. Jake Stoneburner dumped Gatorade on Meyer. Zach Boren gave him a long embrace.

"I turned around and looked at the scoreboard," Reid Fragel said. "It kind of took me a second to realize it was over. At that point, my friend and roommate, Jeff Heuerman, was right behind me in the kneeling position. He said it was over. I gave him a hug. By the time I was done hugging him, everyone was swarming around us. It was kind of a hectic moment, but at the same time one I'll never forget."

Fragel hugged Meyer, who then was enveloped in a sea of scarlet. Eventually, Fragel made his way to the south stands for "Carmen Ohio."

"I had tears in my eyes when I was singing it," Fragel said. "I'm not going to lie. It's one of those things that doesn't really hit you until you go through it. It was a special moment, for sure."

For Sabino, who wouldn't have still been on the team if he hadn't volunteered to redshirt as a junior, it was almost surreal.

"I kind of saw the whole season flash by in a quick instant," he said. "Being on the field, the fans rushing the field, the joy of everyone so happy and thinking this was my last game as an Ohio State Buckeye.... I'm on a 12–0 football team. Life couldn't be better. It was truly like a dream."

Simon, who'd spent the game on the sideline giving pointers to his teammates, found himself surrounded by the swarm.

"I was fired up," he said. "Then the crowd stormed the field. That's one of the best feelings in college football. But I was having trouble walking and got stuck in there."

Fortunately, teammate Steve Miller was nearby, and the defensive lineman was able to keep him from being trampled. "He led the way and was blocking people," Simon said. "I was following him back to the locker room as best I could. Having that moment and excitement is something I'll never forget."

Meyer briefly looked for Hoke, who decided—wisely, probably—to make a beeline for the exits rather than take his chances amid the onrushing crowd. Meyer found his daughters, Nicki and Gigi.

"I grabbed my [security] cop, and they're like pushing through people, almost knocking people over," Meyer said. "So I said, 'Just stop right here.' I was high-fiving the students. We stayed there for about 20 minutes and kind of worked our way to the band."

Meyer couldn't get over in time for the singing of "Carmen Ohio." Meanwhile, players posed for photographs. A father asked Miller to take a picture with his son, who was wearing a No. 5 Miller jersey. Miller happily complied. Corey Linsley hugged his girlfriend, Anna Gilboy. As Miller made his way up the concourse to the locker room, he was met by Herman, who'd just made it down from the upstairs coaching booth. He embraced Miller and planted a big kiss on his helmet. Nathan Williams, who'd battled so hard to return from his knee injury, had been joined on the field by his girlfriend, Stephanie Siegenthaler, and they and her family took pictures to capture the moment. After "Carmen Ohio," Williams tried to make his way through the crowd toward the locker room. But as the band played "Buckeye Swag," the song that had become a 2012 tradition, a band member handed Williams a drumstick and told him to start playing. Williams couldn't resist.

"I have tremendous respect for our band and love what they do," Williams said. "It was the least I could do. It was awesome. It was definitely a great ending."

As for his musical talent, Williams, never lacking confidence, answered characteristically.

"I think I'm pretty talented," he quipped.

The locker room scene was one of unbridled jubilation. Herman and defensive coordinator Luke Fickell presented game balls to deserving players. Meyer had defensive-line coach Mike Vrabel give one to Simon. Like Simon, Vrabel was injured as well, but his was his own doing. During pregame warmups, he got caught up in the moment and head-butted Linsley, forgetting one thing: players wear helmets, coaches don't.

"I grabbed his helmet and put my forehead right in his face mask and it split my head open," Vrabel said.

His face was bloody, but he was unfazed.

"I look over and it looks like he's got mascara all over his face," Meyer said. "I asked Mick, 'What the hell happened to him?'"

Vrabel would require stitches, a small price for a victory over Michigan.

To Meyer, beating Michigan was the fulfillment of a dream.

"It was just surreal to be out there," he said. "I caught myself a few times thinking, *Oh my gosh, it's right there.*"

The scene in the locker room was as close to heaven on earth as Meyer could imagine. His daughters were in that room for the first time. So was Shelley, whose reluctance to leave Florida seemed a long time ago. So was Nate, whose "I'm with you" soothed Meyer's conscience as he weighed returning to coaching.

The Buckeyes had achieved perfection, however imperfectly.

"An incredible moment, with the journey we'd been through the last three years," Meyer said.

· 23 ·

WHAT IT MEANT

AND JUST LIKE THAT, it was over.

Their magical roller coaster had breezed through the finish line and then—boom—it came to an abrupt end. The Buckeyes celebrated in the locker room and went their separate ways on November 24, 2012. Urban Meyer left the stadium, stopped at Eddie George's Grille 27 restaurant on campus to meet with recruits, and then headed home.

"I had a glass of red wine and enjoyed the moment," he said.

The hard part would come soon enough. The Buckeyes could only be spectators as championships were decided. Speaking on the day of the Big Ten Championship Game between Wisconsin and Nebraska on December 1, Etienne Sabino braced himself for a tough night on the couch. "I'm sick to my stomach knowing we beat both of those teams and we're sitting at home right now," he said. "Regardless of who wins tonight in this Big Ten Championship Game, I feel they know who the real champs are."

Wisconsin would win easily. The Nebraska defense that Ohio State obliterated on that picture-perfect October evening turned in another disappearing act. The Blackshirts had become a black hole once again. But the reality that the rightful champion of the Big Ten would be stuck at home became magnified with Badgers coach Bret Bielema's abrupt departure for Arkansas three days after the game. The coach of the official Big Ten champion wouldn't even lead his team in the Rose Bowl. It only added to the sense of a fraudulent crown. Coached by athletics director and former coach Barry Alvarez, the Badgers would lose to Stanford in Pasadena.

Late in the season, the Buckeyes clung to the hope that they might finish No. 1 atop the Associated Press rankings. The AP poll, done by 60 media representatives, was the only one for which the Buckeyes were eligible. But Ohio State's longshot chance ended when Notre Dame finished the regular season undefeated and Alabama beat Georgia in the SEC championship game. Once that happened, it was clear that a one-loss Crimson Tide team or unbeaten Fighting Irish team would finish No. 1 in the media poll after they met for the BCS championship. Alabama dominated Notre Dame 42–14 to become the unanimous pick among the AP voters and repeat as national champion. Despite its status as the country's only undefeated team, Ohio State finished third behind Oregon, which beat Kansas State 35–17 in the Fiesta Bowl.

Meyer served as a guest analyst for the BCS title game, so he saw Alabama and Notre Dame up close. "I thought I would enjoy it, but it was hard," Meyer said. "But it was good. It lit the fire one more time—to walk into that environment and see what we're all shooting for. ESPN asked me to do it, and I don't say no to them. It was hard during the hype for the pregame, watching those kids and their families and the fans. Then it's just football. But the hour leading up to it was very hard."

Adding to the emotion was the site. Florida had beaten Oklahoma in Miami to win its second national title under Meyer four years earlier. Asked how Ohio State might have fared against the Crimson Tide, Meyer was diplomatic.

"We could have competed," he said. "I would never say we could beat them because I don't know if we could and it wouldn't be fair to Alabama. They won the game soundly. But how you compete in major college football is playing really good defense, taking care of the ball and finding creative ways to move it. At the beginning of the season, we would have gotten murdered. We'd have been slapped around. But by the end of the year, we could compete against anybody then."

Whether the Buckeyes could have beaten Alabama may have been irrelevant had they been eligible. Their more likely matchup would have been against Notre Dame. Considering how poorly the Irish played—the soon-to-break bizarre Manti Te'o fake girl-friend story partially explained why—it didn't take much of a leap to see how Ohio State could have beaten them and won the national title.

"From the first touchdown Alabama scored—and it just got uglier and uglier from there—" Christian Bryant said, "I thought, *Man we really could have been national champions this season.* Going 14–0, I don't even know how it would have felt. I was talking with Mike Doss about their season when they won the national championship, and he said it was like no other season he'd ever been through."

Others were more philosophical about not getting a chance to play for the national championship.

"That's life," John Simon said. "Things aren't always going to go your way. We dealt with the sanctions in the off-season and made sure they weren't going to affect us. We were going to take advantage of our opportunities [to play]. We absolutely did that. As a senior class we set the foundation well for Coach Meyer and Ohio State in the future."

But there's little question that the inability to play beyond November meant that the Buckeyes' season slipped from the nation's consciousness. "The quietest undefeated team to ever go through college football was Ohio State in 2012," Nathan Williams said in January while working out for the NFL Combine. "You turn on *SportsCenter* and get the BCS rankings, and we were never in there. I'm training with a lot of guys out here in Arizona who, strange as it is to say, don't know that we were undefeated. I think everyone knew we had a bowl ban, and no one took us seriously who didn't play us and didn't give us the credit that we deserved from that."

Even when the All–Big Ten teams were announced, the Buckeyes didn't get the recognition many expected. The Big Ten has separate coaches and media all-conference teams, and league coaches did not see fit to have Braxton Miller or Ryan Shazier as first-team selections, though John Simon, Johnathan Hankins, and Bradley Roby were. The media picked Miller, Shazier, Simon, Roby, Andrew Norwell, and Travis Howard as first-team picks.

Simon, who finished with nine sacks and 14½ tackles for loss, was named the Big Ten Defensive Player of the Year. Despite the snub by the coaches, Miller was named the conference's Offensive Player of the Year. He set school records in total offense with 3,310 yards and rushing yards by a quarterback with 1,271. Miller finished fifth in the Heisman Trophy voting.

Meyer was a finalist for several coach of the year awards, but came up empty. He didn't even get Big Ten Coach of the Year. That went to Penn State's Bill O'Brien. Meyer said such awards don't matter to him.

"I just want to win and have our kids do well," he said. "People will say, 'Can you believe that [you didn't win Coach of the Year]?' I don't care, and my wife doesn't care."

What Shelley—and others close to Meyer—cared about much more couldn't be measured with a trophy. To them, there would always be two ways to judge whether Meyer had succeeded in 2012. The first was the one by which every coach is judged—his team's record. Obviously, that was perfect, however imperfectly it was achieved. But the second measure, the one that may signal how sustained Meyer's success at Ohio State can be, would be how well he'd handle the stress of returning to coaching in such a high-profile, high-pressure environment. It's one thing to agree to a Pink Contract written by a daughter. It's another to cope with the myriad of real and potential crises that confront every coach in the course of a season.

Even Shelley didn't know when he took over in Columbus how he'd answer that question. "I played devil's advocate with him for so long when he started talking about going back to coaching," she said. "I wanted to know, 'What's your plan? What's going to be different? How are you going to handle these certain situations differently so you don't get like you were?' He had thought it out very well. He always had an answer."

But Shelley wanted to see whether he could stick to the plan. She wanted to know if he could maintain a healthy lifestyle—eating three meals a day, working out regularly, sleeping well at night. He had done that for a while at Florida before it came crashing down.

"Can he still be successful and not get to the point he was in 2009 when it just took over?" Shelley said she wondered.

The answer was yes, with an asterisk.

"He didn't lose one pound this season," Shelley said. "That's the first time ever. He made sure he ate and he slept pretty well all season. But again, what's there not to sleep about when you're 12–0? He did fantastic, but we went 12–0. He didn't get tested. The Purdue game was almost a test, but we still won. Wisconsin was a test, but we still won. What I wanted to see was how would he handle a loss. That's the thing that put him over the edge before—losing a darned game. He worked out. He followed everything on the contract really well. But he didn't have to face losing a game. I still believe that he will handle a loss better than he used to. I really believe that. We've talked about it. He has a different perspective about what losing a game is now."

But accepting a loss in the abstract is not the same as confronting it in reality. Urban Meyer knows that remains a major test. "We didn't hit the speed bump," he said. "The speed bump is the loss. It's the greatest job in the world until you lose."

Even Meyer himself doesn't know for sure how well he'll handle that. "Oh, there's still questions," he said shortly before National Signing Day. "It's a daily challenge. We all have challenges. We have losses. I lost a recruit the other day. I didn't handle it real well, but it wasn't [too] bad."

Shelley even acknowledged that she "sorta kinda" wouldn't have minded a loss in 2012, only to see how her husband would handle a defeat in a season when a championship wasn't at stake. Safe to say that's not a bridge Meyer has any desire to cross.

"I'm not looking forward to that day," he said. "Losing sucks, man. But it is what it is. We work so hard not to let that happen."

But he understands that day will come. He knows he can't revert to the obsessive guy who thought he could overcome failure with one more stab at drawing a new punt-block scheme.

"I feel pretty good," Meyer said. "I think the mechanisms are in place. I let myself go health-wise [at the end in Florida]. I saw how that hurt people. I'm not as worried about myself. I saw my daughters and son [suffer]. I saw my wife. I don't want to have that happen again. There are a lot of things in place to make sure that doesn't happen again. I'm not talking about winning every game you play. I'm talking about handling situations."

During a break in spring practice, he got a visit from an NFL coach who's a friend. They discussed satisfaction, and whether that was attainable. For someone as intense as Meyer, that may be a loaded question.

"Happiness is fleeting," he said. "Peace and joy is a state of mind. I'm at peace and have joy in my heart right now. That's because of the health of my family. I see my girls and boy doing well. I see a program built on the foundation of truth. I see a lot of character. I see a lot of integrity. I see stability. I walk in this place and I feel really good. I walk into my house and see my daughters and son and feel good."

Nicki Meyer said that her father was "flawless" in following the dicta of her Pink Contract. Urban flew to Atlanta to watch her first volleyball game of the season—staying the whole weekend—and then flew in for her Senior Night during the Buckeyes' off week.

Meyer left the office every Sunday at noon so that he could watch Nate play football, something he wouldn't have done before.

"I believe 150 percent that he is healthy and has changed his ways of being a control [freak]," Nicki said. "I think he's hired a really amazing staff. Being able to trust them with their responsibilities, that's making all the difference. He's coaching back where he grew up and for a team that he's loved forever. He absolutely loves the guys he's coaching. I've heard him say that more this year than ever. This was probably one of the happiest years he's ever had."

Meyer does believe that he's a different man than the one who became a head coach in 2001 with a single-minded mission. Back then, he considered himself in a nonstop sprint toward the national championship crystal ball. It wasn't that he had a complete disregard for anything else, but nothing would interfere with that pursuit.

"I don't want to say I'm not still sprinting for that," Meyer said, "but I have a better understanding of what's really important. The crystal ball is very important, but the process to get to that crystal ball and the relationship side of it is very important, because you can't do one without the other."

But the relationships aren't just a means to facilitate victories. He said that his one season of coaching Etienne Sabino will be the basis of a lifelong relationship with him. He considers John Simon to be a virtual son. He has deep affection and respect for many others. And it is reciprocal, which is not something many players would have said during the grueling early days of the Meyer regime.

"Earlier in the year, no one really knew too much about him as far as his personal life or what type of coaching style he would have," Christian Bryant said. "But throughout the year, everything just shot up through the roof—our love for him, our affection for him. We just wanted to play our hearts out for him and the team."

"People might not see his caring side," Sabino added. "People outside of the program who don't know him think of him as this great coach who [only] cares about winning. I truly feel Coach Meyer has a reason for everything he does. There's tough love, but he also lets you know he cares about you. As long as you're working and you show your commitment and dedication to get better, he has a lot of love."

Perhaps no player was more transformed by his time under Meyer than Zach Boren. He was so moved by his experience during the 2012 season that he wrote a poem to express his feelings. The player who'd been marked as a negative guy, who'd asked Meyer to relent on his practice demands, found himself wishing he could go through that grind again.

"You get such an appreciation for everything that he does and he puts you through. It makes you so much stronger as a person," Boren said.

Boren hopes to make it in the NFL. He was listed at the NFL Combine as a fullback, and it might have helped his pro prospects if he'd played a full season there. But Boren has no regrets. He believes his experience at Ohio State under Meyer will help him compensate for that—or anything else he'll face.

"I'm coming from a program that's competitive 365 days a year, that totally pushes you to the max," Boren said. "Your body can't take it anymore, but you go a little bit further. You teach yourself to go beyond the limits. Now that I've gone through that and see how much it changed me as a person, I'm going to forever remember that and I'm going to push myself beyond the limits from here on out, no matter what I do. I think I'm going to have a stronger family and stronger family relationships just because of the stuff I went through with him. I'm going to push myself to go beyond the limits in whatever I do."

*   *   *   *

NO TEAM in the history of major college football had ever gone 12–0 or better the year after having a losing season. That is part of the 2012 Ohio State Buckeyes legacy. But for the legacy of 2012 to be of lasting significance, the Buckeyes have to build on that success. The landscape of college football is filled with teams that caught lightning in a bottle for a season and then disappeared back into the ether. As soon as the 2012 season ended, Meyer declared himself on guard for any sign of complacency. Mickey Marotti vowed to make off-season conditioning at least as rigorous.

On paper, the Buckeyes are well-positioned to have another banner year in 2013. If anything, the schedule is even easier, with Legends Division teams Nebraska and Michigan State cycling off the schedule and Iowa and Northwestern coming on. Ohio State returns several starters on offense, including Heisman Trophy contender Braxton Miller and four starters on the offensive line. On defense, Ryan Shazier and Bradley Roby will be All-America candidates, and the loss of all the defensive-line starters shouldn't be as daunting as some fear with talented young players like Noah Spence and Adolphus Washington ready to emerge.

Bolstering the talent level is an incoming freshman class regarded as one of the best in the country. If the Class of 2012 was a successful scramble, 2013's was the product of a detailed, well-executed plan. Offensive coordinator Tom Herman used his Texas ties to snare three blue-chip players. Everett Withers' successful pursuit of five-star safety Vonn Bell from Chattanooga, Tennessee, may have been the *coup de grâce*. Withers pursued Bell with such vigor that he even got to know the barber in Bell's circle.

"Chris the barber," Withers said with a satisfied smile on Signing Day after Bell picked Ohio State over Alabama and Tennessee, which had been regarded as the front-runner.

Meyer called Withers' recruiting job to get Bell "from start to finish, as good as I've ever seen." Meyer believes that the ability to lure a top-rated recruiting class was directly related to the undefeated season. "You don't do that without having a great year," he said. "You'd have to fight through that negativity."

There's a sense among Buckeyes fans that 2012 was only a prelude. Meyer's history provides support for that contention. At each of his stops, Meyer's second season surpassed his first. At Bowling Green, the Falcons went 9–3. His second Utah team went 12–0. At Florida, the Gators won the national title in his second season.

Meyer is not predicting a national title. He may sell recruits on the idea of that and he strives for that, but a conference title is the first priority.

"Our goal is to be competitive in November for championships," he said. "You never say 'national championship' to players. You don't say that. Think about how hard that is. We're always talking about November around here. You might stumble, and you don't want kids to quit playing. I think that happens sometimes. You start talking about national championships and you lose two games, and it's like, 'Why play?'"

Meyer will probably amass more talented teams in Columbus than he had in 2012. But Ohio State didn't win in 2012 because of its raw ability. The Buckeyes went undefeated and untied for only the sixth time in school history because their players, led by the seniors, invested so much of themselves in the program that they lifted the play of their teammates.

It was Orhian Johnson, who embraced a part-time role and made key plays throughout the season.

It was Storm Klein, who played through pain while vindicating Meyer's decision to give him a second chance.

It was Jake Stoneburner, who accepted constructive criticism and adapted to a redefined position.

It was Garrett Goebel, the unsung captain who did his grunt work with little fanfare.

It was Ben Buchanan, who endured a difficult final season before finishing with the punt of his career against Michigan.

It was Zach Domicone and Taylor Rice, who took on a special-teams leadership role on a young unit desperate for it.

It was Travis Howard, whose development allowed Buckeyes coaches to put more responsibility on his and Roby's shoulders.

It was Nathan Williams, who fought through his microfracture surgery to play his senior season and complete a strong defensive line.

It was Reid Fragel, who shed his previous indifference to become the final, critical piece for the offensive line.

It was Etienne Sabino, who returned early from a broken leg to make pivotal plays against Wisconsin.

It was Zach Boren, who switched sides of the ball in the middle of his senior season to stabilize a defense.

It was John Simon, who, at Marotti's behest, brought younger players along to his pre-dawn workouts and excelled despite pain that would have felled most players. And then, when he faced an injury that even he couldn't overcome, his teammates won the biggest game of all for him.

No two teams are alike. Each must develop its own identity. The players who will form the nucleus of the 2013 team have quite a legacy to uphold. But the foundation has been established.

"The most overused word in athletics is leadership," Meyer said. "One of the most undervalued principles of team is leadership. This team was all about that. For as long as I'm alive, I will always talk about this '12 team, because they deserve that."

ACKNOWLEDGMENTS

WHEN OHIO STATE'S 2012 season began, it never occurred to me that I'd want to write a book about it. But as fall progressed and the Buckeyes got to the brink of an undefeated season, the idea of chronicling such an unlikely feat became appealing. As beat writer for the *Columbus Dispatch*, I knew the potential was there to shed more light on the season. When the Buckeyes beat Michigan to finish 12–0, I knew it was something I wanted to pursue.

But I also knew it would not be easy. I was determined not to write a mere rehash of the 2012 season. I needed to get inside the minds of the main figures, to reveal what they were thinking and feeling, to get well beyond the Xs and Os. Time would not be my ally. I was cautioned by my writer friends and publishers that the window to report and write the book would have to be compressed if the book was to be released before the start of the 2013 season. To do the book I envisioned, I would need much help, and I was quite fortunate to get it.

I should start with Urban Meyer, because without his cooperation this book would have been virtually impossible. He was receptive to the idea from the start and quite generous with his time and insights. So were Urban's wife, Shelley, and daughter, Nicki, whose candor and observations were crucial to fleshing out the personal side of the coach.

I spoke to every Ohio State assistant coach at length, and their observations were instrumental. Defensive coordinator Luke Fickell was particularly insightful, detailing the emotional roller coaster of the 2011 season and his adjustment to being an assistant coach again after a year as the head man. Mickey Marotti took me inside the process of getting the Buckeyes' bodies and minds geared to the new regime.

I interviewed almost all of the key players from the 2012 team, and they were all cooperative and candid. Zach Boren, John Simon,

Etienne Sabino, Travis Howard, Reid Fragel, Nathan Williams, Corey Linsley, Jack Mewhort and Braxton Miller were especially helpful. After getting to know them better, it's easy to understand how their chemistry and leadership allowed the team to be so successful.

All those coaches and players made time for me thanks mainly to Jerry Emig, Ohio State's football communications representative. His help in arranging interviews went well above the call of duty.

I also want to thank so many of my writer friends for encouraging me when the odds looked to be against success. John U. Bacon, Ken Denlinger, Lonnie Wheeler, Jeff Snook, Dave Buscema, Dick Weiss, Scott Kindberg, Josh Katzowitz, and Paul Daugherty provided much needed guidance and moral support. So did Buddy Martin, whose excellent book, *Urban's Way*, detailed Meyer's time at Florida.

I would like to also thank my colleagues at the *Columbus Dispatch*. Editor Ben Marrison, sports editor Ray Stein, and assistant sports editor Scott Davis were behind the project from the start, and their encouragement helped immensely. Tim May has been invaluable as my beat partner and friend. Columnist Bob Hunter has imparted wisdom from his experience as an author, as did my beat predecessor, Ken Gordon.

I owe a particular debt of gratitude to Noah Amstadter at Triumph Books. He saw the potential in the book from the start, despite the many obstacles, and was a constant source of support and expertise. When he came on as my editor, I knew the book was in good hands, and it was. After the manuscript was submitted, Alex Lubertozzi did an excellent job editing and reviewing it.

Most important of all has been my family. My parents, who met as Ohio State students in the 1950s, have always been my biggest supporters. My children, Katie and Michael, have provided inspiration in so many ways. And then there is my wife, Erin. She's the best editor I know, but more important, she's my best friend. I absolutely could not have done this without her constant encouragement and support.